The New
Encyclopedia of
Modern Sewing

This felt bag is simple and smart . . . one of the many accessories included in the Encyclopedia . . . every one of them a natural compliment collector! See instructions on page 166.

The New Encyclopedia of Modern Sewing

Edited by

FRANCES BLONDIN

Published by

WM. H. WISE & CO., INC.

NEW YORK

1946

Through special arrangement made with

THE NATIONAL NEEDLECRAFT BUREAU, INC.

WISE books are trademarked

Look for the WISE old bird!

PRINTED IN THE UNITED STATES OF AMERICA
AMERICAN BOOK—STRATFORD PRESS, INC., NEW YORK

Preface

So much has already been said about the practical advantages of sewing that it scarcely seems necessary to add to it. As an accessory to economy, a first aid to thrift, a boon to the budget, sewing comes well at the head of the average woman's list of accomplishments preferred.

But there is another aspect of sewing which has been less generally recognized, at any rate, less generally publicized. Every woman who sews has experienced the glow of pleasure, the pride of accomplishment with which she says "I made it myself," when somebody compliments her on her suit or her dress and when friends admire the handsome draperies and the flower strewn slipcovers in her living room. Whether or not we are aware of it, most of us sew as much for the pleasure of making something as for sober reasons of economy. There is a definite creative satisfaction in making a smart costume, in converting an ancient closet skeleton into something new and wearable or in making home a more enjoyable place, with one's own hands and skill and taste.

Many people, quite mistakenly, are under the impression that the design is the only original ingredient in sewing. Actually, even following a pattern demands a considerable amount of creative collaboration. Choosing the pattern style that is most appropriate and becoming, marrying it to a suitable fabric, adjusting the pattern to one's measurements, selecting the trimming, blending the colors—all are a challenge to a woman's ingenuity. A dozen women may choose the same dress pattern, but when they have finished, there will be twelve completely different dresses. Each will have added her own individual touch—created, in a sense, her own original design.

One of the major satisfactions of being able to make one's own clothes is having a wardrobe styled to one's own personality. Added to this, is the possibility of having good fit, a distinct advantage when planning to be well dressed. In her children's clothes and in the accessories of her home, the woman who sews has more chance than most to express herself creatively. It is hoped that this book will help many women discover the hidden assets and *pleasures* in their thimbles.

For invaluable assistance in compiling the technical matter in this book, grateful acknowledgement and thanks are given to Jane Chapman, Joan Frye, Mary Harrell and Elizabeth Mathieson, of the Educational Bureau of the Spool Cotton Co.; to American Viscose Corp.; the Butterick Co.; Botany Worsted Mills; Celanese Corp.; E. I. du Pont de Nemours & Co., Inc.; William Skinner and Sons; Arthur Bier Co.; Singer Sewing Machine Co.; and to The American Home; Woman's Home Companion; Simplicity Pattern Co.; J. Wiss & Sons Co.

Frances Blondin

Contents

The New
Encyclopedia of
Modern Sewing

Striped taffeta evening skirt with a peplum . . . the familiar dirndl done in a new version . . . easy to make and fun to wear! See instructions on page 178.

1. Off to a Flying Start

If you've been feeling wistful about the pretty clothes in the shops . . . if you've been down in the dumps because your home is turning seedy at the seams, wearing shabby around the edges . . . if you've been wondering how you're going to juggle the budget into keeping your small fry in clothes, your troubles are over. To live better on less, look lovely on next-to-nothing, take to your thimble!

To start with, let's puncture a myth. You don't need any special talent or ability to make a dress or a slip cover. All it requires is the normal amount of fingers and a fair quota of patience. While most books on sewing assume that you're acquainted with the fundamentals, this one starts out on the premise that you're innocent as a new-born babe about selvages and seams. You begin at the beginning, learn step by step. You learn by doing, and with each step your confidence grows. In the very first lesson you make an attractive and wearable pinafore. In other words, you reap as you sew!

All the important things that you want to know about sewing are described in this book. The construction details are shown in connection with interesting things to make for yourself, your home and your family. If you have a question about a special technique, consult the index in the back of the book which contains a complete list of all the subjects covered.

Sewing is not difficult but, like all skills, it requires practice. Practice may be both pleasant and profitable if an attractive, usable article is made while trying out the construction details given. The purpose of the book is to teach the most fundamental operations of sewing in this way. For example, the basic steps in sewing are taught while making a simple pinafore. This begins on page 27.

Sewing has some tools and equipment which are *Sewing Equipment* indispensable, others which contribute greatly to convenience and efficiency. In Chapter 1, only the essentials are mentioned. In succeeding chapters, additional items appear and are described as they are needed. So as to make it easier to check supplies and to add to them from time to time, the furnishings for the perfect sewing room—the place where every conceivable help for sewing is assembled—are reviewed on pages 309 to 313.

The kind of needle and the size of needle to use de- *Needles* pend on the weight of the fabric and the type of sewing being done. Before beginning to sew, it is advisable to turn to the Thread and Needle Chart on page 315 where there are full particulars as to the proper needle sizes as well as a description of the various types of needles. In buying a package of assorted sewing needles to keep in a work basket, sharps, sizes 3 to 9, is a good general assortment.

purpose. Buy a very cheap pair of scissors for paper, cord and the like, as nothing dulls and spoils the edge of a good scissors as quickly as cutting things of this nature. For good "all around" shears use a *bent trimmer — 8″* long. Keep the blades clean, for dust and dirt dull them rapidly. Apply a drop of oil at the joint occasionally, to keep them running freely. When they become dulled through use, they should be resharpened by a competent grinder. (See page 310 for a good line of scissors and shears.)

Careful measurement is one of the requisites for sewing well. An *oilcloth tape measure* which may be read from both ends is the most practical. A *six-inch ruler*, with markings up to ⅟₁₆″, will serve many purposes where a longer one would be cumbersome. The newest ones are transparent, making it possible to see the grain of the fabric. The *yardstick* is used for measuring fabric and hems and for marking long straight lines. Make sure it is a good durable one with well turned, smooth edges and clear markings.

Measuring Helps

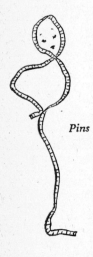

Pins

Buy good quality brass dressmaker pins, size 4 or 5, by the half pound box. Steel pins are also good, but they are apt to rust. Poor quality pins will mar the fabric in which they are used. A convenient method for using pins is to have them in a small pincushion held at the wrist by an elastic. Another type is the wall pincushion which may be hung near the work. A pincushion is sometimes strapped around the arm of the sewing machine.

There are many devices for marking on fabric, but

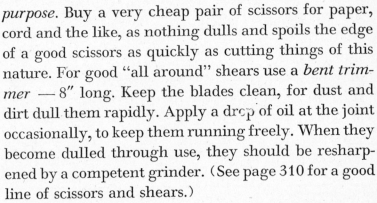

the beginner will find tailor's chalk most useful. The *Marking Aids*
chalk is just what its name implies—a chalky sub-
stance made in a flat or crayon shaped piece—and it
may be used on silk, rayon, cotton, linen and wool.
It comes in white, red and black for use on all colors
of fabric. There is another kind of tailor's chalk, a
wax, but this is for wools only. It will leave a mark on
other fabrics. For other marking aids, see page 311.

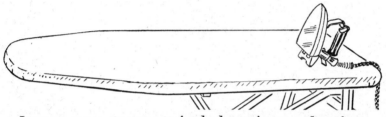

It may seem strange to include an iron and an iron- *Pressing Equipment*
ing board as essential pieces of sewing equipment, but
pressing is an important part of good sewing, not
merely a finishing touch. Each seam of the garment
should be pressed after it has been stitched and the
bastings removed. A good ironing board should be
well padded. Removable slip covers for the ironing
board make it possible to have clean covers at all
times and so prevent any possibility of soiling fabric
while pressing. A press cloth, that is, a cloth which is
placed over the fabric before the iron is applied, should
also be on hand. For pressing cottons and linens, which
will be worked on at first, a piece of cheesecloth or
muslin is best. Remove all sizing first by rinsing several times in clear water. On page 313, further details
are given on pressing.

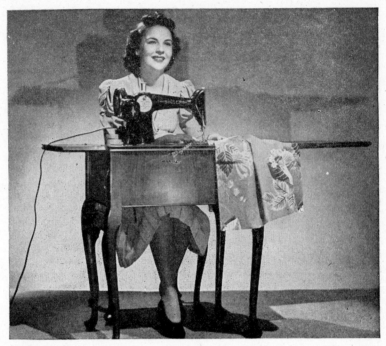

Sewing Machine   The first simple problems of sewing may be done entirely by hand. A sewing machine, however, is a great time saver. Its operation is so simple, that, in this day and age, when automobiles and even airplanes are familiar to us, no woman should have to confess ignorance of the sewing machine.

For those who have never used a sewing machine, there is usually a local sewing machine shop where at least elementary instruction is available. In any case consult the manual which comes with the machine, checking carefully with the machine. Find out how to set the needle, how to thread the machine, how to wind the bobbin. The simple explanations which follow may help also. Read them before beginning to work.

The modern sewing machine has two sets of mech- *Mechanism*
anisms. One set is located in the upper part, or *head,*
and feeds the thread from the spool down through the
needle. The other is located in the lower part, or *bed,*
and regulates the bobbin thread. The two mechanisms
are kept in motion by the balance wheel (the large
wheel on the right side of the machine). The balance
wheel is started by turning the wheel in the proper
direction. From then on it is kept in motion by the
motor or the foot treadle.

The purpose of the machine is to make strong inter-
locked stitches. Because two threads are used the
stitching is uniform on both sides. The thread for the
upper part of the stitch is fed from the spool through
the mechanism in the head to the needle. The lower
part of the stitch is formed with the bobbin thread,
fed by the mechanism in the bed. The two threads
meet and are locked together in a stitch as the needle
goes down through the needle hole in the throat plate.

In order that the stitch be perfectly formed, the first *Stitch*
requisite is that the thread from the spool to the
needle and the thread from the bobbin be arranged
exactly as directed in the manual furnished by the
manufacturer. The size of the thread and the size of
the machine needle should be chosen in accordance
with the fabric used (see Thread and Needle Chart
on page 315). The needle, which should be perfectly
straight, must be inserted according to instructions
(see machine manual). Stitching over a pin will
sometimes bend a needle slightly. This slight bend

may cause irregularity in the stitches. To test a machine needle for straightness, place the flat side of the needle against a perfectly flat solid surface to see that they align.

Tension   Correct tension is another important factor in getting a perfect stitch. The thread coming from the spool is controlled by the tension regulator on the head of the machine (see machine manual). The thread coming from the bobbin is usually controlled by the screw which holds the spring under which the thread passes (see machine manual). Stitches are lengthened or shortened by means of the stitch regulator (see machine manual). The number of stitches to the inch depends on the type of work which is being done. See Thread and Needle Chart on page 315 for correct number of stitches per inch for all kinds of sewing.

Stitch Regulation   For a perfectly regulated machine stitch remember that fine materials need a fine needle, a fine thread, a short stitch (more to the inch) and a tight tension. Heavier materials need a coarser needle, a coarser thread, a longer stitch (less to the inch) and a looser tension.

Follow these steps in regulating the stitch:

1. Use the size of machine needle and thread suited to the fabric (see Thread and Needle Chart on page 315).

2. Regulate the machine so that it has the correct number of stitches per inch. (See Thread and Needle Chart on page 315.)

3. Regulate the tension, keeping the presser bar

down. As a rule, once the bobbin has been properly adjusted, it is seldom necessary to change it. A correct stitch may usually be obtained by varying the tension on the needle thread.

4. Make a sample of stitching on a double thickness of the fabric to which the machine is being regulated. *Figures 1, 2 and 3* show clearly the differences between correct and incorrect regulation of stitches.

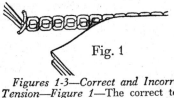

Fig. 1

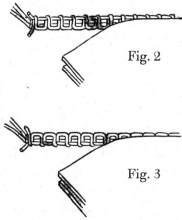

Fig. 2

Fig. 3

*Figures 1-3—Correct and Incorrect Tension—Figure 1—*The correct tension of thread on the sewing machine means that the threads coming from both the spool and bobbin pull evenly as shown. *Figure 2—*When the needle thread on the sewing machine is too tight, the needle thread lies flat along the top of the material as shown. *Figure 3—*When the needle thread on the sewing machine is too loose, the bobbin thread lies straight along the under side as shown.

To sit at the machine correctly and comfortably, *Position at Machine* use a straight chair of convenient height so that, without stooping, the elbows rest comfortably on the machine. The chair should be pulled close and placed directly in front of the machine so that the person using the machine is in line with the presser foot.

If you have never sewed on a machine before, you *Practice Stitching* will need a little preliminary practice. Mark a small piece of fabric with parallel lines extending to the edge. Place another piece of fabric underneath (do not sew on a single thickness of fabric). Proceed according to the directions given below. The following rules will make sewing easy at any time.

Before putting the fabric in the machine—

1. Thread the machine and the machine needle as directed.

2. There should be about 8″ of thread beyond the needle.

3. If there is not enough, pull the thread between the head of the machine and the eye of the needle, and then pull it through the needle. (This lessens the possibility of bending the needle. A bent needle may cause your thread to break or your stitches to slip.)

4. Hold end of thread in left hand.

5. With the right hand, move the balance wheel so that the needle goes down through the hole in the throat plate. Continue moving wheel until needle comes back up into position, bringing the under thread through the needle hole.

6. Lay both ends back under the presser foot before starting to sew.

To put the fabric under the presser foot—

1. Lay the edge of the practice piece to be stitched just far enough under the presser foot so that the first stitch will go through the fabric (on the marked line). It is important to remember that the first stitch must never be taken beyond the fabric.

2. Lower the presser foot and practice stitching on the marked line.

To stop the machine—

1. Just before reaching the end of the line of stitch-

ing, slow up the motor or the pedaling and stop the machine by placing the hand on the balance wheel.

2. Raise the presser bar.

3. Raise the needle up as high as it will go by turning the balance wheel.

4. Give the thread above the needle a little pull. (This prevents bending the needle.)

5. Take the fabric away by pulling it straight back.

6. Cut the thread on the thread cutter usually attached to back of presser foot. (See machine manual.)

Repeat until a straight line is stitched successfully. Then practice stitching squares, triangles and curves to gain perfect control of the machine.

Some Do's and Don'ts

Machine Sewing Rules

1. Do use needle and thread of good quality and correct size.

2. Do set needle correctly.

3. Do thread machine according to directions.

4. Do regulate stitches to the proper length (if stitch regulator is turned back too far, the machine will not feed).

5. Do test tension on a small piece of the fabric to be sewed.

6. Do oil machine regularly (see machine manual).

7. Don't wind bobbin too full.

8. Don't sew over pins unless machine has a presser foot designed to stitch over them.

9. Don't pull fabric while sewing.

10. Don't allow fabric to drag over back of machine.

Place a chair there to hold it as it is being sewed.

11. Don't allow machine belt to become too tight (see machine manual).

12. Don't permit mechanism to become dusty or gummed up (see machine manual on oiling).

Proper Lighting Proper lighting is mentioned last, but is second to nothing in importance. Whether light comes from a window or an electric light bulb, the best light for working comes from over the left shoulder. When sewing, an adjustable light fixture on the machine is a necessity. If the machine does not have an electric light, a small lighting attachment may be purchased and easily attached to it.

HOW TO MAKE A PINAFORE
*Practice Piece for Fundamental Steps
in Sewing, Including Finishes and
Techniques Suitable for Cotton Fabrics*

Certain fundamental processes of sewing are combined in the construction of this pinafore. These processes may be followed in connection with the directions given in the succeeding pages, or they may be used in connection with a commercial pattern.

Fabric

The fabric recommended for the pinafore is percale. Choose a plain or an all-over print so that no matching of pattern is necessary. The adult's size (14-18) requires 2¾ yds. The girl's size (8-12) requires 2¼ yds. The child's size (3-6) requires 1½ yds. If the fabric has a label which indicates that it is pre-shrunk, begin cutting at once. Otherwise it is best to wash the fabric in cold water, hang it up until it is partially dry and then press it. If white thread is used, *size 60* six cord is suitable. Mercerized sewing thread, which comes in size 50, may be used to match the fabric for color. For hand sewing this fabric, use a *size 7* needle; for machine sewing, use a medium sized needle.

To make full-sized patterns from *pinafore patterns No. I, II and III* on page 29, follow the directions accompanying *figure 4* on the same page.

General Cutting Instructions

Cutting Instructions

Any surface which is smooth, firm and flat and sufficiently large is suitable for cutting. A kitchen or dining room table usually provides plenty of space to work on. A good table should be protected by a pad. On the market there is a cutting board made of composition, so designed that it can be folded and put away when not in use (see page 310). It may be used on the floor or the bed, or on any steady flat surface.

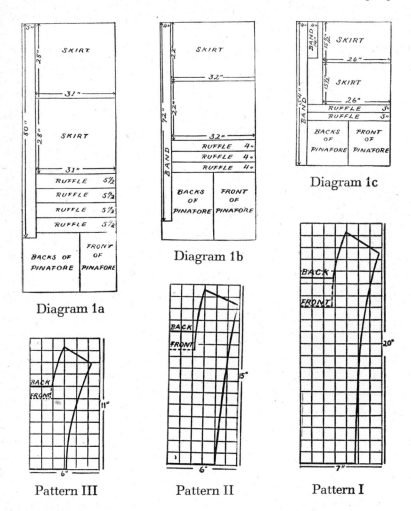

Diagram 1a

Diagram 1b

Diagram 1c

Pattern III

Pattern II

Pattern I

Figure 4—To enlarge to actual size patterns given to scale on small squared sections, follow these directions. Each small square on diagram represents a 1″ square in actual size. To make pattern, use smooth brown paper, pencil and ruler. Note number of inches as marked in length and width of pattern you wish to make. With ruler draw box of length and width needed. Mark off 1″ spaces around all sides of box. Use ruler to join corresponding marks with straight lines. Use squares, thus made, as guide and draw lines to correspond with those given in diagram. *To use pattern,* cut it out around outline made. Pin pattern to fabric. When section of pattern is marked "On Fold," that edge must be laid directly on straight fold of fabric and fold *must not be cut.* Transfer all marks on pattern pieces to fabric pieces.

Fig. 4

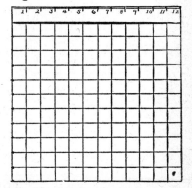

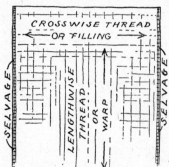

Figure 5—Selvage is the name given to the woven edges on the length of the fabric. "The lengthwise grain" means the lengthwise threads or warp threads and is, of course, parallel to the selvage edge. "The crosswise grain" means the crosswise or the filling threads. "On the grain" or "on the straight" of the goods means to be straight with either of these threads.

Fig. 5

Grain of Fabric   Take the fabric and notice that, on each of two sides, there is a group of closely woven threads. These are known as the selvages and run along the length of the fabric *(figure 5)*. Notice also that the fabric has lengthwise or warp threads and crosswise or filling threads. It would be impossible to overemphasize the importance of knowing about these threads. When sewing, everything must be cut in relation to them. Other expressions often used are "the lengthwise grain," "the crosswise grain," "on the grain," "the straight of the goods." Anything which is not cut in proper relation to the grain will not hang or lie properly. *(See figure 5)*.

Cutting Directions   To cut *adult's* size pinafore, cut the pieces listed below according to *diagram 1a* on page 29. Follow the *Cutting Directions* given on page 31.

Band and Tie—1 piece, 5″ by 80″.

Skirt—2 pieces, each 28″ by the remaining width of fabric.

Ruffles—4 pieces, each 5½″ by 31″.

Front Bib—1 piece, *pattern No. I* (pattern placed on fold).

Back Bib—2 pieces, *pattern No. I* (½″ allowed at center for seam).

To cut *girl's* size pinafore, cut the pieces listed below according to *diagram 1b* on page 29. Follow the *Cutting Directions* given below.

Band and Tie—1 piece, 4″ by 72″.

Skirt—2 pieces, each 22″ by remaining width of fabric.

Ruffles—3 pieces, each 4″ by 32″.

Front Bib—1 piece, *pattern No. II* (pattern placed on fold).

Back Bib—2 pieces, *pattern No. II* (½″ allowed at center for seam).

To cut *child's* size pinafore, cut the pieces listed below according to *diagram 1c* on page 29. Follow the *Cutting Directions* given below.

Band and Tie—1 piece, 4″ by 68″.

Skirt—2 pieces, each 15½″ by 26″.

Ruffles—2 pieces, each 3″ by 32″.

Front Bib—1 piece, *pattern No. III* (pattern placed on fold).

Back Bib—2 pieces, *pattern No. III* (½″ allowed at center for seam).

Cutting Directions for Pinafores

(*Diagrams 1a, 1b* and *1c* on page 29 serve as guides for cutting adult's, girl's and child's sizes, respectively. The following measurements are for the adult size only. In cutting other sizes merely substitute correct measurements given above.)

Fig. 6

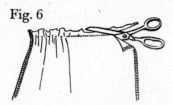

Figure 6—To straighten the end of fabric, pull carefully (until it breaks) the first crosswise thread which extends all across the piece. Cut along the line it makes. Continue to pull and cut in this manner all across width of piece.

Figure 7—To tear across to straighten the end of certain firmly woven cotton fabrics, such as percale, clip the selvage at a crosswise thread. With the left thumb on the top of the material and the right thumb underneath, tear quickly, straight across.

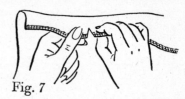

Fig. 7

1. Be sure that the edge of the fabric is straight, that is, that the same crosswise thread marks the entire top edge. If not, straighten the edge as shown in *figure 6 or 7*.

2. For the band, measure down 80″ on the selvage and across 5″ on the width and mark. If using percale, clip at the marks. Tear down as far as the 80″ mark and tear or cut across. If weave is less firm, it is advisable to pull a thread and cut as in *figure 6*.

3. For the skirt, measure down 28″ along selvage, mark. Tear across or pull thread and cut. Repeat.

4. For the ruffles, measure down 5½″ along selvage and mark, tear across or pull thread and cut. Repeat this 3 more times.

5. For the back, fold the remaining fabric over about 7½″. Be sure that the fold is on the straight of the goods (*see figure 5*). Place the center edge of the pattern about ½″ from fold and parallel to it. Pin pattern to fabric with pins placed at right angles as shown in *figure 8*. Cut around edge of pattern. Slit the fabric along the fold (the extra allowance will

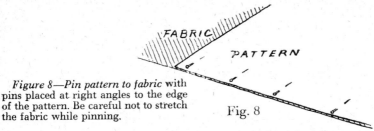

Figure 8—*Pin pattern to fabric* with
pins placed at right angles to the edge
of the pattern. Be careful not to stretch
the fabric while pinning.

Fig. 8

provide for a seam allowance at the back opening).

6. For the front, fold the remaining fabric over about 7". Be sure that the fold is on the straight of the goods. Place center edge of the pattern on the fold, placing pins at right angles (*figure 8*). Cut around edges and be sure to cut neck lower as indicated on pattern.

7. If any of the edges are fluffy and pulled from tearing, trim and press before sewing.

Place all cut pieces and sewing materials on a table of convenient height; a card table is good for this purpose. A comfortable chair of a suitable height for the table will eliminate the tiresome necessity of stooping over work. Get the habit of working on a table.

Sewing Directions for Pinafore
(All pattern pieces allow ½" for seams.)

Sewing Directions

Skirt and Band

1. Working on a table, take the two pieces cut for the skirt.

2. Since there is no pattern to be matched in the fabric, place the two pieces right sides together, selvage edge to selvage edge to make a plain seam.

3. Pin two pieces together as shown in *figure 9*, edge to edge.

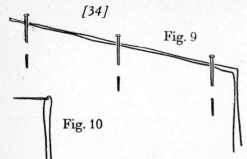

Fig. 9

Fig. 10

Figure 9—Pin edges to be seamed to-gether with pins placed at right angles to the edge about 2" apart.

Figure 10—The correct length for thread is 18" (or about the distance from forefinger to elbow). A longer thread is apt to knot or tangle, or even break. Thread should be cut, rather than broken; then end will be sharp and will pass more readily through the needle.

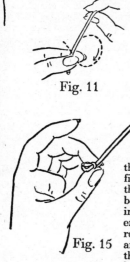

Fig. 11   Fig. 12   Fig. 13   Fig. 14

Fig. 15

*Figures 11–15—How to make a knot—Figure 11—*Grasp the thread about ½" from end between thumb and fore-finger of left hand. *Figure 12—*With the right hand, bring the long end of thread around the left forefinger and in between the forefinger and the left thumb (which is hold-ing down the short end). *Figure 13—*Still holding the long end between the thumb and the forefinger of right hand, roll the short thread end forward between the left thumb and forefinger. *Figure 14—*Continue rolling end through the loop and off the forefinger. *Figure 15—*The resulting loop is pulled down into a knot by the thumb and fore-finger of the left hand.

4. Take the marking chalk and the 6" transparent ruler and mark ½" from edge at fairly close intervals. The ½" is the seam allowance, and it will be the same wherever there is a seam on the garment.

5. To baste, cut off 18" of thread or basting cotton (*figure 10*). Thread the needle and make a knot (*fig-ures 11–15*).

Figure 16—To hold a needle and thimble correctly, first place the thimble on the middle finger of the right hand. Hold the needle between thumb and forefinger, so that the eye is near the thimble finger, and the point is poised in the direction of the work. Needle should be braced against side of thimble, about in position of fingernail.

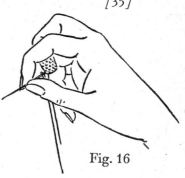

Fig. 16

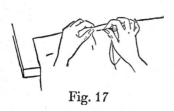

Fig. 17

Figure 17—To hold work properly, rest the left arm on the table. Grasp work with left hand, thumb on top of the end of the work where stitching is to begin. Use the left thumb and forefinger as a guide for work. The work is always between the hand and the body. Sew towards the left shoulder. Place needle in work from the right side for basting and from the wrong side for final stitching.

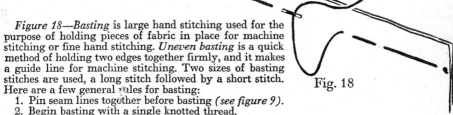

Fig. 18

Figure 18—Basting is large hand stitching used for the purpose of holding pieces of fabric in place for machine stitching or fine hand stitching. *Uneven basting* is a quick method of holding two edges together firmly, and it makes a guide line for machine stitching. Two sizes of basting stitches are used, a long stitch followed by a short stitch. Here are a few general rules for basting:

1. Pin seam lines together before basting *(see figure 9)*.
2. Begin basting with a single knotted thread.
3. Make basting stitches ⅛" nearer edge than desired finished seam line.

6. Hold needle and work as shown in *figures 16 and 17*. Use an uneven basting *(figure 18)*. Baste just outside the marked line ½" from edge.

7. Stitch on marked line by machine (see pages 20 to 26 for general instructions on using a sewing machine). This is a plain seam *(figure 20)*. Since one end of the seam will be included in the hem and the other

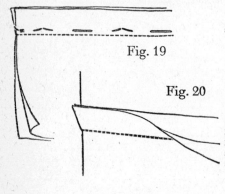

Figure 19—To remove bastings, clip stitches at short intervals so that fabric will not be drawn.

Fig. 19

Fig. 20

Figure 20—To make a plain seam, pin, baste *(see figure 18)* and stitch two pieces of fabric right sides together. The distance from the stitching line to the edge of the fabric is known as the seam allowance. Remove bastings *(see figure 19)* and press open *(see figure 26).*

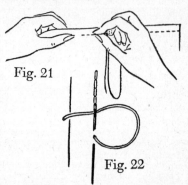

Figure 21—Hand running stitch is used where there is not much strain on a seam. To begin, fasten thread as in *figure 24.* Guide the material in the left hand as for basting. Take very small stitches (4 to 6 threads) of equal length, holding the portion worked taut with the right hand. Several stitches are taken on the needle before it is pulled through. Fasten off thread as in *figure 25.*

Fig. 21

Fig. 22

Figure 22—A back stitch is used where firm hand sewing is needed. The work is held as shown in *figure 23.* Fasten the thread as directed in *figure 24* and take one running stitch. Take the second stitch back over the first one, bringing the needle through to the right side the length of a stitch (4 to 6 threads) ahead of the first stitch. Repeat. Fasten off thread as in *figure 25.*

Figure 23—To hold work for a back stitch, place the fabric over the forefinger of the left hand and hold it firmly with the middle finger and thumb of the left hand.

Fig. 23

Fig. 24

Figure 24—To begin a line of hand stitching, put the needle in from the right side and take a short stitch. Draw the thread through until only a very small end shows. Take a stitch or two back over stitch just made. This fastens the thread securely.

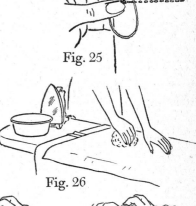

Figure 25—To finish off a line of hand stitching, take one or two stitches back over last stitch and bring the needle to the wrong side. Hold the thread down close to the fabric with the left thumb and pass the needle under the thread. Draw thread up tight to make a knot, still holding thread close to fabric with thumb. Repeat two or three times for stronger knot and clip.

Fig. 25

Figure 26—To press a seam open on cotton fabric, open seam allowance out by creasing along seam with thumb nail. Lay press cloth over opened seam and moisten it with a sponge over seam line. Press over moistened line. Pressing is not ironing. The weight of the iron and the steam do the work. Do not push the iron as if to smooth out wrinkles.

Fig. 26

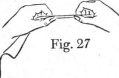

Fig. 27

Fig. 28

Fig. 29

*Figures 27-29—How to Turn a Narrow Hem—Figure 27—*Hold fabric at the right hand end of the edge to be turned between thumb and forefinger of left hand. With the thumb and forefinger of the left hand, turn in edge ¼" and crease with thumb nail for about 2". *Figure 28—*Make a pleat of the creased portion and hold it between thumb and forefinger of right hand. Continue turning hem, creasing with left hand and catching pleats in right hand until there are about three pleats. Give these a hard pinch, release the pleats and go forward repeating the process. *Figure 29—*The edge is turned again in the same manner for the whole length. Baste through all thicknesses. The hem may be stitched by hand *(figure 30)* or by machine.

gathered into the waistband, clip ends of thread close to fabric.

If stitching is done by hand use either plain running stitch *(figure 21)* or back stitch *(figures 22 and 23)*. Begin and finish off hand stitching as in *figures 24 and 25.*

8. Clip basting *(figure 19)* and press seams open *(figure 26)*. With this cotton fabric a press cloth is not necessary, but the seam should be opened out and moistened with a sponge or a cloth thoroughly wet and wrung out. Because the two edges of the seam are

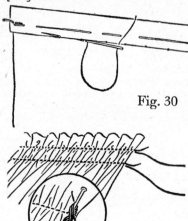

Fig. 30

Figure 30--To do blind hand hemming, hold fabric the same as for a back stitch *(figure 22).* Fasten thread under fold. Take a very small stitch, catching 2 or 3 threads of fabric at edge of fold. Slide point of needle along under fold for about 1/8" and bring needle through the edge of fold. Repeat. Stitches should be small, straight and barely visible.

Fig. 31

Figure 31—To gather by hand or by machine, at least two rows of gathers are made, one on the seam line and another 1/4" nearer edge. Before gathering, divide the edge to be gathered and the edge to which it is to be applied into the same number of equal sections. Mark points with pins or with a few running stitches at right angles to edge. *To make hand gathers,* use a thread at least 6" longer than the distance to which piece is to be gathered. It is not advisable to use a thread more than a yard long. When gathering a longer piece, use a separate thread for each section of gathers. Fasten thread at the beginning *(see figure 24).* Take short, even, running stitches, then push the fabric back on thread without removing the needle. When the end of the row has been reached, draw fabric up to the desired length and wind excess thread around a pin until gathered edge is fitted exactly to the ungathered edge *(see figure 32).* *To machine gather,* adjust machine to six or eight stitches to the inch. Run two rows of stitching along the edge to be gathered, one row on the seam line and one row 1/4" nearer edge. Do not gather more than a yard or so with one continuous thread. Pull stitching up to proper measurement by pulling the under (bobbin) threads of both rows of stitching at the same time. Pull top threads through to wrong side. Wind both threads around a pin until the gathered piece is fitted exactly to the ungathered edge *(see figure 32).*

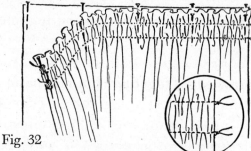

Fig. 32

Figure 32—To apply gathered piece to ungathered edge, match markings on ungathered edge to corresponding markings on gathered edge. Distribute the gathers evenly between markings. Baste edges together along line of gathers on seam line. Fasten off hand gathers as in *figure 25.* Fasten off machine gathers by knotting two threads together as shown, or thread the ends in a needle and take a few stitches. Stitch along gathering line on seam line.

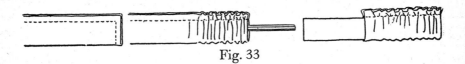

Fig. 33

Figure 33—To turn a belt, insert the blunt end of a pencil into the seamed end. Work the fabric over the pencil until opposite end opening is reached. Then pull the belt through. (If both ends are open, use a safety pin.)

selvages, it is not necessary to finish the edges.

9. On the two short sides turn a narrow (¼") hem *(figures 27–29)*. This may be stitched by machine or hemmed by hand *(figure 30)*.

10. Gather *(figure 31)* the top edge of the skirt to 26" (24" for girl's size, 22" for child's size).

11. The band should be marked at the center and at points 13" to each side (12" for girl's, or 11" for child's).

12. The center seam will serve as a mark on the skirt. Apply band to gathered edge of skirt, edge to edge and right side to right side. Match centers and pin together. Match ends of skirt to marked points on band. Proceed as directed under *figure 32.*

13. Pin, baste and stitch along gathering line which is on seam line.

14. Fold entire band in half lengthwise, right side inside and raw edges together. Pin and baste all raw edges together except across gathered edge of skirt.

15. Stitch on ½" seam line around ends of band (ties) up to skirt. Trim seam to ¼".

16. Turn stitched ends of band (ties) to right side *(figure 33)*. Crease along seam line and baste close

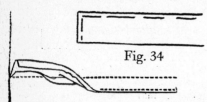

Fig. 34

Figure 34—To finish a turned belt, work out the corners sharply by using an orangewood stick from the inside, or a pin from the outside. Be careful not to pull threads of fabric. Crease edges exactly on seam line and baste close to crease. Press.

Fig. 35   *Figure 35—A flat fell seam* is a strong, tailored seam. Stitch seams on the right side, edge to edge. Trim one edge (the edge towards the back of a garment) ⅛" or less from stitching. Bring longer edge over, creasing at seam line. Turn under raw edge so that finished seam will be ¼" wide. Baste flat to garment. Edge stitch *(see figure 38)* close to fold.

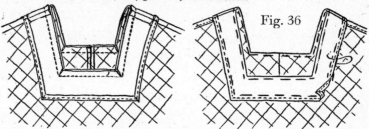

Fig. 36

Figure 36—To finish the neckline with a facing cut to fit, take the patterns used for front and back of the garment and pin to fabric. Cut out front and back neck opening. Cut about 2" across the shoulder edges and down center (unless it is a fold). Mark 2" away from cut neck edges (use ruler and tailor's chalk). Cut around this line. Join facings at shoulder seams in a plain seam *(see figure 20).* Stitch and press open. Turn under outer raw edge ¼" and edge stitch *(see figure 38).* Baste and stitch the entire facing to the neck edge (right sides together). Be sure to take full designated seam allowance. Trim seam to ¼" and clip seam in to stitching line at corners and along curved edges to insure a neat turn. Turn to wrong side, crease at seam line, baste close to crease, press. Slip stitch *(see figure 39)* to garment around outer edge.

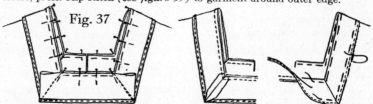

Fig. 37

Figure 37—To finish the neckline with a mitered facing, cut a straight strip of fabric 2" wide and long enough to fit around neck edge. Turn under ¼" along one edge and edge stitch *(see figure 38).* Pin raw edge of strip to neckline, right sides together. Leave a triangular fold at corners. Pin along this fold so that the facing lies perfectly flat. Baste and stitch at corners as shown. Cut away excess fabric to ⅛" and press seam open. Baste and stitch facing to entire neckline, taking full designated seam allowance. Trim seam to ¼" and clip seam in to the stitching line at mitered corner. Turn to wrong side, crease at seam line, baste close to crease, press. Slip stitch *(see figure 39)* to garment around outer edge. (The facing strip may also be made on the bias. See page 48 for instructions on how to cut and join bias strips.)

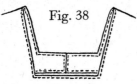

Fig. 38

Figure 38—Edge stitching is a line of machine stitching applied on the right side very close to a fold edge (or to one edge of a seam).

Figure 39—Slip stitch is used for a hem invisible from both sides. Insert needle in fold, slip it along ¼″ or more and bring it through. Take up 1 to 3 threads of fabric directly under the point where the needle comes through. Draw thread through and begin next stitch.

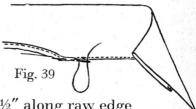

Fig. 39

to crease *(figure 34)*. Turn under ½″ along raw edge that has been left open and baste.

Front and Back of Bib

1. Finish straight opening of back with a narrow (¼″) hem *(see figures 27–29)*.

2. Join back to front at shoulders with a flat fell seam *(figure 35)*.

3. Face neck edge. This may be done in several ways. Two are given under *figures 36 and 37.* The neck may also be finished with a bias strip or with prepared bias binding. (See page 49.)

4. Edge stitch on right side *(figure 38)* and press.

Ruffles

1. Take strips for ruffles. Sew ends together with narrow French seams *(figure 40)*.

2. Cut the long strip thus formed in half and shape the ruffles as shown in accompanying diagram. Note that the centers are marked on three sides.

CENTER CUTTING LINE   CUTTING LINE CENTER
CUT AWAY   CENTER   CUT AWAY

3. On shaped edges of both ruffles make a narrow (⅛″) hem *(see figures 27–29)*.

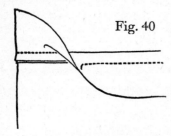

Fig. 40

Figure 40—A French seam is a strong seam, especially adapted for long straight seams on garments of sheer fabrics that do not have any particular fitting problems but need frequent launderings, such as lingerie and baby clothes. Stitch seam on the right side, taking ¼" less than seam allowance designated. Trim seam to ⅛" from stitching line. Turn to wrong side, crease along seam line and baste close to crease. Hand sew or machine stitch ⅛" to ¼" from fold edge, depending on type of fabric and fineness of seam desired.

Figure 41—An overcast finish can be made on a plain seam without pressing the seam open. Trim seam edges evenly and finish by sewing the two edges together with slanting overcast stitches taken from right to left. Make stitches firm, short and about ¼" apart.

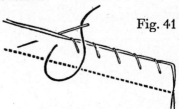

Fig. 41

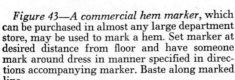

Fig. 42

Figure 42—To take a hem with a yardstick, decide the height from the floor at which dress is to be worn. Have someone mark this distance from the floor with a yardstick at short intervals around the bottom of the skirt, inserting pins parallel to the floor. Person upon whom dress hem is being taken should not turn around but should remain in one spot. Baste on pin line.

Fig. 43

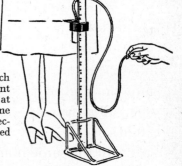

Figure 43—A commercial hem marker, which can be purchased in almost any large department store, may be used to mark a hem. Set marker at desired distance from floor and have someone mark around dress in manner specified in directions accompanying marker. Baste along marked line.

Fig. 44

Figure 44—To mark hem when it is impossible to have any assistance, stand close to a table and mark a line (with chalk or pins) around the skirt where it touches the table. This line must come below the hips so that the skirt will hang straight. Measure the height of the table. Subtract from this figure the distance from the floor at which skirt is ordinarily worn. Measure this distance down from the marked line. For instance, if table is 30" high and skirt is normally worn 17" from floor, mark for hem line 13" down from marked line. Baste along marked line.

4. Mark center on straight edge of each ruffle and gather (*see figures 31 and 32*).

5. Place gathered edge of one ruffle against each side edge of bib, raw edge to raw edge, and right sides together.

6. Pin centers of ruffles to shoulder seams and pin edges together at each end.

7. Draw gathers to fit side of bib (*see figure 32*) and distribute them evenly.

8. Baste, stitch and overcast raw edges of seam together in an overcast seam (*figure 41*).

9. Press seams so that the seam edges turn in toward bib.

10. Edge stitch the side edges of bib on the right side (*see figure 38*).

Attaching Bib to Skirt and Finishing

1. Mark center of lower edge of bib front and center of skirt band.

2. Insert lower edge of bib front ½" under opening in skirt band wrong sides together, matching centers, pin and baste.

3. Slip stitch (*see figure 39*) free edge of band (fold) over the bib, catching stitches through to skirt.

4. In the same manner, insert lower edges of back pieces of bib ½" under opening in skirt band so that the back edges of the bib are at the ends of the opening. Pin, baste and slip stitch.

5. Press bib up and baste top edge of band to bib.

6. Edge stitch (*see figure 38*) all around band.

7. Fasten at back opening (*figure 103*, page 177).

Fig. 45

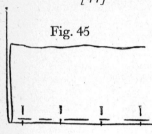

Figure 45—To turn hem, lay garment on table wrong side out and turn hem up on inside of garment along basting line. Place pins at right angles to fold. Baste close to fold. Press on the wrong side and trim to desired width, using a gauge *(see figure 46)*.

Figure 46—This hem gauge is an invaluable aid in marking a hem. It is made available by the publishers of *The New Encyclopedia of Modern Sewing* as a supplement to this book. To use, place lower edge of gauge against fold of hem. Set the handy movable indicator at the correct measurement for a hem, usually about 2″. Mark the fabric with chalk in line with the pointer as shown. Move gauge along hem, continuing marking. It has many other uses, such as keeping an even distance between buttonholes or any fastenings such as hooks and eyes or snaps. It is also used to measure buttonholes and to ensure evenness of width in tucks, pleats and ruffles.

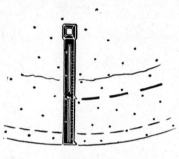

Fig. 46

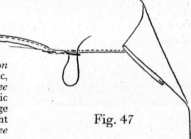

Figure 47—To finish a plain hem on a straight skirt made of cotton fabric, turn in top of hem ½″. Edge stitch *(see figure 38)*. Trim raw edge of fabric close to stitching. Pin and baste edge of hem to skirt, easing in any slight fullness. Slip stitch hem to skirt *(see figure 39)*.

Fig. 47

Hem

1. Put on the pinafore and take the hem *(figures 42, 43, or 44)*.

2. Turn up a 2″ hem *(figure 45)*.

3. Mark and finish hem as shown in *figures 46 and 47*. Press.

2. Sew a Straight Seam

Well, here you are, ready to go on to bigger and better things. Chapter 1 took care of your elementary education! Now you're going to put it to work and learn some new tricks as you go along. In this chapter you'll still be sticking pretty much to the straight and narrow — that is, things which are made largely from straight pieces. You'll be surprised at how many gay and attractive things come under this category — brighteners for the kitchen scene — aprons, pot holders; attractive accessories for the dining table — luncheon and bridge sets, scarves, napkins. Even the bedroom can have its face lifted with simple-to-sew, delightful-to-live-with bedspreads, bureau and dressing table covers. What are we waiting for? Let's get going!

When the fundamentals of sewing have been mastered, there are many simple and attractive articles which may be made for the home. On the pages following, each important room in the house is considered, and suggestions are given for articles to be made. The important subjects of curtains and slip covers are treated separately in Chapters 3 and 4.

USEFUL KITCHEN ACCESSORIES

Pot Holders

Pot Holders   Pot holders are always a necessity in the kitchen, and they may be made in many shapes and forms. Use bright scraps of washable fabrics such as gingham and percale. Cotton batting or scraps of woolen fabric are used for padding.

Round or Square

Pot Holders

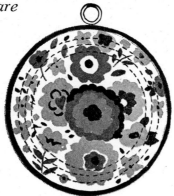

Material (for two):

Plain or printed percale or gingham — ¼ yd.; percale bias trim *(see figure 52)* or a bias strip cut from fabric *(figures 48–51)* — 2 yds. of same or contrasting color; cotton batting or scraps of heavy woolen fabric—¼ yd.

Directions for cutting:

Round Pot Holder — 2 circles of fabric, each 8″ in diameter, and 1 similar circle of cotton batting or of several thicknesses of woolen fabric.

Square Pot Holder — two 8″ squares of fabric and 1 similar square of cotton batting or of several thicknesses of woolen fabric.

Directions for making:

1. Place batting or woolen pieces between two fabric pieces (right sides out) and baste through all thicknesses close to edge.

2. Bind edges with bias trim or bias strip *(figures 53–59)*.

3. Make two or more rows of machine stitching ½″ apart toward center, following edge of binding as a guide.

Fig. 48

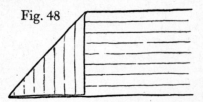

Figure 48—*The true bias grain* is found by folding a lengthwise thread to meet a crosswise thread. The selvage edge of the fabric is always straight, and before trying to find the true bias, the crosswise edge should be straightened (*see figure 6, page 32*). Fold one corner of the fabric so that the selvage edge (or a lengthwise thread) lies along a crosswise thread. A right angle is formed by the selvage. The long side (fold) of the triangle is the true bias. Fabric cut on the true bias can be curved or fitted more easily than pieces cut on the straight thread. For this reason, bias cut strips are frequently used for finishing raw edges. A bias strip may be made from self fabric, or bias may be purchased already cut and folded on cards. In this form it is usually known as bias trim (*see figure 52*).

Bias Finishes

Figure 49—To cut bias strips, find the longest possible true bias (*see figure 48*). Press along fold and cut along crease. This edge is a true bias edge, and strips are cut parallel to it. The width of the strip is determined by the width of the trimming or facing desired, plus seam allowances. When the bias strip is to be used for a facing (bias will not show on right side), determine the width of the facing and add ½" for seam allowances. When bias strip is to be applied as binding over a raw edge (bias will show on both sides of edge), the cut width of the bias strip should be twice the width of the finished binding showing on the right side, plus ½" for seam allowances. Mark off lines desired width away from the true bias edge and parallel to it. Mark with tailor's chalk, using a ruler or yardstick. Cut along these lines.

Fig. 49

Fig. 50

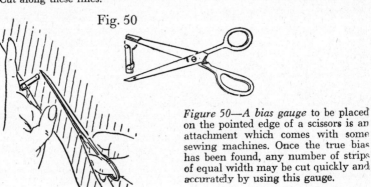

Figure 50—*A bias gauge* to be placed on the pointed edge of a scissors is an attachment which comes with some sewing machines. Once the true bias has been found, any number of strips of equal width may be cut quickly and accurately by using this gauge.

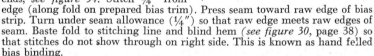

Figure 51—To join bias strips, place the straight lengthwise ends of two strips at right angles to each other, right sides together. The points of the angles should extend just enough at each end so that the bias edges meet exactly on the ⅛" seam line. Baste the strips together and stitch with a ⅛" seam on the straight of the goods. Be

Fig. 51

careful not to sew the lengthwise grain to the crosswise grain, but always match lengthwise to lengthwise and crosswise to crosswise. Stitch together enough pieces to make the desired length, following the rules given. Snip selvage edges (if there are any) to avoid pulled seams. Press seams open and carefully clip the small triangles extending beyond strip.

Fig. 52

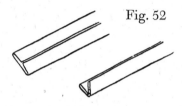

Figure 52—Commercial bias trim may be purchased already cut, folded and wound on cards. It is usually made in either percale or lawn. Bias trim is cut 1" wide. "Single fold" bias trim has ¼" turned under along each edge. "Double fold" bias trim is folded again through the center so that it is all ready to apply as binding over a raw edge.

Bias Finishes

Figure 53—To apply a bias strip as a binding, cut a strip as long as the edge to be bound plus 2", to allow for a joining. If binding is to be applied to an edge (such as a neck edge) where there is a seam allowance, first trim seam allowance from edge. Place edge of bias strip against edge to be bound, right sides together. Baste to edge, shaping it if the edge is curved. Be careful not to pull the binding as it is applied, because the edges are easily stretched. To make a joining at the ends, *see figure 54.* Stitch ¼" from

Fig. 53

edge (along fold on prepared bias trim). Press seam toward raw edge of bias strip. Turn under seam allowance (¼") so that raw edge meets raw edges of seam. Baste fold to stitching line and blind hem *(see figure 30, page 38)* so that stitches do not show through on right side. This is known as hand felled bias binding.

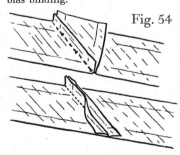

Fig. 54

Figure 54—To join ends when applying bias binding, trim strip diagonally at beginning on the straight grain. In basting the binding to the article, leave this end free for about ½" and stop just before reaching the end. Smooth out the binding so that it meets the other end and seam the ends diagonally on the straight grain of the fabric *(see figure 51)*. Press the seam open so that the joining is perfectly flat.

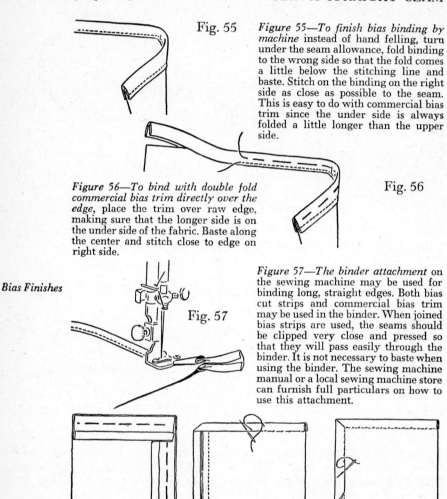

Fig. 55

Figure 55—To finish bias binding by machine instead of hand felling, turn under the seam allowance, fold binding to the wrong side so that the fold comes a little below the stitching line and baste. Stitch on the binding on the right side as close as possible to the seam. This is easy to do with commercial bias trim since the under side is always folded a little longer than the upper side.

Figure 56—To bind with double fold commercial bias trim directly over the edge, place the trim over raw edge, making sure that the longer side is on the under side of the fabric. Baste along the center and stitch close to edge on right side.

Fig. 56

Bias Finishes

Fig. 57

Figure 57—The binder attachment on the sewing machine may be used for binding long, straight edges. Both bias cut strips and commercial bias trim may be used in the binder. When joined bias strips are used, the seams should be clipped very close and pressed so that they will pass easily through the binder. It is not necessary to baste when using the binder. The sewing machine manual or a local sewing machine store can furnish full particulars on how to use this attachment.

Fig. 58

Fig. 59

Figures 58 and 59—How to Turn a Square Corner with Bias Binding—Figure 58—Baste to within the seam's width of the corner. Fold corner as shown. On the other side of the fold bring the thread through at the point where basting stopped and continue basting seam of the same width around the next side. Stitch. *Figure 59*—Turn binding to wrong side, fold corners in a miter as shown and fell down binding with blind hemming stitches (*see figure 30, page 38*).

Double Oven Mitt

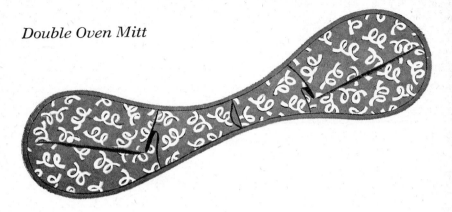

Material:

Plain or printed percale or gingham — ½ yd.; percale
bias trim *(see figure 52)* or a bias strip cut from fabric *Pot Holders*
(see figures 48–51) — 2 yds. of same or contrasting
color; cotton batting or scraps of heavy woolen fabric
— ½ yd.

Directions for cutting:

Pattern No. IV (see figure 4, page 29, for directions
for enlarging pattern from diagram) — 4 pieces of
fabric, 2 pieces of cotton batting or several thicknesses
of woolen fabric.

Pattern No. V (enlarge as above) — 2 pieces of fabric.

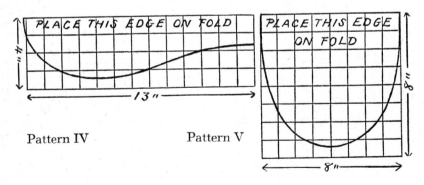

Pattern IV   Pattern V

Directions for making:

1. Join two No. IV pieces with a plain seam (¼″) along straight edge and press seam open. Repeat for the other two No. IV pieces.

2. Place batting between these two pieces and baste through all thicknesses close to edge.

3. Pin rounded edges of No. V pieces to rounded edges of No. IV pieces, easing in fullness (*figure 61*) and baste.

Fig. 60

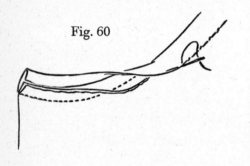

Figure 60—A bias strip used for facing is stitched edge to edge as for binding (*see figure 53*). Take a ¼″ seam. Turn strip to other side on the stitching line, baste close to fold, press. Blind hem (*see figure 30*, page 38), or stitch flat by machine. If there is a corner it is mitered as shown in *figure 59*. If the facing is to be on the wrong side of the article, apply the bias strip to the article right sides together. If the facing is to be brought to the right side of the article (to form a trim) apply the right side of bias strip to the wrong side of the article.

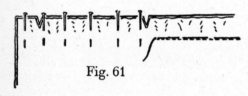

Fig. 61

Figure 61—Easing in fullness means that fullness is eased into one edge of a seam without gathering the fabric. In pinning, basting and stitching, keep the full side of the joining on top. Pin with fullness distributed as desired. Baste on the seam line with small stitches, spaced very closely together to hold the fullness in evenly.

4. Cut a 4″ strip of bias trim, fold in half and stitch fold edges together. Baste at center seam for loop. Ends are caught in binding.

5. Bind all around with bias trim or bias strip (*see figures 53–59*).

Aprons

Aprons are a necessity in the kitchen and they may be pretty as well as practical. They should be made of fabrics which launder easily and well, such as gingham, percale or unbleached muslin. Dainty party aprons may be made of organdie or dotted swiss. Bias trim in various combinations makes an easy and attractive trimming. There are many commercial patterns for aprons. The directions on page 54 for a simple apron made without a pattern may be applied to any of the fabrics mentioned.

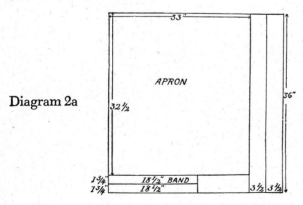

Diagram 2a

Organdie
Apron

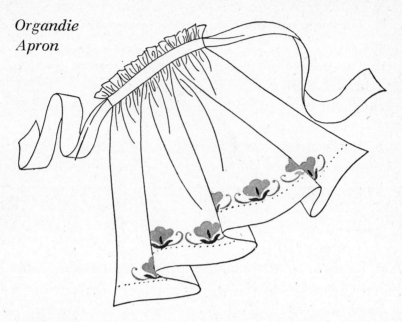

Material:

Organdie—-1⅛ yds. of white; scraps of light weight cotton fabric in a pretty color for appliqué.

Directions for cutting (see diagram 2a, page 53):

Skirt—1 piece, 32½″ by 33″
Ties—2 pieces, each 3½″ by 36″
Bands—2 pieces, each 1¾″ by 18½″

Directions for making apron: (½″ seams allowed)

1. On the band pieces, turn under and press ¼″ around all sides.

2. On the ties, make a narrow hem (*see figures 27-29, page 37*) along two long sides and one short side.

3. On the skirt, make a narrow hem along each long side.

4. On one short side, fold 1¼" to wrong side, baste and press.

5. On the same side, make two rows of gathers (through both thicknesses) (*see figure 31*, page 38), the first row 1" from the fold edge and the second row 1" below.

6. Pleat unfinished ends of ties to measure 1" and baste to skirt on the right side between the lines of gathers, lapping ends of ties ½" over side edges of skirt.

7. Baste band to right side of skirt over the rows of gathers, covering the tie ends. Edge stitch all around (*see figure 38*, page 41).

8. Baste the other band piece to the wrong side of skirt over the gathers and slip stitch in place (*see figure 39*, page 41).

9. Make a 2½" hem at lower edge of apron (*see figure 47*, page 44). (For most adults, a 2½" hem will make the apron the correct length. Pin this amount up and try on apron, adjusting as necessary.)

10. Trim just above hem line with a dainty appliqué (see pages 268 and 270 for design and directions).

Potholder Apron
Unbleached Muslin Apron with Bias Trim

These two aprons are pictured on page 56. They are variations of the same design that is used in the organdie apron and can be made from the same directions. The potholders button on and have an extra flap added for a pocket.

Pot Holder
Apron

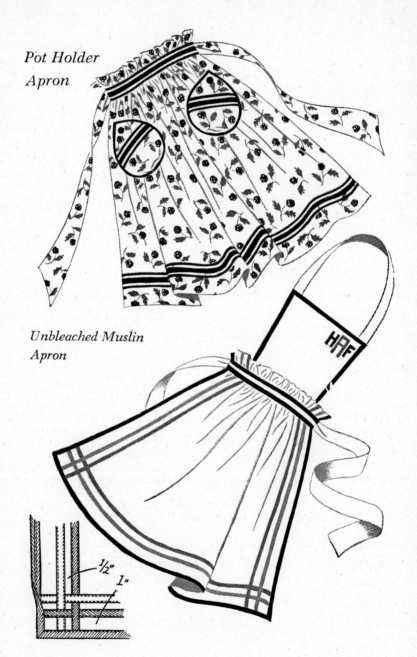

Unbleached Muslin
Apron

Mother and Daughter Aprons

Size 14 and Size 8
Picture and patterns, pages 58 and 59

Materials:

Plain fabric (linen like rayon)—(mother) ¾ yd.;
(daughter) ½ yd. . . . Flowered Chintz—(mother) ⅝
yd.; (daughter) ⅜ yd. . . . Percale bias trim, double fold
(*see figure 52,* page 49) in contrasting color—
(mother) 11 yds.; (daughter) 9 yds.

Directions for Cutting: (*See figure 4,* page 29.)

Patterns (page 59)	Mother	Daughter
Bodice Front (plain)	1 piece (Pattern VIa)	1 piece (Pattern VIc)
Bodice Back (plain)	2 pieces (Pattern VIb)	2 pieces (Pattern VId)
Apron Skirt (chintz)	1 piece (21½" x 36")	1 piece (10½" x 36")
Bottom Band (plain)	1 piece (6" x 36")	1 piece (3¼" x 36")

Directions for making either apron: (½" seams are
allowed)

1. Baste and stitch the darts on bodice front, right sides
together, as shown by X's; graduate to single X at
points. Press darts to one side. Stitch darts on back
bodice in same way.

2. Baste and stitch side seams of bodice, right sides
together. Press open.

3. Press out center fold of bias trim for about 32"
(mother), 26" (daughter). Pin in crisscross design
down center front of bodice, taking in fullness on inner
curved edge by making a small dart. Baste and top
stitch close to each edge.

4. Bind edges of back opening and neckline of bodice

Mother and Daughter Aprons
Directions for making given on page 57.

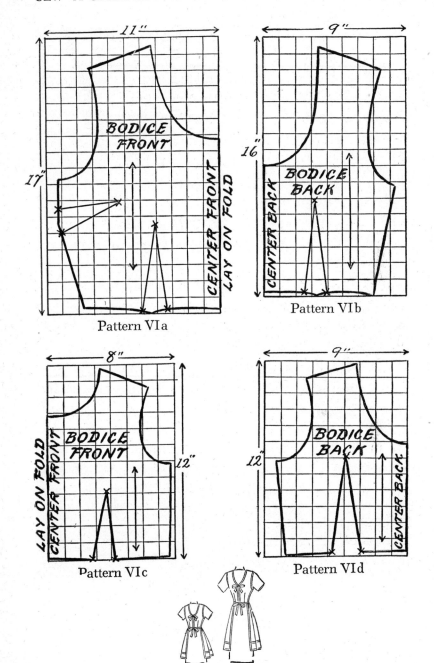

Pattern VIa

Pattern VIb

Pattern VIc

Pattern VId

with bias trim. Bind armholes in same way. (See *figure 56*, page 50.)

5. Baste and stitch bottom band to lower edge of apron, wrong sides together. Press seam open. Turn seam allowance on lower edge of band to right side; press.

6. Press out center fold of bias trim for 2 yds. and baste over seam joining apron and bottom band and again across lower edge of bottom band. Top stitch close to each edge of bias trim.

7. Bind side edges of apron with bias trim.

8. Run gathering stitches at upper edge of apron (*see figure 31*, page 38).

9. Baste and stitch gathered apron to bodice front, wrong side to wrong side, adjusting gathers evenly (*see figure 32*, page 38). Trim seam to ¼″.

10. Bind seam joining bodice and apron skirt.

11. For ties, fold a piece of bias trim about 2 yds. long on the length so that the right side is inside and raw edges are even. Sew twice close to raw edges. Turn to right side.

12. From this piece, cut 20″ for a bow at center front waistline and divide remainder into four parts for ties at neck and waist. Finish ends by folding under raw edges and slip stitching.

Fig. 62

Figure 62—Whip stitch is used to catch an edge to another piece of fabric. It is done with small slanted stitches. Catch through only a few threads of the under piece of fabric and then through the edge which is being whipped down. Whip stitch is also used for joining edges (see index).

Kitchen Tablecloths

Tablecloths for the kitchen should be bright and cheerful. Indian Head, a firmly woven linen-like cotton is a good inexpensive fabric to use for these cloths. Linen, sailcloth, percale, or unbleached muslin may also be used. Since these fabrics are usually 36″ wide, a small size cloth 36″ by 36″ may be made from 1 yd. An additional ¾ yd. will make 6 napkins, 12″ by 12″. To insure a straight edge when cutting linens, always measure, draw a thread and cut along it *(see figure 6, page 32)*. Finish in any of the ways under *Suggested Finishes for Table Linens*, beginning on page 65.

A larger luncheon cloth, 72″ by 72″, may be made from 4 yds. Cut the fabric into yard lengths (see above). Turn a narrow hem *(see figures 27–29, page 37)* along two adjacent sides of each piece. Stitch by hand. Fagot the four pieces together along the finished edges *(figures 63, 64 or 65)*. Finish the edges with a napery or damask hem *(figure 66)* or a narrow machine hem *(see figures 27–29, page 37)*. To get more wear from worn linens, cut them into squares, cutting away the worn spots, and piece them together again in this manner.

Kitchen Tablecloths

Fig. 63

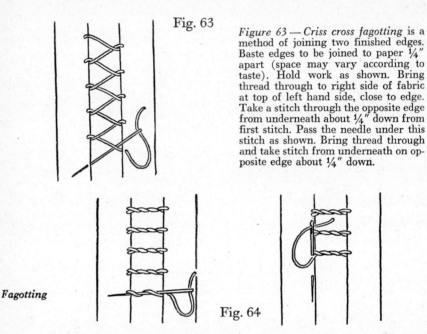

Figure 63 — Criss cross fagotting is a method of joining two finished edges. Baste edges to be joined to paper ¼" apart (space may vary according to taste). Hold work as shown. Bring thread through to right side of fabric at top of left hand side, close to edge. Take a stitch through the opposite edge from underneath about ¼" down from first stitch. Pass the needle under this stitch as shown. Bring thread through and take stitch from underneath on opposite edge about ¼" down.

Fagotting

Fig. 64

Figure 64—Bar fagotting is prepared and started as in *figure 63*. **Take first stitch straight across opening and bring needle through right edge from underneath. Twist the needle under and over thread. Put needle into the fabric on the left side from top, slide through fold ¼" and bring through to start next stitch.**

Fig. 65

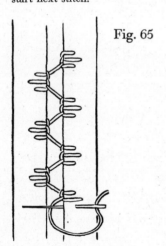

Figure 65 — To use grouped blanket stitches like regular fagotting on an open-work seam, prepare edges as in *figure 63*. Work blanket stitches alternately on either side of opening.

FINE LINENS FOR THE DINING ROOM TABLE

Damask Linen Cloth and Napkins

For special occasions and family gatherings there Damask Cloth
is nothing to surpass a damask linen tablecloth and
napkins. Unhemmed cloths may be purchased in regulation sizes 72″ by 72″, 72″ by 90″, 72″ by 108″, 72″
by 126″, 72″ by 144″. The napkins are usually 22″ by
22″ and are purchased uncut by the dozen. The raw
edges are always finished with a napery or damask
hem (*figure 66*). Since it takes quite some time to pre-

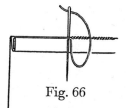

Figure 66—Napery or damask hem is used for hemming linens, especially fine table linens. Turn hem
twice as for a narrow hem (*see figures 27–29, page
37*), making the complete hem less than ¼″ wide.
Crease hem back (to right side) at fold of hem.
Catch both creases together with a small overhand
stitch made at right angles to the fabric edge, as
shown. Take up only two threads of fabric.

Fig. 66

pare this hem for hand sewing, the attachment on
the sewing machine known as the foot hemmer (see
machine manual) may be used to very good advantage. Set the hemmer for the desired narrow width
(¼″). Remove the thread from the machine needle
but do not remove the needle. Run the edges to be

turned through the hemmer, and the hem will be evenly turned. The needle softens up the edges of the fabric, making it easy to do the hand sewing.

Luncheon Sets

Luncheon sets are the special joy of the homemaker. They are easy to launder and permit variety in table settings. Fabrics may range from unbleached muslin, percale and heavy linen to fine linen, dotted Swiss and organdie. A luncheon set consists of one runner; place mats, usually four, six or eight; and napkins, the same number as the place mats. The sizes are as follows: Runner   — 14″ x 24″ (or 36″)
Place Mat — 12″ x 18″
Napkin   — 16″ x 16″

Various finishes for luncheon sets are given next. The cut sizes above allow for fringing a narrow hem, or binding, but if the finish decided upon has a deeper hem, add the necessary number of inches all around.

To insure a straight edge when cutting linens, always measure, draw a thread and cut along it *(see figure 6, page 32).*

Suggested Finishes For Table Linens

The finishes which follow may be applied to luncheon sets or cloths, or to any sort of a doily or runner. Where edge finish is plain and further decoration is desired, use appliqué, embroidery or embroidered monograms (see index).

Finishes for Linens

1. The edge may be fringed *(figure 67)*.

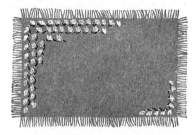

2. A narrow hem may be hand rolled *(figure 68)*.

3. The edge may be bound *(see figures 49–54)*.

4. The edge may be scalloped and bound (*figure 69*), in the same or contrasting color.

5. The hem may be hand hemstitched (*figures 70–79*).

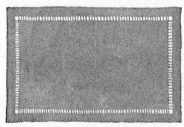

6. The edge may be finished with a hand hemstitched hem and the body of the runner, place mat or napkin divided into sections as shown and double hemstitched by hand (*see figures 70–79*). After hems have been basted, clip threads as shown and draw threads through body of piece. Turn clipped thread ends under into hem and finish this space in hem as a corner.

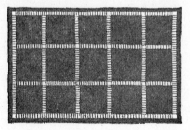

7. A hem 1″ to 2″ wide may be finished with napery or damask stitch *(see figure 66)*. The corners may either be mitered *(see figures 70–73)*, or the hems may overlap *(figure 80)*.

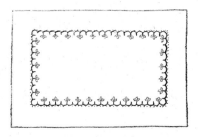

8. A hem 1″ or 2″ wide may be turned to the right side and edge stitched *(figure 81)*. The corners are mitered.

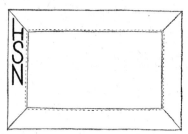

9. A hem turned to the right side may be piped with a contrasting color *(figure 82)*.

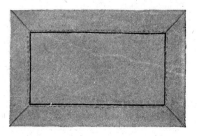

10.   A hem turned to the right side may be scalloped at the edges and piped (*figures 83 and 84*).

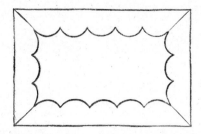

11.   The edge may be piped and faced at the same time with a contrasting color (*figure 85*).

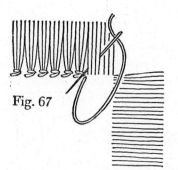

Fig. 67

Figure 67—Fringing may be used best on fabrics which have fairly heavy threads, such as heavy linen, monk's cloth and Indian Head. Pull threads to make fringe of desired width. The fringe may be strengthened to prevent threads from pulling out by hemstitching (*see figures 70–79*).

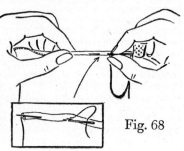

Fig. 68

Figure 68—A hand rolled hem gives a fine professional finish. First, machine stitch very close to edge of fabric to give it body. Roll edge with thumb and forefinger of left hand and slip stitch (*see figure 39, page 41*). The finished hem should be less than $\frac{1}{8}$" wide.

Figure 69 — Scallops of any size or depth may be marked on fabric by making a pattern of desired size from cardboard. Mark edge to be scalloped into sections equal to size of scallop and mark a scallop in each section by drawing around pattern with chalk. The edges are bound as in *figure 53,* page 49. Clip points between scallops when turning binding. Scallops look best when they are finished by hand.

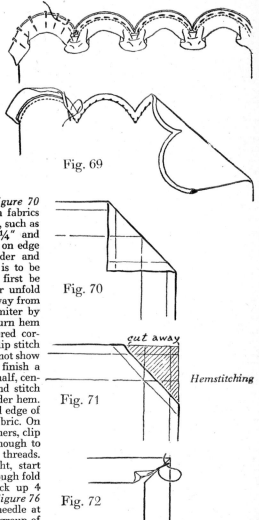

Fig. 69

Figures 70-79—How to Hemstitch—Figure 70 —Hemstitching can be worked only on fabrics from which threads can be easily drawn, such as linen, monk's cloth, etc. Turn under ¼" and crease *(see figures 27 and 28,* page 37) on edge or edges to be hemstitched. Turn under and crease hem of desired width. If piece is to be hemstitched all around, corners must first be mitered. *Figure 71*—To miter a corner unfold creased hem and cut away corner ¼" away from crease. *Figure 72*—When finishing a miter by hand, turn in ¼" along corner edge, turn hem under again all around, bringing mitered corners together and finish corner with a slip stitch *(see figure 39,* page 41). Stitches should not show through on right side. *Figure 73*—To finish a miter by machine, fold corner crease in half, center exactly at point of inside corner and stitch by machine. Press seam open. Turn under hem. *Figure 74*—Baste hem. Be sure that fold edge of hem follows a straight thread of the fabric. On the wrong side close to fold edges at corners, clip the number of threads to be drawn (enough to make a space ⅛" to ¼" wide). Draw threads. *Figure 75*—Working from left to right, start hemstitching by bringing needle up through fold of hem and draw thread through. Pick up 4 threads with needle from right to left. *Figure 76* — Circle group of threads and insert needle at back of hem, emerging just to right of group of threads. *Figure 77*—To make corner of hemstitching secure, use a blanket stitch worked closely to hold edges together. *Figure 78*—For plain double hemstitching, repeat the operations on other side of drawn threads as in *figures 75 and 76. Figure 79*—For diagonal hemstitching, divide groups of threads (taking 2 from each) when hemstitching other side of drawn threads.

Fig. 70

cut away

Hemstitching

Fig. 71

Fig. 72

Fig. 73

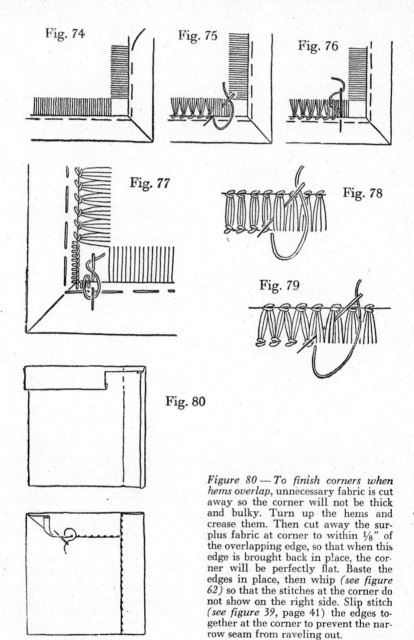

Fig. 74   Fig. 75   Fig. 76

Fig. 77   Fig. 78

Fig. 79

Fig. 80

Figure 80 — To finish corners when hems overlap, unnecessary fabric is cut away so the corner will not be thick and bulky. Turn up the hems and crease them. Then cut away the surplus fabric at corner to within ⅛" of the overlapping edge, so that when this edge is brought back in place, the corner will be perfectly flat. Baste the edges in place, then whip *(see figure 62)* so that the stitches at the corner do not show on the right side. Slip stitch *(see figure 39,* page 41) the edges together at the corner to prevent the narrow seam from raveling out.

Figure 81—A hem turned to the right side makes a decorative band effect. This may be done only on fabrics which have no right or wrong side. If there is a seam in the fabric that is to be hemmed in this way, clip the seam a little below where the top of the hem is to come and seam the part that is to be inside the hem on the right side. The corners are mitered by machine *(see figures 70–73)* to make a neat finish on the right side.

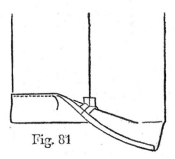

Fig. 81

Fig. 82

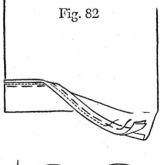

Figure 82 — A piping is a narrow bias fold of the same or contrasting fabric used to decorate edges and seams. Use a 1″ bias strip *(see figures 48–52)* folded in half. When using commercial bias trim, press flat and fold through center. Baste the bias fold under the fold edge of hem so that only a narrow edge is visible. Machine stitch close to fold edge of hem.

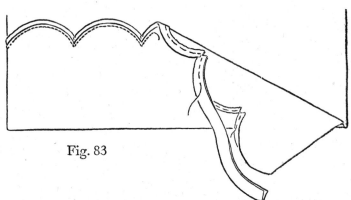

Fig. 83

Figure 83—Piping may be used to trim a convex scalloped edge, turned to the right side as a hem. Mark and cut scallops in same manner as in *figure 69.* Clip in ⅛″ at each point between the scallops. Turn the scalloped edge under ⅛″ and baste close to the turned edge. Prepare piping as in *figure 82* and baste the bias fold in place under scalloped edge so that only a narrow edge is visible, clipping it at the point of each scallop. Machine stitch close to fold edge of scallop, lifting the presser foot and pivoting the work on the machine needle at the points between the scallops.

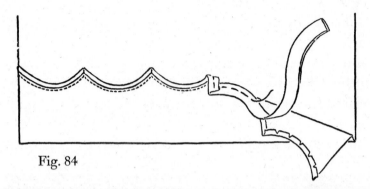

Fig. 84

Figure 84—For bias trim piping for concave scallops, mark and cut scallops using a cardboard guide as in *figure 69.* Clip the edge, as shown, making the slashes not more than ⅛" deep. Turn edge under ⅛" as shown, being careful to make the points of the scallops sharp and true. Prepare piping as in *figure 82* and baste bias fold in place so that only a narrow edge is visible. Fold bias as shown at points. Stitch as in *figure 83.*

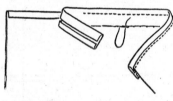

Fig. 85

Figure 85—To combine piping and facing, cut a bias strip *(see figures 48–52)* and press the edges under, making the fold on one edge twice as deep as on the other. Turn under ¼" along edges to be finished with facing. Place the wide fold of the bias under the folded edge of the fabric, so that it shows about ⅛". Baste and stitch on the right side of fabric close to fold edge. Slip stitch *(see figure 39,* page 41) the opposite edge to fabric on wrong side.

Figure 86—For a piped seam, prepare piping as in *figure 82.* Baste bias strip to right side of one edge of fabric to be seamed so that the fold is ⅛" inside seam line and raw edges of piping are against raw edge of fabric. Apply the other piece of fabric as for a regular seam. (Where seam allowance is ½", if bias strip is cut 1¼" wide, raw edges of seam and piping will be even.)

Fig. 86

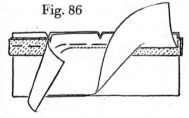

Directions for several complete luncheon sets of various types are given in the following pages. The *Luncheon Set* fabrics and colors mentioned are those which are used in the illustrations. Any other suitable fabrics in any desired colors may be substituted except in the *Monk's Cloth Set*, page 77. For this, monk's cloth is the only fabric which can be woven in the manner described.

Appliqué Luncheon Set

Material (for four settings):

Pastel linen (36″ wide)— 1½ yds.; organdie — ¾ yd.; chintz — floral design to blend with the pastel, enough yardage for 6 flower motifs, each roughly about 5″ or 6″ in diameter, and 4 smaller flower motifs about 1½″ in diameter.

Directions for cutting:

Cut from linen *(see diagram 2e):*

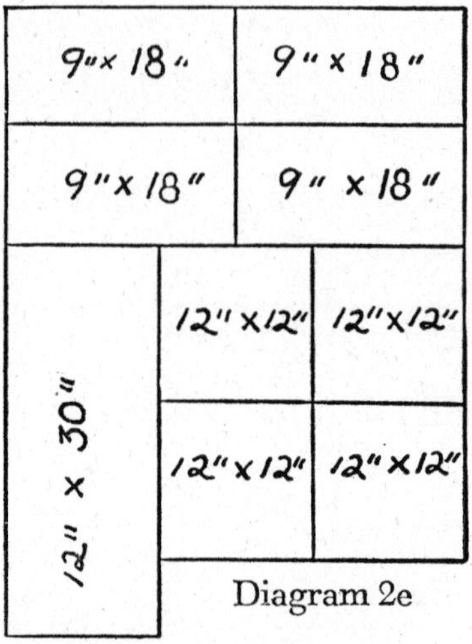

Diagram 2e

Place Mats — 4 pieces, each 9″ by 18″
Center Runner — 1 piece, 12″ by 30″
Napkins — 4 pieces, each 12″ by 12″
Cut from organdie:
Place Mat Trim — 4 pieces, each 7″ by 18″
Center Runner Trim — 2 pieces, each 7″ by 12″
Napkin Trim — 4 pieces, each 3″ by 12″
Cut from chintz:
Flower Motifs — 6 large motifs, 4 small motifs (leave ¼″ around outer edges to turn under).
Directions for making:
Place Mat

1. Hand roll hem *(see figure 68)* one long side and **two** short sides of each place mat piece.

2. Place raw edge against one 18″ raw edge of a 7″

by 18″ piece of organdie, right sides together. Ends of organdie will extend over finished sides of linen piece. They should extend the same amount at each side. Baste.

3. Stitch together with 2 rows of stitching, ¼″ and ⅛″ from edge.

4. Trim seam close to ⅛″ stitching line and press seam toward organdie.

5. Turn under ⅛″ along 18″ edge of organdie and baste.

6. Fold organdie to meet seam line, right side inside. Stitch ends together on a straight line with sides of linen.

7. Turn to right side.

8. Slip stitch fold edge to stitching line (see figure 39, page 41). Make stitches very fine; be sure they do not show on the right side.

Center Runner

1. Hand roll hem both 30″ edges.

2. Finish ends of runner with 7″ by 12″ pieces of organdie in same manner as for *Place Mat* above.

Napkin

1. Hand roll hem all edges.

2. Fold 3″ by 12″ piece of organdie in half lengthwise, right side inside.

3. Stitch 1½″ ends together so that this piece when finished is the same length as one side of hemmed napkin.

4. Turn to right side, press.

5. Turn in raw edges ⅛″, baste and press.

6. Place fold of organdie strip edge to edge with one side of napkin. Pin in place all along edge.

7. Baste and slip stitch (*see figure 39*, page 41) opposite edge and ends to linen.

Where To Apply Motifs

Apply motifs partly on organdie and partly on linen (see photograph on page 73). Place Mats — Upper left hand corner; Center Runner — Upper left hand corner and lower right hand corner; Napkins — Lower right hand corner.

How to Apply Motifs

Turn raw edges to wrong side all around outline of motif and baste. Where indentations in outline occur, clip in to outline to make a sharp corner. Blind stitch (*see figure 30*, page 38) to fabric.

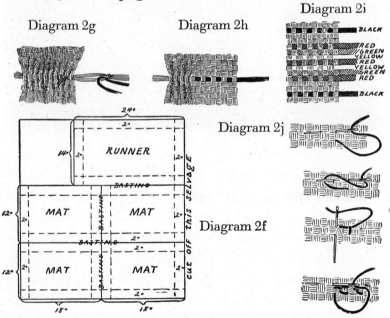

Diagram 2g   Diagram 2h   Diagram 2i

Diagram 2j

Diagram 2f

Monk's Cloth Luncheon Set with Woven Trim
Material (for four settings):
Monk's cloth (36″ wide) — 1¼ yds.; cotton rug yarn
— 1 ball each of red, green, yellow, black or any four
contrasting colors; Indian Head or linen to match one
of contrasting colors — ¾ yd. (to make 4 napkins, each
12″ by 12″).

Directions for Making

1. Cut off one selvage edge and pull out two or three strands each made up of 4 threads. (The single threads are used later for hemstitching.)

2. By means of bastings, mark cloth off for a runner and four place mats *(see diagram 2f)*.

3. Before cutting the pieces apart the contrasting threads are woven in:

a. Measure up 2″ from lower edge of piece along the side where selvage was cut, and at that point pull one strand (made up of 4 threads). The fabric will pucker slightly, since the other end of the strand is still caught in the opposite selvage edge.

b. Make a knot in the end which is pulled out *(diagram 2g)*.

c. Insert black rug yarn through strand under knot as if through the eye of a needle *(diagram 2g)*.

d. Pull out opposite end of strand at selvage, weaving the rug yarn through as the strand is pulled out *(diagram 2h)*. Ease the knot through with thumbnail as yarn is pulled through.

e. Thread the black rug yarn through in this manner 2″ to each side of basting lines which mark off mats and runner, as indicated by dotted lines on *diagram 2f*.

f. In the same manner, work the pattern *(diagram 2i)* in toward center of mats from each of these lines of black rug yarn.

g. Work same pattern 2″ in from side edges.

h. Cut the runner away from group of four mats along basting line. Work same pattern in on either side of the basting line which marks the ends of the mats.

   i.   Work pattern at other end of runner.

   4.   Cut out mats and runner along basting lines and hemstitch *(diagram 2j)* all around each piece, 1¼″ in from edge, using a single thread from strands of thread pulled out previously *(step 1)*.

   5.   Fringe edges up to hemstitching.

   6.   Fringe napkins *(see figure 67)*.

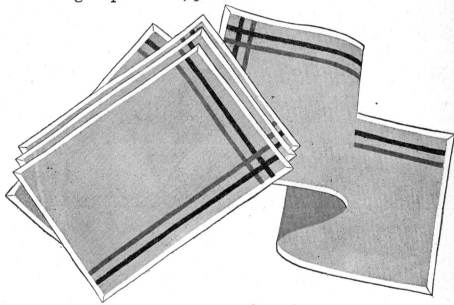

Unbleached Muslin Luncheon Set
with Bias Trimming

Material (for four settings):

Unbleached muslin (36″ wide)—1 yd.; percale bias trim—5 yds. each of black and aqua, 10 yds. of red (color used to bind outer edges), or any other colors; Indian Head to match one of contrasting colors—¾ yd. (to make 4 napkins, each 12″ by 12″).

Directions for cutting (see diagram 2k):
Cut from unbleached muslin:
Place Mats—4 pieces, each 12″ (selvage) by 18″
Center Runner—1 piece, 12″ (selvage) by 36″
Cut from Indian Head:
Napkins—4 pieces, each 12″ by 12″
Directions for making:

1. On one long and one short edge (lower and right hand edges of place mats), mark a line with tailor's chalk 3″ in from edge and another line 2″ in from edge. These lines will cross at corners.

2. On 3″ line baste aqua bias trim flat so that the edge toward center is directly on marked line. Cross strips at corners as shown in *diagram 2l.*

3. On the 2″ line do the same with black bias trim and cross at corners as in diagram.

4. Machine stitch close to both edges of all strips.

5. Apply red bias trim to edge as facing on the right side *(see figure 60).*

6. Fringe napkins *(see figure 67).*

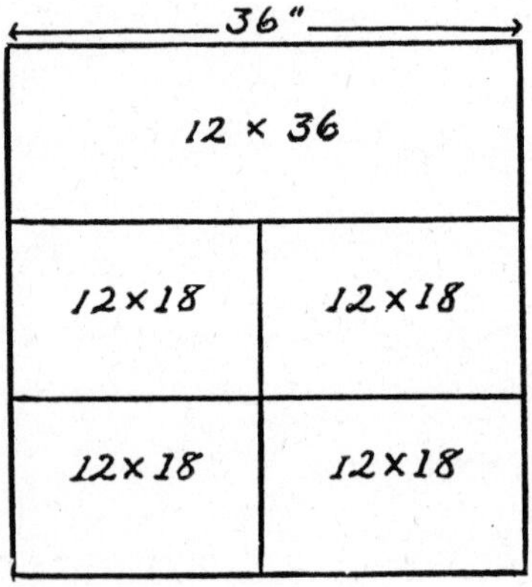

Diagram 2k

36″

12 × 36

12 × 18   12 × 18

12 × 18   12 × 18

Diagram 2l

1″

½″

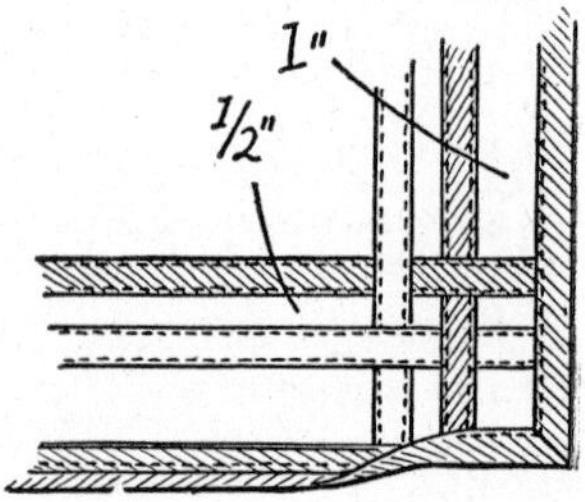

Table Scarves

Scarves which may be used on serving tables are made in the following sizes: 16" by 35", 16" by 44" and 16" by 52". Fabrics are the same as those suggested for luncheon sets (see page 64). For finishes, see *Suggested Finishes for Table Linens*, beginning on page 65.

Cocktail Napkins

The correct size for cocktail napkins is 6" by 9". Fine ones are made of handkerchief linen. A fringed hem that is hemstitched *(see figure 67)* or a hand rolled hem *(see figure 68)* is the easiest finish, but many of the finishes under *Suggested Finishes for Table Linens*, beginning on page 65, are suitable. Napkins can be made amusing and gay with appliqués, or with embroidery, see index.

Bridge Cloths

Bridge Cloths   A dainty cloth to fit a bridge table should measure 36″ by 36″. The napkins are 11″ by 11″. Linen makes a fine cover, but almost any other fabric may be used. Sheer fabrics make dainty, feminine cloths. See *Suggested Finishes for Table Linens*, beginning on page 65, for suitable edge finishes. The napkins may be finished to match the cloth, or they may be finished with a napery hem *(see figure 66)*, or with fringing *(see figure 67)*.

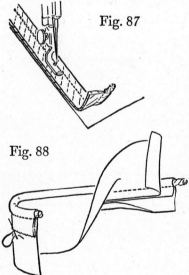

Fig. 87

Fig. 88

Figure 87 — Corded piping makes an attractive trimming. Cover cable cord with a bias strip or bias trim *(see figures 48–52)*, using a cording foot as shown to stitch the covering close against the cord.

Figure 88—To combine a corded piping and a facing, cut a fairly wide bias strip (1½″) and make corded piping *(see figure 87)*. Cut one edge to within ⅛″ of stitching line. Baste piping to right side of fabric with narrow raw edge of piping against raw edge of fabric. The long edge extends beyond edge of fabric. Stitch close to cord with cording foot *(see figure 87)*. Bring the long edge to wrong side. Turn under raw edge, baste and blind hem *(see figure 30, page 38)*.

NEW COLOR FOR THE BEDROOMS

Bedspreads

Bedspreads are the most important item to consider *Bedspreads* in dressing up a bedroom, and it is fun to make them. Measurements for beds vary, but a good standard size is 39″ wide by 75″ long for a single bed, and 54″ wide by 75″ long for a double bed. Any measurements given are based on these figures. If the size of the bed differs, it is easy to make the necessary adjustments. Suitable fabrics for bedspreads are chintz, cretonne, organdie, dotted Swiss, gingham, percale, taffeta. See pages 292 to 303 for descriptions of these fabrics. Some of these fabrics come in both 36″ and 50″ widths. Before computing the necessary yardages, it would be well to check with local stores as to what is available.

Figure 89 — To insert corded piping in a seam, make corded piping as in *figure 87.* Baste piping to right side of one edge of fabric to be seamed so that the stitching line on the piping is on the seam line, and edges of the piping are against the raw edge of fabric. Apply the other piece of fabric as for a regular seam and stitch close to cord with **a cording** foot.

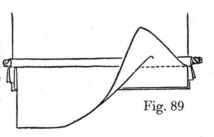

Fig. 89

Directions for Making a Plain Bedspread

Plain
Bedspread

For a single bed, the standard size for a plain bedspread is 72″ by 108″. This type of spread may be made
from 6 yds. of 36″ fabric. Cut it in two sections of 3
yds. each. One section will be the center panel. The
other section is divided into two strips, each 18″ wide
by 108″ long. These are stitched to either side of the
center panel. For decoration, contrasting piping *(figure 86)* or corded piping *(figures 87 and 89)* may be
inserted in these seams. When the seams are completed, the seam allowance should be overcast together
(see figure 41, page 42). If bedspread is made of a
sheer fabric, it must be lined. The lining is made in
exactly the same manner as the spread, and the two

thicknesses are sewed together when the edge finish is applied.

For a double bed, a plain spread measures 90″ by 108″. To make a spread similar to the one described before, it is necessary to use 6 yds. of 50″ fabric. Cut the fabric into two 3-yd. sections. From the selvage edge of one section, remove a strip 9″ wide. (If fabric has a pattern which should be centered, take 4½″ strips from each side.) This makes a center panel of 41″. Split the other 3-yd. section into two strips each 25″ wide. Stitch these strips to the center panel as for the spread for a single bed. To make this spread of 36″ fabric, 9 yds. are needed. The center panel, 36″ wide by 3 yds. long, is stitched to two side strips, each 27″ wide by 3 yds. long.

Suggested Finishes for Bedspreads

1. The edges of the spread may be finished with a contrasting piping and facing (*see figure 85*). If a corded piping is used in the seams, this piping should also be corded (*see figure 88,* page 82).

Finishes for Bedspreads

2. The edges may also be faced (*see figure 60*) with bias trim or a bias strip.

3. A straight facing of a contrasting fabric may be applied to make a band on the right side. Use a straight strip as wide as desired and long enough to go around edge of spread. Stitch the right side of this strip to the wrong side of the spread. Turn to the right side on seam line. Miter the corners of the facing (*see figures 70–73*). Turn in the raw edge ¼″, baste to spread and machine stitch to fabric along fold.

Dust Ruffle

Directions for
Making a Dust Ruffle

Some beds look very attractive with a short spread used with a dust ruffle attached to the box spring or wire spring. This spread should hang over the side of bed just enough to cover the mattress by a few inches. To make a continuous dust ruffle for a bed with a box spring, without a footboard, remove the mattress and measure the top of the box spring. Cut a piece of strong white fabric to these measurements, allowing ½" all around for seams. Unbleached sheeting comes wide enough so that it will not have to be pieced. Sateen and unbleached muslin may be pieced together and used also. The ruffle is usually made of chintz, sateen, percale or a similar fabric with enough body to stand out crisply. The depth of the ruffle will equal the distance from the box spring to the floor plus 2" (½" for seam allowance and 1½" for hem). To determine the length of the ruffle, add together the lengths of two sides and the end of the bed and multiply this figure by 2. To determine how many yards will be needed, divide the number of inches needed for the ruffle by either 36″ or 50″, according to the width of fabric used. To make ruffle piece, measure down along selvage the depth of ruffle plus 2″. Clip selvage and tear across (see *figure 7*, page 32), or draw thread and cut along it if fabric will not tear (see *figure 6*, page 32). Continue tearing length into pieces this size. Join selvage edges of pieces to make one long strip. Make plain seams and press them open. Make a narrow hem at the short ends and a 1½″ hem along one long side. Gather the other long side by machine (see *figure 31*, page 38). Make a 1″ hem on one short side of the foundation piece. Apply gathered edge of ruffle to the two long sides and one short side of foundation piece. On beds which have footboards or posts (where ruffle cannot go around in one piece), make ruffle in three parts, one for each side and one for foot of bed.

To mount a dust ruffle on a wire spring, measure for the ruffle in the same way as before. Make ruffle in three parts, each part twice the measure of the side of bed to which it is to be attached. Gather to fit corresponding side of bed. Instead of a foundation piece, make a strip 5″ wide and long enough to go around the two sides and the end of bed. Stitch side, end, and side ruffle pieces in this order to one edge of this strip. Turn under the raw edge and stitch to the seam. Sew 8″ cotton tapes at 6″ intervals all around. Tie these tapes to the wire of the spring, 2″ in from edge.

Used with a dust ruffle, a plain spread will be smaller. For a single bed, make a center panel 21″ by 112″. The side strips should each be 18″ by 112″. For a double bed, make a center panel 36″ by 112″. The side strips should be 18″ by 112″. This provides for a 9″ overhang on three sides and for a 27″ over-the-pillow tuck-in. Join strips as described under *Bedspreads* on page 84. Cut a 9″ square out of each lower corner (see illustration) and finish as on page 85.

Variations of Plain Bedspreads

There are many types of spreads that can be made, using the plain spread as a basis. They all use a plain center piece made to fit the top of the bed exactly. The length of this center piece varies according to the type of spread made. To make a spread in 36″ fabric for a single bed 39″ wide, a 26″ center strip is stitched to two outer strips each 8″ wide. For a double bed 52″ wide, 9½″ strips are stitched to a 36″ center strip. See *Directions for Making a Plain Bedspread* on page 84.

A spread may be made with ruffles on the sides, an over-the-pillow tuck-in at the top and a tuck-in at the foot. The length of the plain center piece, which should exactly fit the top of the bed (see above), will be the length of the bed, plus 27″ for the over-the-pillow tuck-in and 18″ for the tuck-in at the foot. A ruffle is placed on each long side of center piece from the top to within 18″ of the bottom edge (18″ allowed for tuck-in). The length of each ruffle must, therefore, be 2 times the length of the side measure (minus the 18″ tuck-in allowance). The depth of the ruffle is the dis-

tance from the top of the mattress to the floor, plus 2″ (1½″ for hem, ½″ for seam allowance). Make narrow hems on ends and on one long side. Gather the raw edge to fit the allotted space on sides of center piece, baste and stitch.

The foregoing spread, when used on a bed that has no footboard, needs a ruffle around the two sides and one end. The length of the ruffle should be twice this measurement. The length of the center piece will equal the length of the bed, if separate pillow cases are used. If a tuck-in for pillows is desired, 27″ is added.

To make a fitted spread with scalloped edges for use with a dust ruffle, make the spread center piece to fit exactly the top of the bed (see directions on page 88). Make a lining that is the same size as the center panel.

From the fabric used for the spread, make a strip 10″ wide and 12″ longer than the distance around the

Fitted Spread

two long sides and one short side of the center piece. Make a similar strip from the lining fabric. Fold the spread fabric strip in the center on the width. From the center fold, mark off 12″ segments along one edge until the entire edge is marked. Cut a paper pattern for a 12″ scallop and in each section mark a scallop. If there is some left over at the ends, mark only part of a scallop. Pin the lining strip under this strip wrong sides together and cut the scallops in both fabrics.

Baste and stitch the straight edge of the strip of spread fabric to the side and end edges of the center panel, made of spread fabric, matching the center fold of the strip to the center of the panel. Cut off any excess at the ends. Repeat with lining strip and panel. Place the lining and spread wrong sides together and pin scalloped edges together. Bind both together around scallops and across top end of spread with a bias strip of the same or contrasting fabric, or with bias trim (*see figure 69*, see page 69).

Dressing Tables

A dressing table may be decorated in many different ways. Chintz or sateen to match bedspreads or draperies may be used. Sheer fabrics, such as organdie or dotted Swiss, make dainty covers. With these, a petticoat of white muslin or pastel-colored sateen is necessary.

Dressing Tables

General Directions for Covering a Table with Arms

For a dressing table which has arms that open out, cover the top with a piece of fabric cut to fit the top, plus 2″ around all edges. Cut a bias strip *(see figures 48–52,* page 48*)*, or use bias trim and bind, or face with bias *(figure 53 or 60,* page 49 or 51). Tack to the top of the table with thumbtacks placed on the underside. Make two covers at the same time, so that the cover may be changed frequently for laundering.

Table with Arms

On this type of dressing table, the skirt is made in two sections and attached to the table so that it may be easily removed. One method of doing this is to cut 2 pieces of buckram each 2½″ wide and long enough

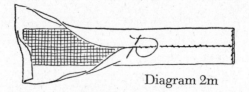

Diagram 2m

to fit each arm. Cover with muslin or sateen, as in *diagram 2m.* When skirt is finished, it is basted firmly to
covered buckram, and the buckram is tacked to
table arms. To remove skirt, clip basting stitches. The
arms may also be covered by winding with a strip of
fabric, and the flat half of a strip of snap tape slip
stitched *(see figure 39,* page 41) to front of each arm.
The matching half of tape is sewed to each skirt section.

Corded Skirt

Corded Dressing Table Skirt

To make the type of skirt pictured for a table with
arms, measure the length of the arm. A strip twice
this measurement will allow for ample fullness. To
find the width of the strip, measure the distance from
the top edge of the arm to the floor. Add to this 1¾″

for top heading, 2½" for tucks (½" each for 5) and ½" for lower hem. Make 2 pieces to these measurements, piecing if necessary to make strip long enough. Finish the center edges with a narrow hem. Along the top, turn in the raw edge ¼" and then turn a ¾" hem. Baste and stitch. On the right side, make a ¼" tuck just below the stitching line for the hem and another ¼" tuck 3" below the first tuck *(see figure 90)*. About 20" down make 3 tucks, each ¼" wide and 2" apart. Make a narrow hem along the lower edge.

Fig. 90

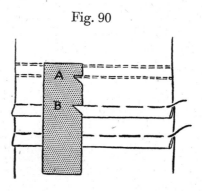

Figure 90 — A cardboard gauge for measuring tucks is made by cutting a notch (A) into a strip of cardboard at the width of the finished tuck and then cutting another notch (B) at the distance between tucks (stitching lines). When making tucks, be sure to start measuring from a straight line where first tuck is to be. Mark the width of the first tuck with notch (A) on the gauge (using tailor's chalk). Fold on marked line and baste tuck in. Place notch (B) on the basting line, as shown. At notch (A) and at the end of gauge, mark stitching line and fold of next tuck.

The top is gathered to fit the table. Insert ¼" cable cord in a safety pin or bodkin (see page 312) and run it through tuck at top of the skirt, pushing the fabric back on the cord *(diagram 2n)*.

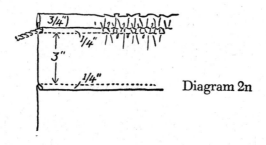

Diagram 2n

Cable cord is also inserted in lower tucks, but here the fabric is only slightly gathered. Baste skirt to buckram, allowing the hem to stand above it as a heading, and tack to arms. Snap tape may be slip stitched to wrong side of skirt to match snap tape sewed to arms.

To make this type of skirt for a table which does not have arms, make strip in one piece, twice the length of the outer edge of table. Finish and attach in same way.

Scalloped Cover

Scalloped Cover for Table without Arms

This is an attractive cover for a table top to be used over a plain skirt. Cut a piece of fabric to fit top of table, plus ½" seam allowance all around. Cut a lining the same size. Stitch two pieces together along back. Turn and press. Cut a strip of fabric 6" wide by the length of the outer edge of table. Mark off one edge into 6" sections. Make a pattern for a 6" scallop and

BRIGHT CLOSET ACCESSORIES

There is every reason why a closet should be bright and interesting. There are many articles which can be made easily that are useful and yet decorative.

Closet Accessories

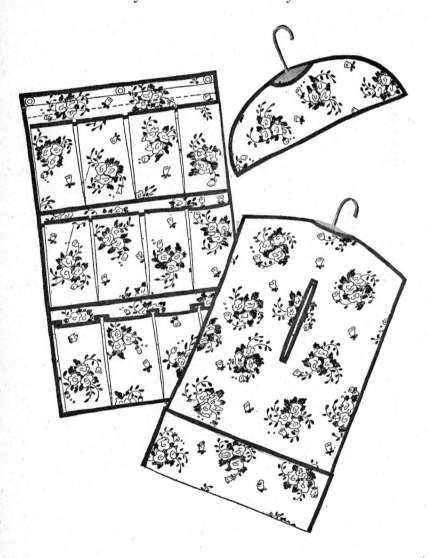

Shoe Bag

Material:

Percale or chintz—1½ yds.; percale bias trim in contrasting color—8 yds.; wooden slat—16″ by ½″ by ¼″; metal rings (¾″ diameter)—3.

Directions for cutting:

Foundation—1 piece, 17½″ by 30″ (selvage)

Pockets—1 piece, 24″ (selvage) by 33″, cut in three equal lengths, each 8″ by 33″

Directions for making:

1. Bind one 33″ edge of each pocket piece.

2. Mark off this edge into 4 sections, each 8¼″. Divide each section into 3 parts, 2″, 4¼″, 2″, respectively.

3. Each 2″ section is made into a pleat 1″ deep. Each 4¼″ section is the face of a pocket. Between the faces of the pocket the pleats are pinned and folded with edges facing, making box pleats *(see diagram 2o)*.

4. Baste pleats across bottom (raw) edge.

5. Place wrong side of one pocket at bottom of foundation piece against right side, raw edge to raw edge.

6. Baste around sides, across bottom and between box pleats.

7. Place lower edge of second pocket piece ¾″ above first, baste as for first pocket piece. Repeat for third pocket piece.

8. Starting at top edge, stitch pockets in place between pleats, continuing line of stitching from top to bottom *(see diagram 2p)*.

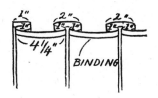

Diagram 2o

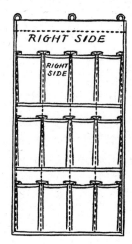

Diagram 2p

9.   Cover lower raw edge of top and center pockets with bias trim, stitched flat.

10.   Make 1½″ hem at top. Slip wooden slat into open hem at top.

11.   Bind *(see figure 53)* sides and lower edge with bias trim.

12.   Fasten rings securely to top with loops of bias trim.

Hanger Cover

Material:

Percale or chintz—¼ yd.; percale bias trim in con- trasting color—2 yds.; wooden coat hanger.

Directions for cutting:

Paper Pattern—Lay hanger flat on a piece of wrapping paper. Trace around top edge. At sides, draw straight vertical lines, 5″ deep. Connect vertical lines by a horizontal line. Cut out pattern, making a slight curve at point where wire hook occurs.

Fabric—2 pieces from paper pattern. Allow ¼″ all

Hanger Cover

around edges for seam allowance.

Directions for making:

1.   On one piece bind *(see figure 53)* curve for wire hook with bias trim.

2.   On each piece bind straight (lower) edge.

3.   Place pieces wrong sides together and join by binding around sides and top edge.

Laundry Bag

Material:

Laundry Bag Percale or chintz—1 yd.; percale bias trim in contrasting color—3 yds.; coat hanger.

Directions for cutting:

Bag—2 pieces, each 16″ by 31″ (selvage). Shape top (16″) edge by placing the two pieces wrong sides together, edges even. Lay coat hanger against one 16″ end. Draw curve to correspond and cut. On front piece, 4½″ down from top edge, cut an 8″ slit lengthwise through the center.

Directions for making:

1.   On front, bind *(see figure 53)*, slit and make a 5″ hem at lower edge.

2.   On back, bind lower edge and bind a 1½″ section at center of top edge.

3.   Place front and back pieces wrong sides together with top and side edges even (back extends 5″ beyond lower edge of front). Pin.

4.   Turn up 5″ back extension over front, pinning at each side edge (see diagram 2q).

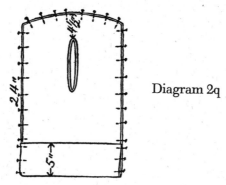

Diagram 2q

5. Bind raw edges together all around.
6. To hang, insert hanger in hole left at top edge.

Traveling Slippers

Material:

Percale or chintz, plain and printed—¼ yd. of each; *Travelling Slippers* denim or drill cloth—¼ yd.; cotton batting or scraps of heavy woolen fabric—¼ yd.; percale bias trim in contrasting color—2 yds.; elastic (⅜″ wide)—½ yd.

Directions for cutting:

Sole—3 pieces, *pattern No. VII*, 1 denim, 1 plain percale, 1 cotton batting (*see figure 4*, page 29, for directions for enlarging patterns from diagrams).

Top—3 pieces, *pattern No. VIII*, 1 plain percale, 1

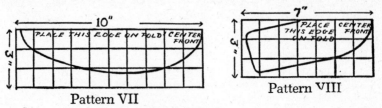

Pattern VII   Pattern VIII

printed percale, 1 cotton batting (or several thick-nesses of woolen fabric). (Enlarge as above.)

Ties—2 pieces, each 2″ by 12″, printed percale.

Directions for making:

1. Place batting (or woolen) between denim and percale pieces of sole (No. VII), and between plain and print pieces of top (No. VIII), right sides of fabric out.

2. Baste layers together and machine quilt. To ma-chine quilt, mark off diamond shapes by marking lines about ¾″ apart to cover piece. Machine stitch along these lines (see illustration).

3. Bind *(fig. 53)* edges of both pieces with bias trim.

4. Top stitch another piece of bias trim over bind-ing just applied around rounded edge of top piece on printed side, turning under ½″ at each end.

5. Baste top to upper side (percale) of sole, match-ing center fronts.

6. Whip *(see figure 62)* free edge of bias trim to under (denim) side of sole.

7. Fold 2″ by 12″ strips in half lengthwise (right side inside).

8. Stitch edges together along 12″ side.

9. Turn *(see figure 33,* page 39), insert 8″ of elastic in each and whip ends of elastic to ends of strip. Turn under ends of strip and whip to slipper top at each side of center notch (see illustration, page 101).

3. Window Dressing

In the theater, "curtain" means the end — the act is finished, the play is over. But in a home, curtains are the beginning, an invitation to enter and linger if they're sparkling, fresh and crisp. Decoratively speaking, half your battle is won if your windows get the treatment they deserve, if the curtains or draperies are suitable, colorful and ample. There are two important rules to observe. The first is to choose a suitable style — formal draperies in a formal room, informal curtains for a more casual setting. The second thing to remember is that yards and yards of the most inexpensive fabric make for a more gracious effect than a more expensive material used skimpily.

Types of Curtains   Curtains are usually divided into two types, glass curtains and draperies. Some of the ordinary types of glass curtains are plain straight curtains, sash curtains, cottage or Dutch curtains, casement curtains and ruffled curtains. Each type is discussed in this chapter. Draperies vary in fabric, length and top finish, but basically, they are similar.

Necessary Equipment   It is very important to have good sewing and pressing equipment to make professional looking curtains. Sewing and pressing equipment are described in detail on pages 309 to 315. See index for directions for pressing various types of fabrics. A steel tapeline or an extension ruler is necessary for taking accurate measurements.

GLASS CURTAINS

Glass Curtains   Glass curtains are made in lightweight fabrics, mostly sheers, because they are meant to subdue strong light and to give privacy without cutting off the view or the light entirely. However, in certain cases, when greater privacy is desired, or when curtains are pushed aside during the day and drawn only at night, non-transparent fabrics are used. The sheer fabrics generally used are cheesecloth, dimity, dotted Swiss, marquisette, net, ninon, organdie, scrim, theatrical gauze or novelty curtain fabrics. The non-transparent fabrics are batiste, casement cloth, handkerchief linen, pongee and shantung. See pages 292 to 303 for descriptions of these fabrics. When buying, it is advisable to inquire whether the fabric is washable, and if it is washable, whether it has been pre-shrunk. If it has not been pre-shrunk, it will be necessary to leave a 2″ shrinkage allowance on the length. This is concealed as a tuck at the top of the curtain.

How to Measure for Glass Curtains

Measuring Curtains

On a plain curtain the top hem must be made wide enough so that a rod may slide through easily. This is known as a *casing*. The top hem may, however, be made wider so that it includes enough fabric, not only for the casing, but also for a tuck known as the *heading (diagram 3a)*. This tuck is formed by making a line of stitching above the top hem line stitching and parallel to it. The rod is inserted in the lower opening (casing), the tuck on top making an attractive ruffled edge. A heading is always used when there are no draperies. Another method of finishing the top of a curtain when there are no draperies is a *French heading* or "pinch pleats" *(diagram 3b)*. Directions for making a French heading are given on page 119. The finished lower hem is usually 2″ wide, and this hem

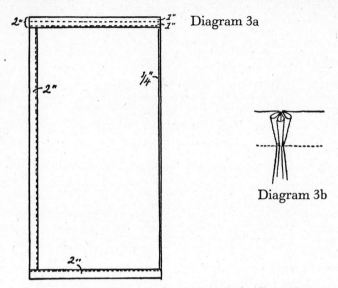

Diagram 3a

Diagram 3b

is made double to give body to the curtain and also
to prevent the raw turn-under edge from showing on
a sheer curtain. The finished center hems look well
when they are of the same width as the lower hem.
These are also finished double. The finished side hems
are ¼″. The lower and center hems are sometimes
omitted when trimmings are used (see page 115 for
making a trimmed curtain).

Width of
Curtain   The width of the curtains should be at least one and
one half, but preferably twice, the width of the window. For an average size window, 72″ high by 34″
wide, two lengths of 36″ fabric are considered ample.
If the window is exceptionally wide, measure horizontally from the inside of the frame on one side to
the inside of the frame on opposite side and estimate
how much more fabric will be needed to give the
proper fullness. It is often possible to take one more

length of curtain fabric, cut it in half and join each half to a full width of fabric to make a curtain of ample width. When any joining is done, narrow French seams are used (*see figure 40*, page 42).

Glass curtains may come to the sill, to the window apron (the lower edge of the window frame), or to the floor. When combined with draperies, the glass curtains usually come to the sill. When there are no draperies, the glass curtains extend to the apron. Long curtains which extend to the floor are used to give a luxurious touch, or to add height to a room. The total length of a curtain is derived from a combination of several measurements. The list of these measurements is given below, and directions on how to find them follow. Always check back against this list, because all subsequent directions for glass curtains will be given with reference to these measurements. The total of all these measurements is the proper cut length of most glass curtains (exceptions will be noted as they occur).

Length of Curtain

1. Measurement of the window (see below)
2. Allowance for top hem (see page 108)
3. Top hem seam allowance of ½"
4. Allowance for 2" lower hem — doubled
5. Allowance of 2" for shrinkage

The measurement of the window should be taken with a steel tape or an extension ruler. *Sill-length curtains* are measured from the bottom of the rod to within 1" of the sill. (The casing allows curtains to drop down slightly and curtains stretch somewhat after hanging.) This type of curtain is often hung from a round rod set inside the window frame 1" down from top, especially when draperies are used. However, both draperies and glass curtains may be hung from a double rod fastened to the window frame. *Apron length curtains* are measured from the bottom of the rod to the bottom of the apron. *Floor length curtains* are measured from the bottom of the rod to within 1" of the floor. These last two types are always hung from rods fastened to the window frame. Tieback curtains are always apron or floor length. *See diagram 3c* for all measurements.

The allowance for top hem depends on the size of the rod and whether there is to be only a casing *(diagram 3d)*, or a casing and a heading *(diagram 3e)*. Since the measurements for the window are taken from the bottom of the rod, the allowance for the finished top hem is doubled. The measurements given below for allowances for the top hem are based on the various widths of rods most likely to be used. They do not include the seam allowance.

When rod is ½" wide (1" casing):

    For casing alone, add 2" for top hem.

    For casing and a 1" heading, add 4" for top hem.

When the rod is 1" wide (1½" casing):

    For casing alone, add 3" for top hem.

    For casing and a 1" heading, add 5" for top hem.

When the rod is round (casing—twice the diameter):

    For casing alone, add 4 times the diameter of the rod for top hem.

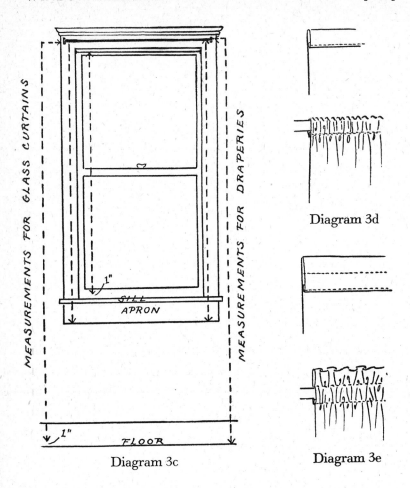

Diagram 3d

Diagram 3e

Diagram 3c

For casing and a 1″ heading, add 4 times the diam·
eter of rod plus 2″, for top hem.

Sash curtains, cottage curtains, casement curtains
and ruffled curtains are similar to plain glass curtains
so that most of the directions already given apply to
them as well. The special characteristics of each are
taken up in the following paragraphs.

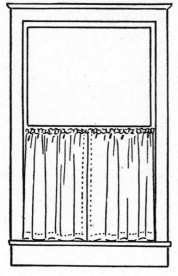

Sash Curtains   Cottage Curtains

Sash Curtains   Sash curtains are mounted on a narrow brass rod fastened to the top piece of the lower sash, so that the curtains may move up and down with the raising and lowering of the window. A sash curtain is measured like the plain glass curtain, from the bottom of the rod to within ½″ of the sill *(diagram 3f)*. The same allowances are made as for plain glass curtains (see page 107). A heading is usually used on a sash curtain.

Cottage Curtains   Cottage curtains or Dutch curtains are a combination of sash curtains and of short curtains placed on a rod mounted at the top of the window frame. The top curtains may be made with ruffles or without. These curtains are very practical because the lower section can be drawn together to give complete privacy, while the upper section can be tied back to admit more light.

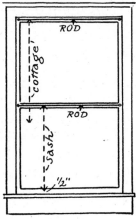
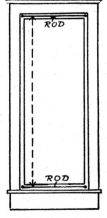

Diagram 3f   Diagram 3g

The sash curtains are measured as directed above. The top curtains are measured from the bottom of the rod to about 5″ below the top of the lower sash *(see diagram 3f)*. The same allowances are made as for plain glass curtains.

Casement curtains are for casement windows which open in and out, instead of up and down as regular windows. For casement windows which open toward the inside, the curtains are often attached directly to the window. Two rods are used, one at the top and one at the bottom of the window. The width of the curtain is, as usual, twice the width of the window. The measurement for the length of the curtain is taken from under the top rod to the top of lower rod *(diagram 3g)*. Add to this figure an allowance for a casing and a 1″ heading (see page 109), and the same amount for the lower hem, as a casing and heading are used both at the top and the bottom. If it is not desirable to attach the curtains directly to the window, it is possible to

Casement Curtains

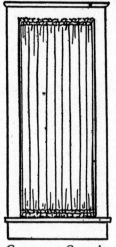

Casement Curtains   Ruffled Curtains

make a plain glass curtain and mount it on a swinging rod which moves with the sash. When the casement opens out, the best method is to make a plain glass curtain and mount it on a rod placed on the window frame. These curtains are usually mounted on rings or hooks and opened and closed by means of a pulley and cord. For these latter two kinds of curtains, a French heading (pinch pleats) is preferable (see page 119).

Ruffled Curtains   *Ruffled curtains* follow the same rules for width as the other glass curtains (see page 106). For length, they are measured from the bottom of the rod to the apron or to the floor *(see diagram 3c, page 109)*. The allowance for the top hem is the same as for plain glass curtains with a 1″ heading. There is no allowance made for a lower hem, only the ½″ seam allowance. For cutting the ruffles, see page 116. For applying the ruffles, see page 116.

How to Prepare and Cut the Fabric for Glass Curtains

For all types of curtains, the fabric is prepared and cut in the same way.

1. Straighten the fabric. Sometimes the fabric is rolled unevenly on the bolt so that it is pulled more tightly on one side than on the other. If this is so, grasp the end of the fabric with one hand at either selvage, holding a good amount of fabric. Have someone else grasp a good handful of fabric at either selvage further on. Pull diagonally first one way and then the other to stretch the fabric. Work down the fabric in this way until the entire piece is straightened.

2. Straighten the top edge of the fabric. This is done by pulling a thread and cutting on this line *(see figure 6,* page 32). If it is not possible to pull a thread, mark a straight line with a yardstick and tailor's chalk and cut.

3. Measure the length of one curtain along one selvage and mark with chalk or a pin. It is best to measure this length with an oilcloth tape measure, because it will not stretch the fabric. At mark, pull a thread to show cutting line, or measure curtain length on opposite selvage and mark the cutting line with a yardstick and chalk. Cut on line made.

4. Use first length as a pattern for cutting all other curtain lengths. Pin it to the fabric carefully, cut edge against cut edge and selvage edges together. Do not pull the fabric. Draw a thread or mark a line to cut along each time a curtain is cut.

5. Trim off all selvages. These edges are more

tightly woven and will cause the edges of the curtain to draw when it is hung. Selvages will also shrink more than the rest of the fabric when curtain is washed.

6. Fold curtains in pairs.

7. For ruffled curtains, cut ruffles (see page 116).

8. Before beginning to sew, it is well to mark off width of hems (allowance for hem plus seam allowance). Use a hem gauge (*see figure 46*, page 44) and tailor's chalk for marking. Remember that the hems on each curtain of a pair must be made to face each other.

How to Finish Glass Curtains

Finishing Curtains On glass curtains, the hems may be stitched by machine or by hand. When stitched by machine, at the end of each line of stitching turn and stitch back 4 to 6 stitches instead of tying the ends. If hems are done by hand, a slip stitch is used (*see figure 39*, page 41). On curtains with no trimming, the procedure is as follows:

1. Make a pair of curtains at one time. Measure them against each other for length as hems are made. Make sure that the center hems face each other.

2. Make the narrow outside hems first. Turn the edge twice, ¼″ each time (*see figures 27 and 28*, page 37). Baste, stitch and press.

3. On the center hems (which should be the same as the lower hem), the raw edge is turned in the width of the hem, basted and pressed. Then this edge is turned back (*diagram 3h*). Baste, stitch and press.

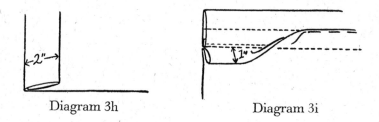

Diagram 3h   Diagram 3i

4.   The lower hems are done next in the same way.

5.   The top hems are done last. Before putting in the top hem, check both curtains of a pair against each other for length. Turn under ½" and then turn under one half of the amount allowed for top hem. Baste, stitch and press. If there is to be a casing, make a line of stitching above and parallel to the stitching line of the hem. See page 108 for width of casings to be used with different rods.

6.   To hide the 2" shrinkage allowance, make a 1" tuck on the wrong side close to the stitching line of the top hem, turn it up and catch it to the back of the casing with long stitches *(diagram 3i)*. On French headings, it is awkward to make a tuck at the top. In this case, make an extra turn of the bottom hem to allow for shrinkage, sewing it with long stitches for easy ripping.

How to Make Trimmed Glass Curtains

The easiest way to trim glass curtains is to use ready-made trims, such as fringe, pleating and ruffling. Trims are usually applied to the center and lower edges. Allow only a ½" seam allowance at the lower edge of the curtain when cutting. All other

Trimming Curtains

measurements are taken in the same way (see page 107). To estimate the necessary amount of trimming needed, measure down the center and around the lower edge of one curtain and multiply by the number of curtains to be trimmed. Curtains are finished in the same way as on page 114. Trim is applied instead of making center and lower hems in steps 3 and 4. Turn the lower and center edges in ½" either to right or wrong side, depending on trim. If the trim has a decorative edge, turn the raw edge to the right side, baste trim over it on the right side. Slip stitch (*see figure 39*, page 41) or machine stitch both edges of the trim to the curtain (*diagram 3j*). If the trim edge is to be hidden, turn the raw edge of curtain to the wrong side and slip stitch or machine stitch this edge over the trim edge (*diagram 3k*). Also slip stitch (or machine stitch) opposite edge of trim to curtain on the wrong side.

How to Cut, Finish and Apply Ruffles to Glass Curtains

Applying Ruffles To estimate the amount of fabric needed for ruffles, measure around the center and lower edge of the curtain. For ruffles of organdie and chintz, 1½ times the measurement of curtain should be allowed. For dotted Swiss, net and voile ruffles, allow twice the measurement of the curtain. Multiply the amount needed for one curtain by the number of curtains to be trimmed.

Cutting ruffles lengthwise means that fewer joinings are necessary. To find out the amount of 36" fabric needed for the ruffling, divide the total yards of ruffling needed by 12 for 3" ruffles, by 9 for 4"

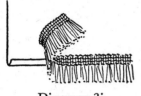 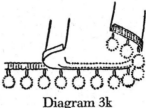

Diagram 3j   Diagram 3k

ruffles. Measure piece off into 3″ or 4″ strips and either draw threads at markings and cut along them (*see figure 6*, page 32), or mark strips with a yardstick and tailor's chalk and cut. The pieces are joined together by very narrow French seams (*see figure 40*, page 42). Join strips to make ruffle length for each curtain separately.

Hem one long edge and ends of the ruffle pieces with foot hemmer on the sewing machine (see machine manual), with a narrow hem (*see figures 27 and 28*, page 37) stitched by machine, or with a narrow hand rolled hem (*see figure 68*, page 68). These edges may also be machine hemstitched and the hemstitching clipped through the middle to get a picot edge. Gather raw edges of ruffles by machine or by hand (*see figure 31*, page 38). Make rows of gathers ¼″ and ½″ from edge. Pin and baste gathered edge of ruffle to curtain, wrong side to wrong side, ¼″ in from edge (*see figure 32*, page 38). Be careful not to stretch the fabric. When turning a corner, make sure that the gathers are full enough so that the ruffle will stand out straight. Stitch on ¼″ gathering line. Press on right side so that edge of curtain lies over top of ruffle. Turn edge of curtain in ⅛″ at edge. Baste and stitch to ruffle *(diagram 31)*. Finish the top of the curtain like a plain glass curtain (see page 115).

Diagram 31

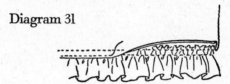

To make an easy valance finish for a ruffled curtain, make a strip of fabric twice as long as the entire curtain rod. The width of this strip should equal the width of the ruffle, plus the same allowance as on the curtain for top casing, heading and seam allowance. Finish two short sides and one long side with a narrow hem. Make casing and heading like that on the curtain (see step 5, page 115). Using double rods, mount the ruffled curtain on the inner rod and the valance piece on the outside rod.

How to Make Tie-backs

Tie-backs   An attractive tie-back for a ruffled curtain is made by cutting a band of fabric 3″ by 12″, and a ruffle 2″ by 18″ or 24″, depending on how much fullness was allowed in the ruffle of the curtain. Hem the ruffle except on one long side. Gather and stitch this edge to one long side of the band piece, right side to right side and edge to edge. Turn in ends of band. Turn in and baste free edge of band to seam line of ruffle. Stitch all the way around straight strip and press. Sew small rings or loops to the short ends.

The simplest kind of tie-back is made by cutting a straight piece of curtain fabric 4″ by 12″. Seam the two long sides together right side inside. Turn to right side, turn in ends and edge stitch all around. Sew small rings or loops to the short ends. Ball fringe, ruffling or plain fringe may be applied to plain tie-backs.

How to Make French Headings

In order to describe the making of a French heading or "pinch pleats," it is necessary to use an actual curtain as an example. To fit other cases not described here, insert figures to fit individual measurements. The figures are given for a curtain made from fabric 36″ wide, from which ½″ has been cut away (when selvages were trimmed) and 4½″ has been used for hems (4″ for center and ½″ for outside). This leaves 31″ available for pleating. Pleats are made from inside 2″ center hem to within 2″ of outside edge. *French Headings*

1. When measuring for curtains, make the allowance for top hem to include a casing and a 1″ heading (see page 109).

2. Insert a strip of crinoline in top hem of curtain and finish without stitching a casing.

3. Measure curtain rod from bracket to bracket (32″ in this case) and take half of it, 16″.

4. Measure curtain across the width, 31″.

5. Subtract (3) from (4). This gives 15″, the amount available for pleats. Since 4 pleats are usually sufficient, divide this amount (15″) by 4. Each pleat will be 3¾″.

6. There will be three spaces between the pleats. The amount for spaces is 16″ (the measurement found in step 3). From this, subtract the width of the center

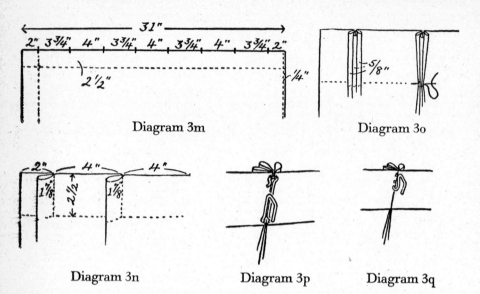

Diagram 3m   Diagram 3o

Diagram 3n   Diagram 3p   Diagram 3q

hem (2″) and an equal amount (2″) to be left at outer edge of curtain. This leaves 12″. Divide the 12″ by 3 to find the amount for each space, 4″.

7. The top of curtain is then divided as shown in *diagram 3m.*

8. Bring pleat markings together to make a pleat on the right side. Stitch pleat down the width of the hem *(diagram 3n).* (On draperies, stitch down 3″.)

9. Divide pleat evenly into three parts and pass needle through and over the pleat several times and catch down with two or three stitches on the right side *(diagram 3o).*

10. Rings or hooks are stitched to the back of the finished pleat so that the curtain may be moved back and forth on rods *(diagram 3p).* Or use the type of hooks which stick into top of drapery *(diagram 3q).*

DRAPERIES

The fabrics suitable for informal draperies are *Draperies* chintz, cretonne, percale, gingham, linen, monk's cloth, quilted cottons, sateen. For formal draperies use bengaline, damask, moire, satin, taffeta, velvet and velveteen. (See pages 292 to 303 for descriptions of these fabrics.) Draperies are usually lined. Sateen is a suitable fabric for lining most draperies. For formal draperies, taffeta may be used. When making draperies of heavy fabrics, use a heavy duty sewing thread. (See Thread and Needle Chart on page 311).

How to Measure for Draperies

*Measuring
Draperies*   One width of 36″ fabric for each side of the window is generally used for draperies. One width of 50″ fabric is not too wide for a large window.

Draperies are most attractive when they are floor length. Short draperies should come to the window apron (lower edge of window frame). To get the proper length for draperies, measure from top edge of rod (attached to window frame) to the floor or to the lower edge of the window apron (*see diagram 3c,* page 109). Add 9½″ to the window measurement (4″ for the top hem, 2″ for heading and 3½″ for the lower hem).

Draperies are frequently used with a valance, and, in that case, they are made straight and then gathered when placed on the rod. Directions for a few simple valances are given on page 128. On one arrangement, the glass curtain is placed on a rod inside the window frame. A double rod is used for the drapery and the valance. For another arrangement, a double rod is used for the glass curtain and the drapery, and the valance is tacked to a valance board (*see diagram 3w,* page 130). Draperies sometimes have French headings.

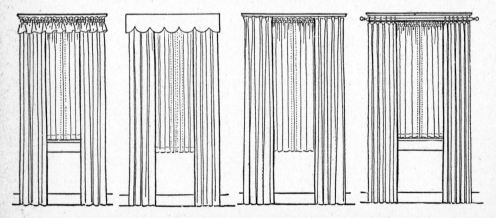

In such a case, the glass curtain is mounted on a regular rod, and the drapery is placed on a swinging crane arm. If a second rod were used, it would not be entirely covered and so would be unsightly.

Occasionally a decorative wooden pole is used for draperies. Rings are sewed to the top of the drapery at equal intervals and are strung on the pole. Four to five inches is a good allowance between each ring, depending on the amount of space to be covered. Measurement for this drapery should be taken from under the pole to within ½″ of the floor, and no allowance is made for a heading.

How to Prepare and Cut the Fabric for Draperies

1. Before measuring for cutting, straighten the top edge of the fabric by pulling a thread and cutting along it (*see figure 6*, page 32). If it is not possible to pull a thread, mark a straight line with a yardstick and marking chalk and cut. *Cutting Draperies*

2. Measure the required length along both selvages and mark with chalk or a pin. At mark, pull a thread, or mark with chalk and cut.

3. Use the first drapery as a pattern for the others so that no variation in size will occur. Pin to next length of fabric (cut edges and selvages together) and pull thread, or mark before cutting.

4. If the fabric has one of the large floral designs now so popular, or any kind of a repeated design, carefully match the drapery already cut to the fabric to be cut. The cut drapery piece is not pinned against cut edge of fabric. It must be pinned at exactly the

same point in the design. It is quite possible that a small strip will have to be discarded, but this excess fabric may be used for valances or tie-backs.

5. The lining is cut the same width as the drapery and 3″ shorter than the measured length of the drapery, without allowing for any hems.

6. Cut a piece of buckram 36″ by 5″ to go under the top hem of each drapery.

7. Trim off all selvages from both drapery fabric and lining.

8. Fold draperies in pairs.

How to Make Draperies

Making Draperies

1. Make a pair of draperies at one time, measuring against each other for length. Make sure that center hems face each other.

2. Lay the drapery fabric on a large table, right side down.

3. Turn in and baste 1½″ along the outside edge of drapery, making only a single turn, catch stitch (*figure 91*) and press.

4. Turn in and baste 2″ along the center edge of

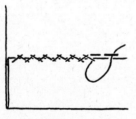

Figure 91 — To catch stitch a hem, work from left to right. Take up a few threads of fabric, being careful not to have stitches show on the right side. Take a similar stitch in the hem about ½″ to the right. Continue making zig-zag stitches as shown.

Fig. 91

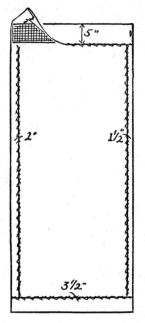

Diagram 3r

drapery (single turn), catch stitch in place and press.

5. Turn in and baste 3½″ for lower hem (single turn). Catch stitch in place and press.

6. For top hem and a 1″ heading, turn down 5″ over the 5″ strip of buckram and baste *(diagram 3r)*. Catch stitch in place and press.

7. On the lining, turn up and baste a 2″ hem (single turn). Catch stitch in place and press.

8. Place the sateen lining on top of the drapery with wrong sides facing.

9. Turn the top of the lining in ½″ and pin in place ½″ above lower edge of the top hem of the curtain.

10. If the drapery fabric is heavy it should be tacked to lining. Smooth lining over drapery so that side edges are even. Pin lining to drapery down the center. Unpin

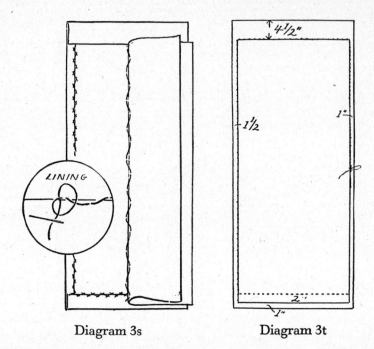

Diagram 3s   Diagram 3t

the lining across half the top. Fold the lining back
along the center and catch the two fabrics together
with a long, loose basting stitch that does not show on
the right side of either fabric or lining. Thread is
knotted about once every 2' as shown in *diagram 3s*.

11. Repin across top and fold under side edges and
pin to the drapery so as to cover the raw edges of side
hems by ½".

12. Baste and slip stitch *(see figure 39*, page 41) the
lining to the drapery around sides and top *(diagram
3t)*. Stitches should not show through on the right
side of the fabric.

13. The lining should not be attached along the
lower edge. So that it does not show, tack it to the

Fig. 92

Figure 92 — To make a French Tack,
make a stitch about 1″ long from several strands of thread, to connect lining
and drapery. Buttonhole stitch closely
together around these threads.

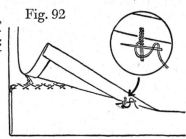

drapery hem about every 6″ with French tacks *(figure 92).*

14.   Attach a weight to each lower corner of drapery.

15.   Finish the top of the drapery with a French
heading (see page 119), or if it is to be used with a valance, sew hooks 1″ down and 4″ apart *(see diagram
3p, page 120).*

How to Apply Trimmings on Draperies

Lined draperies are usually untrimmed. However, *Trimming*
Draperies
fringe, pleating and similar decoration may be easily
applied. Finish drapery completely. If the trimming
has a decorative edge, baste trimming to the edge of
the drapery on the right side and slip stitch both edges.
These edges may also be stitched by machine *(see
figure 38,* page 41). If the edge of the trimming is to
be hidden, press drapery with a warm iron. Slit the

Diagram 3u

center and lower edge of the drapery along the crease. Turn in raw edges of the drapery ⅛" along the crease. Insert the fringe between the edges and baste (*diagram 3u*). Stitch the three thicknesses together with slip stitches that go through all three thicknesses at once, or sew with two closely spaced rows of machine stitching.

How to Make Valances

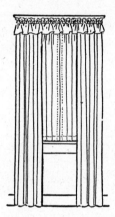

Shirred Valance

An easy valance is one that is shirred on a rod. In this case a double rod is used, one for the drapery and one for the valance. For a valance to be used with floor length drapes on an average size window, 10" is a good width. Add 6" (4" for top hem and 2" for bottom hem). The length of the valance should be twice the width of the window. Piece fabric lengths together to make a strip this size. Make the lining the same length but only 6" wide. On the fabric turn in 1" hems at sides, a 4" hem at top and a 2" hem at bottom. Catch stitch and press. Lay the lining on the fabric wrong sides together, turn under and pin edges so as to cover raw edges of hems by ½". Baste as shown in *diagram 3v*. Make two lines of stitching parallel to

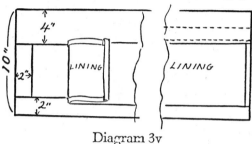

Diagram 3v

the top edge, one 2" down and one 3½" down. This makes a casing for rod. Slip stitch around except over ends of casing. Mount draperies on lower rod and valance on upper rod.

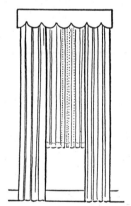

Scalloped Valance

Other valances may be made which can be tacked to a valance board. A valance board can be made by attaching a board (4" wide by 1" thick by the length of the window frame) to the window frame with sev-

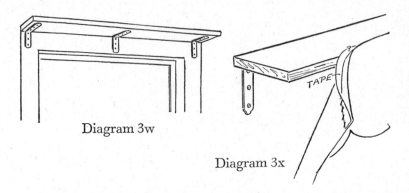

Diagram 3w

Diagram 3x

eral arm brackets as shown in *diagram 3w*. These valances are usually cut about 12″ wide, not allowing for seams. The simplest type is a scalloped valance. It may be made by cutting a piece of fabric long enough to go across the length of the board and around the corners to the window frame. Make it about 11″ wide to allow for seams. Cut the lining the same size, pin and baste the two fabrics right sides together and mark the center on the width. Make a cardboard pattern for scallop 7″ wide and about 2″ deep. Working from the center, mark scallops along one edge of valance by drawing around the pattern. Stitch around scallop markings and along two short sides. Trim scallops close to seam and clip at points. Turn to right side. Crease on seam line, baste close to crease and press. Turn under raw edges at top and slip stitch together *(see figure 39,* page 41). Pin 1″ tape to wrong side with edge even with top edge of valance. Whip lower edge of tape to valance *(diagram 3x)*. Stitches should not show through to right side. Tack valance around board as shown in diagram.

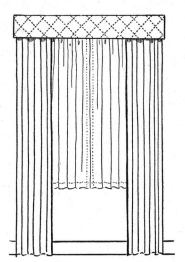

*Quilted
Valance*

Another type of valance tacked to a valance board is made on a buckram foundation. One attractive type of this kind is quilted. Cut a piece of fabric (chintz is good) 12″ deep and long enough to go around valance board from one side of the window frame to the other. Cut lining sateen, cotton batting and buckram stiffening to the same dimensions. If buckram has to be pieced, overlap the edges and stitch each edge flat by machine. Turn under all edges of buckram 1″ and stitch with large stitches, using a coarse needle and a strong thread. Lay batting against wrong side of chintz and lay buckram on top of this. Turn long edges of batting and chintz over buckram and stitch raw edges together with a long catch stitch *(see figure 91)*. Cut out corners to eliminate bulk and catch stitch short ends to buckram. Draw diagonal lines on chintz (see illustration) with marking chalk and quilt with heavy embroidery cotton, using bold running stitches through all thicknesses. Sew large fabric-covered buttons at intersections of quilting lines if desired. Make a lining of sateen cut to fit finished valance. Turn in 1" on all edges and slip stitch (*see figure 39*, page 41) in place on back of valance. Attach tape as in *diagram 3x*. Tack to valance board (*see diagrams 3w and 3x*).

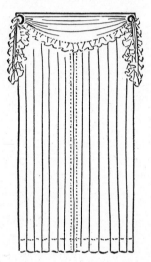

*Swag
Valance*

    Swag valances are also very popular. A ruffled swag for chintz draperies can be made quickly and easily. For an average size window, make a strip of chintz 18" wide and 2 yds. long. Hem one long side. For ruffling, cut a strip 3" wide and 4½ yds. long. Gather to 3 yds. and attach it to the two short sides and one long side of strip, right sides together. Cover seam with a bias strip (*see figures 48–51*, page 48) applied like a facing (*see figure 60*, page 52). Drape the swag over arms or rings screwed to window frame as shown in illustration.

4. Bright Inside Story

Next to the windows, the upholstered furniture is the biggest bugaboo in the average woman's decorating budget. Today many decorators, and the alert women who follow their lead, have found slip covers the perfect — and inexpensive — solution to the problem. A glowing chintz, a bold stripe, a fresh color scheme can put a new face on an old room for the cost of a few yards of fabric. Many people have adopted the idea of having two sets of slip covers, one for winter and one for summer. A room full of shabby upholstered furniture is a challenge to your wit and imagination. Try your hand at slip covering that fading wing chair, and you'll see that there's plenty of life in the old chair yet!

Slip covers may be made in cotton, linen and rayon fabrics. Some of the cottons commonly used are chintz, cretonne, denim, **gabardine**, gingham, Indian Head, percale, piqué, quilted cotton, rep, sateen, ticking, twill. See pages 292 to 303 for descriptions of these fabrics. Chintz comes with a glazed and an unglazed finish. An ordinary glaze will wash out. To assure a permanent glaze, the fabric should be labelled "permanent finish." Plain and printed linens are durable. Most of the rayons used, such as brocade, damask, moiré and cotton-backed satin, even though mixed with cotton, must be dry cleaned. The cottons and linens are washable. When buying cottons which are intended for washing, however, it is necessary to ascertain from the label or to inquire whether they have been pre-shrunk. Otherwise, it will be necessary to wash the fabric, partly dry it in the shade and iron while damp.

Chintz, cretonne, sateen, etc., which are purchased as upholstery fabrics, come in a 50″ width. This width cuts to best advantage for most slip covers. Regulation 36″ or 39″ wide fabrics may be used, however.

Slip covers are sometimes trimmed with binding tape or bias trim, welting, or fringe, or they may be self-trimmed by means of a seam called a boxed seam. A boxed seam is a narrow French seam with the ridge on the right side.

Trimming   For washable slip covers, only colorfast trimming should be used. If trimming is not pre-shrunk, it must be washed before being used. It is much easier to use

binding tape or bias trim, welting and fringes purchased ready-made. However, bias strips for binding
and welting may be made of the same or contrasting
fabric. Bias strips 1¼″ wide are cut and joined together
as shown in *figures 48–51*, page 48. For binding, the
raw edges are folded to meet at the center. Welting is
made by covering cotton cable cord of any size with
the bias strip *(see figure 87*, page 82). Trimming is
applied only on the principal seams and never on the
seams inside the chair, like those inside the seat or
back. See illustrations of chairs of various types on
page 137 for approximate amounts of trimming required for various types of chairs. Measure seams of
chairs to be trimmed as indicated on sketch to figure
exact amount necessary for individual chair.

Proper sewing and pressing equipment is necessary *Necessary*
for making slip covers. Sewing equipment is discussed *Equipment*
on pages 309 to 313. Pressing aids are described on
page 313. The ways to press various fabrics are taken
up in detail *(see index)*. The proper thread, both for
hand sewing and machine sewing, is important also.
A special type of heavy duty mercerized thread is
ideal for this. See Thread and Needle Chart on page
315.

How to Measure Fabric for Slip Covers

Each slip cover should be measured separately as *Measuring*
described in the following pages. In order to provide
a guide against which beginners may check their own
calculations, general estimates are given with the

sketches of various types of chairs on facing page. These estimates are for average type, average-sized chairs in plain, evenly striped or all-over print designs. When the fabric has a large central design or grouped stripes, the design must be centered on all the important sections of the chair. Under these circumstances, at least 1 yd. should be added — more, if the design is very large.

Before measuring the chair, remove the cushion. It is measured separately. Take the measurements of the length and width of each part of chair (*see diagram 4a* and directions following) and note them down as in table on page 143. All seam allowances are 1". This may seem like too much, but it is better to fit the slip cover with generous seams. They can always

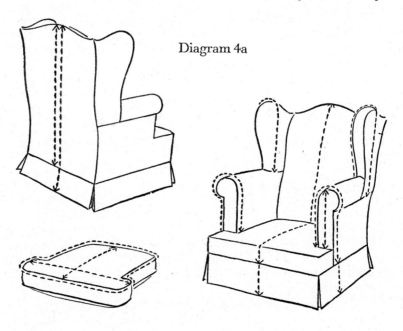

Diagram 4a

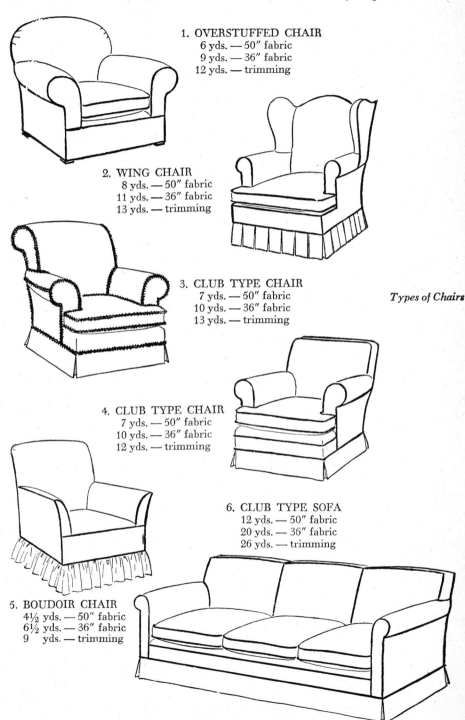

1. OVERSTUFFED CHAIR
6 yds. — 50″ fabric
9 yds. — 36″ fabric
12 yds. — trimming

2. WING CHAIR
8 yds. — 50″ fabric
11 yds. — 36″ fabric
13 yds. — trimming

3. CLUB TYPE CHAIR
7 yds. — 50″ fabric
10 yds. — 36″ fabric
13 yds. — trimming

Types of Chairs

4. CLUB TYPE CHAIR
7 yds. — 50″ fabric
10 yds. — 36″ fabric
12 yds. — trimming

6. CLUB TYPE SOFA
12 yds. — 50″ fabric
20 yds. — 36″ fabric
26 yds. — trimming

5. BOUDOIR CHAIR
4½ yds. — 50″ fabric
6½ yds. — 36″ fabric
9 yds. — trimming

be trimmed after the sewing is completed. Tuck-in allowances are provided around the seat and back sections of the chair (where there are springs) to accommodate the "give" of the springs. Allow 4″ on each edge of the pieces where this tuck-in is to be.

Back of Chair

The back ends at the highest point on the back of the chair. It may be at a seam, at the top of a wooden rim or under a roll, if the upholstery rolls over the top of the chair. Sometimes a straight piece, known as a boxing strip, is inserted between the back and the front (see sketch of chair 4, page 137). If so, the measurement of the back begins at the back of the strip.

Length — This measurement is taken from the highest point to the lower edge of the upholstery (if there is to be a valance around the bottom), or to the floor (if the back is to be straight). Add 2″ for seam allowances at top and bottom.

Width — This measurement is taken at the widest point plus 2″ for seam allowances.

Front of Chair

Length — This measurement is taken from the place where the back ends to the edge of the upholstery in front (if there is to be a valance) or to the floor (if the cover is to be straight). Several additions must be made (totaling from 12″ to 14″ in all): 1″ for top seam allowance (3″ if there is a boxing strip); 8″ for the tuck-in between the seat and the front; 2″ to allow for seams if the apron piece is made separate; 1″ at the lower edge.

Small Home Studios—Barker Bros.

Width — The measurement of the widest point of the front will usually be the measurement of the seat, because 8″ must be added on the sides (4″ on each side) for tuck-in allowance. However, on a chair with a T-shaped cushion, the front edge plus 2″ for seams may be the widest measurement.

Sides

These measurements include only the portion of the sides of the chair below the top of the arms. Allowance must be made for two of these pieces. The depth of the chair back, whether it is a wing or whether it takes some other form, will be measured and made separately.

Length — This measurement is taken from the lower edge of the upholstery at the side (if there is to be a valance) or from the floor (if the cover is to be straight) over the top of the arm down to the seat. The additions will total 7″ or 9″: 1″ at edge; 2″ for seam allowances at joining of outside and inside of arm (4″ if there is a boxing strip); 4″ for tuck-in at the seat.

Width — This measurement should be taken at the widest point according to the chair. Add 2″ for seam allowances.

Wings

Length — This measurement is taken from the point where the wing joins the arm on the inside to where it joins on the outside. There are three seams, one at each joining and one on top (double seam allowance), so 4″ for seam allowances should be added.

Allowance must be made for two of these side pieces.

Width — This measurement is taken at the widest point of the wing from the point where it joins the front on the inside of chair to the point where it joins the back of chair on the outside. Allow 7″ as there will be three seams: 1″ for seam at back corner, 2″ for the edge seam (double seam allowance), and 4″ for tuck-in between wing and back of seat.

Extra Pieces

The extra pieces are those which are often placed at the front of the arm and between the back and front above the arm. Often it is possible to cut these from the scraps left over from the other pieces. Take the length at the longest point and width at the widest point. Make a 2″ allowance on the length and 2″ on the width for seams. Allowance must be made for two of these pieces.

Valance

Length — Measure all around the bottom of the chair at the point where the valance is to be joined (usually at the bottom of the upholstery) to find the circumference of the chair. The amount of fabric needed will depend on the type of valance used.

A shirred valance requires twice the circumference of the chair.

A box pleated valance with the pleats placed edge to edge requires three times the circumference.

A straight valance with box pleats at each corner requires 42″ more than the circumference. This is a popular type of valance which is easy to make.

Width — Measure the distances from upholstery to floor. Add 3″—1″ for seam allowance, 2″ for hem.

The amount of fabric is estimated as follows: The valance may be made on the length or the width. It is best to wait until the yardage is figured out on a chart (see page 144) before deciding which is the most satisfactory way to cut the valance. In 50″ fabric it usually works out that the valance is cut on the length. To estimate the amount needed for a valance cut on the width of the fabric, divide the length needed for valance by the width of the fabric minus 1″, to allow for joining seams. If this comes out with a fraction left over, take the next highest whole number. This gives the number of times the width of the fabric needs to be cut. Multiply this figure (the whole number) by the number of inches in the width of the valance and divide by 36″ to estimate the yardage needed.

Extra Cushion

The length and width of the top are measured. Add 2″ to each measurement for seams. Allowance must be made for two of these pieces. The length of the joining strip is measured around the entire pillow plus 2″ for joining seam. The width is the distance between the top and bottom plus 2″ for seams. This piece may be cut on the length or width, depending on how the rest of the pieces come out of the fabric (see chart, page 144). In 50″ fabric, it is often best to cut it on the length. To estimate the amount of fabric needed to cut this strip on the width of the fabric, divide the length of the strip by the width of the fabric minus 1″ for

seams. If this comes out with a fraction, take the next
highest whole number. Multiply this figure by the
width of the strip.

How to Estimate Yardage for Slip Covers

Put measurements down in a table like the one fol- *Estimating*
lowing. For an example, an average wing chair with *Yardage*
a T-shaped cushion has been chosen. For other chairs
of different measurements, merely substitute individual measurements taken in the manner described
before, beginning on page 135.

Back of Chair........Length — 35" + 2" = 37"

Width — 26" + 2" = 28"

Front of Chair.......Length — 63" + 12" = 75"

Width (at front) — 27" + 2" = 29"

Sides (2)............Length — 31" + 7" = 38"

Width — 23" + 2" = 25"

Wings (2)...........Length — 39" + 4" = 43"

Width — 24" + 7" = 31"

Extra Pieces (Front of Arm) (2)

Length — 9" + 2" = 11"

Width — 4" + 2" = 6"

Valance (Box Pleated). Length — 105" × 3" = 315"

Width — 6½" + 3" = 9½"

Extra Cushion

Top Piece ....Length — 22" + 2" = 24"

Width — 27" + 2" = 29"

Strip ....Length — 96" + 2" = 98"

Width — 3½" + 2" = 5½"

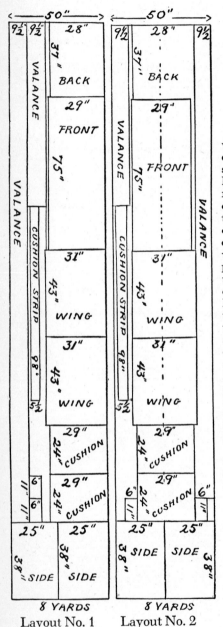

Layout No. 1   Layout No. 2

In order to estimate exactly how much fabric will be needed and where pieces will be cut, it is easiest to make a layout chart. This also will show whether valance pieces should be cut lengthwise or across the width of the fabric. In most cases, main pieces of chair are too wide to enable cutting more than one on the width of the fabric. Follow Layout No. 1 for all fabrics except those with large designs which must be centered, placing all main pieces along one selvage of fabric so that excess will be in the largest possible piece. Strip pieces and extra pieces can usually be cut from this excess and where design of fabric permits, the valance can also be cut lengthwise from this excess. On striped fabric, this means that the stripes will go around the valance, but this variation is often desirable on a striped cover. If the design is one which must be centered, Layout No. 1 would be impossible, since all pieces are cut off center. Follow Layout No. 2 for this type of fabric. For 36″ fabric the same type of diagram can be made. There will not be enough excess on width to cut any but small pieces. Valance must be cut on the width. See page 142 for instructions for figuring out yardage required to cut fabric on width.

To estimate yardage, add up lengthwise measurements of pieces and divide by 36″. Add an extra yard if fabric has a large pattern which may require some shifting to center the design.

General Instructions for Making Slip Covers

There are many types of chairs and couches, and *General* while they all differ in the problems they present, *Instructions* fundamentally, they are similar. It would be impossible to anticipate all the problems of making slip covers of every possible type, so a wing chair with a T-shaped cushion, which contains most of the problems which might be encountered, has been selected as an example. In covering another type, follow the directions given, omitting those steps which do not apply to the chair being covered. Plan the pieces to fit as nearly like the upholstery as possible, seaming and piecing wherever the upholstery underneath is seamed. For a couch, the same procedure is followed as for a chair.

Before beginning to cover any chair, straighten edge of fabric by pulling a thread and cutting on line made (*see figure 6*, page 32). If it is not possible to pull a thread, mark a straight line with marking chalk and yardstick before cutting.

How to Place the Fabric on the Chair

When covering a chair, the fabric is laid on the *Placing* chair lengthwise. The selvages are at sides always, *the Fabric* never at the top and bottom. Always be careful to keep the fabric on the correct grain while pinning and fitting (*see figure 5*, page 29).

Whether the fabric is placed on the chair for pinning right side out or wrong side out is determined by the type of finish desired. Place fabric on chair *right side out* for a bound edge, *wrong side out* for a boxed edge, for a welted edge or for any inserted trimming, such as fringe.

Centering a Design

Centering Design   The directions which are given are for plain, evenly striped or all-over print fabrics. If a fabric with a large design or grouped stripes is used, the directions will have to be adjusted. The pattern or stripes must be centered by placing the fabric on the chair, so that the center of the design is in the center of the pieces. Then adjust it, following the straight of the goods, and proceed as outlined.

How to Fit a Slip Cover for a Wing Chair

Fitting Slip Covers   *Piece 1 — Front of Chair Back and Seat* (with cushion removed)— This piece extends from the top of the chair to the front of the seat. There should be 1″ seam allowances at top and front edges and a 4″ allowance for tuck-in at the sides and 8″ excess to allow for a 4″ tuck-in between back and seat. Follow *diagrams 4b, 4c and 4d* when fitting this piece.

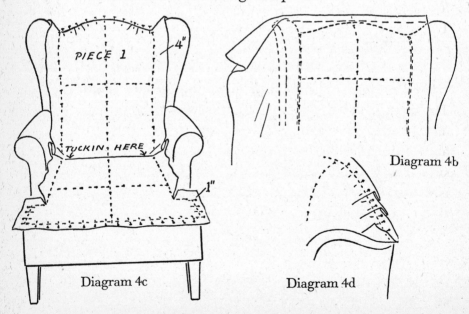

Diagram 4c

Diagram 4b

Diagram 4d

1. Mark a straight line 1″ from the straight top edge of fabric.

2. Place fabric on chair so that the line just marked is at the point at which the back upholstery ends (*see Back of Chair*, page 138). If the back and front chair pieces are joined by a boxing strip with a seam at both edges, the marked line should be at the front edge of the strip.

3. If there is a definite pattern, center the design (page 146). Otherwise take the measure of the widest point across seat (*see Front of Chair*, page 138), plus allowances for seams and divide this measurement in half. Measure this amount across straight edge of fabric and place this point at center back of chair (*diagram 4b*).

4. Be sure that the grain line of the fabric (*see figure 5*, page 29) is straight in relation to the length and width of the chair back. One way to assure this is to adjust the fabric very carefully and pin it to the chair, following a lengthwise thread down the center back. Then pin it on a crosswise thread about half way down the back (*see diagram 4c*).

5. Smooth the fabric up to the top edge from the crosswise pinning and pin it to the upholstery seam. The pins, which are placed with points facing inward, are not put in all the way. If there is excess fabric across the top, pin in corresponding pleats on each side. These pleats should turn toward sides on the finished cover, so if cover is being fitted wrong side out they should be turned toward center (*diagram 4d*).

6.   Smooth the fabric out from the lengthwise pinning and pin along the side edges at the creases where the back and wing meet. Trim edge 4″ from pin line. Do not cut into excess strip at side, as this will be used later. If back and front are joined with a boxing strip, pin the side pieces to the front edge seam and trim 1″ away.

7.   Smooth the fabric down to the seat line and tuck fabric into crease between back and seat as far as it will go.

8.   Smooth fabric across the seat of the chair and pin same straight thread which was pinned to center of back to center of seat. Pin across the center of seat on a crosswise thread also.

9.   Bring the fabric forward to the edge of the chair and pin to the front edge or to the upholstery seam.

10.   Cut off 1″ from pin line.

11.   Smooth fabric to creases at sides and pin along crease. Trim edge 4″ from pin line.

12.   If chair has a T-cushion, fit fabric around chair arm, slashing if necessary, and pin around T of chair seat. Trim this seam to 1″.

Piece 2 — Apron — This piece extends across the front of the chair from the edge of the seat to the bottom of the upholstery (or to the floor if there is no valance). It has a 1″ seam allowance on all sides. Follow *diagram 4e* to fit this piece.

1.   Be sure the cut-edge of fabric is straight, but do not cut through excess strip at side.

2.   Pin straight edge of fabric to the top edge of

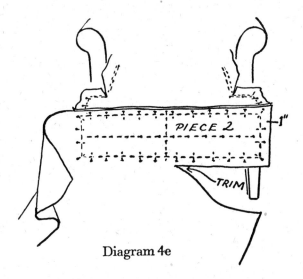

Diagram 4e

apron, leaving 1″ for a seam. If there is a large pattern in the fabric, center the pattern on this strip as before.

3. Pin strip to the upholstery at sides and across bottom. Extend piece to the floor if there is not to be a valance.

4. Trim 1″ beyond the pins.

Piece 3 — Pieces for Inside of Arm — These pieces extend along the arms of the chair on the inside from one end of the arm to the other and from the seat over the top of the arm to the seam in the upholstery. (Sometimes this piece is seamed at the roll of the arm just where it meets the wing. See illustration of chair trimmed with fringe on page 137.) These pieces have 1″ seam allowances on the front and top edges and 4″ tuck-in allowances on the bottom and back edges.

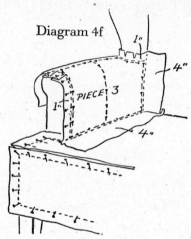

Diagram 4f

Follow *diagram 4f* above. When fitting each piece:

1. Straighten cut edge of fabric (without cutting excess strip).

2. Mark a straight line 4″ in from the straight top edge and crease on this line.

3. Pin this crease along the crease between seat and arm at the side and bring the fabric up and over the top of the chair arm.

4. If there is a large pattern in the fabric, center it, otherwise place the fabric on the arm so that one edge comes out over the front about 1″.

5. To make sure that the fabric is on the straight grain, pin fabric to the chair arm along a length-wise thread up the center of the arm and do the same on a crosswise thread across the top of the arm.

6. Smooth fabric toward the back and pin to the crease where the arm joins the back. Trim this seam to 4″.

7. Pin fabric firmly along upholstery seam where

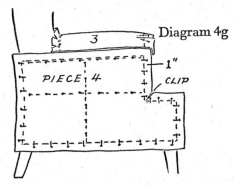

Diagram 4g

arm joins inside of wing. Trim 1″ away from pin line. Clip seam allowance if necessary to make it lie flat where the fabric curves around wing.

8. Smooth fabric toward the front and pin to upholstery around edge of arm. Trim 1″ from pin line. If the arm rolls, pin the fullness into tiny pleats. The pleats should turn down on the finished cover, so if cover is being fitted wrong side out, they should be turned up.

9. Smooth fabric up and pin along the line where the upholstery is seamed to the chair at the outside of the arm. This may be at the top of the arm or under the roll of the arm. If the outside and inside of the arm are joined by a boxing strip with two seams, pin this piece to the inner seam.

Piece 4 — Pieces for Outside of Arm — These pieces extend on the outside under the arms to the bottom of the upholstery (or to the floor if there is no valance) and from the front edge of the arms to the back of the chair. They have a 1″ seam allowance on all sides. Follow *diagram 4g* above. When fitting each piece:

1. Straighten the edge of the fabric (without cutting excess strip).

2. Mark top seam allowance 1″ from straight edge.

3. Place piece against side of chair. Center the design if necessary. If there is no design, extend the front of the piece 1″ beyond front edge of chair and pin 1″ marked line across top on the same upholstery line to which piece 3 was pinned. Extend the piece to back corner of chair.

4. Pin to edge of upholstery at front, back and bottom. Extend piece to the floor if there is not to be a valance. Trim seam allowances to 1″.

Piece 5 — Pieces for Inside of Wing — These pieces have a 1″ seam allowance on all sides except the inner edge where there is a 4″ seam allowance. Follow *diagram 4h.* To fit each piece:

1. Pin fabric on inside of wing so that the grain is straight and the pattern is attractively placed. Pin fabric to the chair along a lengthwise thread in the center and then pin on a crosswise thread. Smooth out to the edges.

2. Pin around all outside edges, making pleats along outer curve if necessary to make it fit. Pleats should turn down on the finished cover, so if cover is being fitted wrong side out, they should be turned up. Trim 1″ away from pins.

3. Pin the fabric to the crease between wing and back of chair and trim 4″ from pin line.

*Piece 6—Pieces for Outside of Wing—*These pieces have a 1″ seam allowance all around. Follow *diagram*

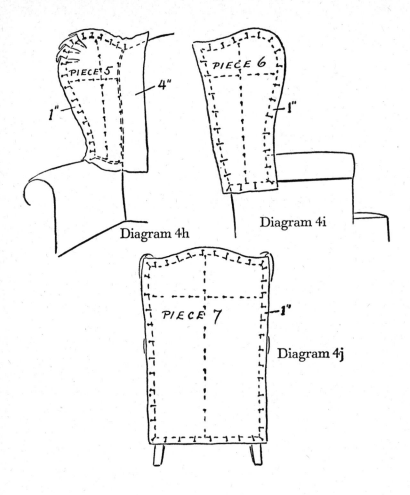

Diagram 4h

Diagram 4i

Diagram 4j

4i. To fit each piece: Fit the same way as for inside wing above. Trim seam allowance to 1″ all around. *Piece 7—Back of Chair*—This piece has a 1″ seam allowance all around. Follow *diagram 4j*.

1. Straighten fabric and mark a line 1″ in from straight edge.

2. Place fabric on chair so that marked line is at the

highest point at which the back upholstery ends (*see Back of Chair*, page 138).

3. Follow steps 3 and 4 under *Piece 1*, page 147.

4. Smooth fabric up to top and pin to top edge of upholstery, making pleats if it is necessary to fit in any extra fullness. Turn pleats same as on *Front of Chair Back*.

5. Smooth fabric out and pin to sides and bottom of chair. Extend piece to floor if there is not to be a valance.

6. Cut around edges, so that there is a 1″ seam allowance on all sides.

Piece 8—Pieces for Front of Arm—These pieces have a 1″ seam allowance all around. Follow *diagram 4k*. To fit each piece:

1. Place the fabric over the surface to be covered and pin in place around edges. Be sure that design is well placed and that the grain lines are straight. Cut two matching pieces.

2. Cut around edges, leaving a 1″ seam allowance on all sides.

Piece 9—Extra Cushion—For each cushion:

1. Cut two pieces, each ½″ larger all around than the top of the cushion. Be sure to center the design and keep the grain lines straight.

2. Cut a strip of fabric, 1″ wider than the width of the pillow and as long as the distance around the pillow plus 2″. (Boxing strip.) Piece if necessary.

Piece 10—Valance—Cut enough strips of fabric of the desired width to make the length needed. These may

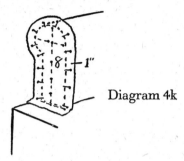

Diagram 4k

be cut on the length or the width (see layouts on page 144) by pulling a thread at the proper intervals and cutting along the line made.

Miscellaneous Pieces on Other Kinds of Slip Covers

On other kinds of slip covers it may be necessary to make a boxing piece or a small piece to cover the depth between the back and front. These are cut in the same way as *Piece 8*. They are pinned on to fit and cut with a 1″ seam allowance.

How to Sew Slip Covers

Before sewing a slip cover, remember that an opening must be left to permit the cover to be removed from the chair. This is usually at one back corner, and it extends from the floor to a point 3″ or 4″ above the arm. *Sewing Slip Covers*

To Finish with Bound Edge (Slip cover was pinned to the chair right side out.) *Bound Edge*

1. Pin all pieces of slip cover together except those edges where 4″ seam allowances were left and edges at opening. Mark these seams with chalk at the lines where they are pinned to chair. Make sure that cover is fitted snugly, adjusting if necessary.

2. Remove cover from chair and baste seams to-

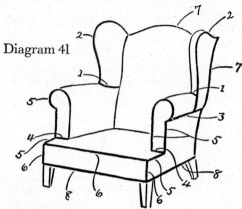

Diagram 41

gether along pinned lines with an uneven basting (*see figure 18*, page 35).

3. When seams are bound, it is easier to stitch, trim and bind each seam before it is stitched to the next piece. Start with the basted seam between the inside of arm and the inside of the wing—the seam marked No. 1 in *diagram 41*. Stitch this seam on basting line. Trim seam to ¼". Baste and stitch binding tape (½" to ⅝" wide) or prepared bias trim over this seam (*see figure 56*, page 50). Continue to stitch, trim and bind basted seams in the order indicated in *diagram 41*. Stitch back seam (7) around to top of opening, trim to ¼" but do not bind.

4. Turn slip cover to the wrong side and pin marked lines of 4" seams together. Trim seams evenly 4" away from pin line. It may not be possible to tuck the full 4" into the crease at the upper part of wing. If so, trim seam allowance so that there is only enough excess to tuck in neatly. A full 4" may be too much all the way down this crease. If so, adjust as necessary.

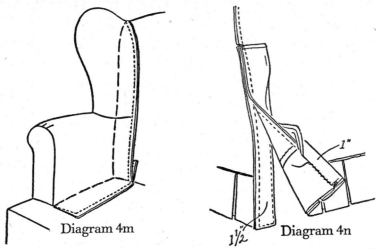

Diagram 4m   Diagram 4n

5. Pin edges together allowing ½″ seam, starting at top of seam between wing and front of chair back. Pin down to corner. Then pin in from corner formed by inside arm piece at front and seat piece. Leave excess on Piece 1 free in a pleat. Stitch edge of pleat together as shown in *diagram 4m*. Then baste seams out to ends from this corner. Stitch seams twice to resist wear.

6. Press all seams made on slip cover and place it on the chair. Turn up lower edge even with chair upholstery and baste.

7. Apply valance as described on page 160.

8. Finish the closing by using a prepared button tape or a zipper, or by placing a facing on the back piece and an extension on the side and closing with large snaps (*diagram 4n*). This is done as follows:

a. Trim seam allowance of opening to ¼″. Clip in to stitching line at end of opening.

b. Cut two bias strips (*see figures 48–51,* page

48) 1½" and 2½" wide respectively and ½" longer than the opening.

    c. Turn in ends ¼" on 2½" strip and place edge to edge (right sides together) against the edge of the opening which comes on the side of chair. Baste and stitch ¼" from edge.

    d. Turn in the raw edge ¼" and machine stitch or slip stitch it (*see figure 39*, page 41) to the seam line on the wrong side.

    e. *For a bound edge,* turn under ¼" along ends and one side of 1½" strip and stitch by machine. Place the raw edge of this piece against back of opening, wrong sides together. Stitch ¼" from edge. Bind entire back seam of chair, binding this edge of opening also (*diagram 4o*). *For a boxed or welted edge,* turn under ¼" along ends and one side of 1½" strip. Place raw edge of this piece against back of opening, right sides together. Stitch ¼" from edge. This will be along stitching line of welting, if edge has been welted. Turn to wrong side, crease along seam line and baste close to crease. For a boxed finish, stitch all around back seam and back of opening as on other seams.

    f. Sew large snaps at intervals to close.

Boxed Edge *To Finish with Boxed Edge* (Slip cover was pinned to the chair wrong side out.)

    1. Pin all pieces of slip cover together except at opening and where 4" seams are allowed. Mark these seams with chalk at the lines where they were pinned. Be sure that the cover fits snugly.

    2. Remove cover from chair and baste all seams

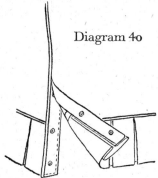

Diagram 40

along pinned lines. Pin marked lines of 4" seams together. Continue as described under step 4 under finish
for *Bound Edge* on page 156.

3. On all seams except where 4" were allowed,
stitch ⅛" from bastings (nearer edge) and trim seams
to ¼".

4. Pin and stitch seams where 4" were allowed as
in step 5 under finish for *Bound Edge* on page 157.

5. Turn slip cover to right side, crease all ¼" seams
back on seam line and baste close to crease. To make
boxed finish, stitch seams ¼" in from crease in the
order specified in *diagram 41*. Do not stitch back
seam (7).

6. Place slip cover on chair. Turn up lower edge
even with chair upholstery and baste.

7. Apply valance as described on page 160.

8. Finish the closing as described in step 8 under
finish for *Bound Edge*, page 157.

To Finish with Welted Seams (Slip cover was pinned   *Welted Seams*
to the chair wrong side out.)

1. Pin all pieces of slip cover together except at
opening and where 4" seams are allowed. Mark these

seams with chalk at the lines where they were pinned. Be sure that the cover fits snugly.

2.   Remove cover from chair. Trim all pinned seams to ½″.

3.   Unpin the seams following the order specified in *diagram 4l* on page 156, insert welting *(see figure 89, page 83)* and baste the seam with all the thicknesses sewed in. At back seam (7), continue welting along back edge of opening on ½″ seam line.

4.   Stitch welted seams with a cording foot *(see figure 87, page 82)* in the same order in which they were basted *(see diagram 4l)*.

5.   Pin marked lines of 4″ seams together. Continue as described under steps 4 and 5 under finish for *Bound Edge*, pages 156 and 157.

6.   Turn slip cover to right side. Place on chair and turn up lower edge even with chair upholstery. Put welting under this edge and baste.

7.   Apply valance as described below.

8.   Finish the closing as described in step 8 un finish for *Bound Edge*, page 157.

How to Make and Attach Valances

To Make a Shirred Valance

Shirred Valance   1.   Seam together pieces cut for valance (see page 154) and press seams open.

2.   Turn up and stitch a 2″ hem along one edge.

3.   Mark off raw edge into spaces, each twice the measurement of side, front, side and back of chair in that order.

4. Gather (*see figure 31*, page 38) raw edge with two rows of stitching, ½″ and 1″ from edge. Make separate gathering threads for each section.

5. Adjust gathers of each section to fit side in the usual manner (*see figure 32*, page 38). Pin gathered edge under lower edge of slip cover on 1″ gathering line. Adjust if necessary.

6. Remove slip cover from chair, baste and edge stitch cover to valance on fold.

To Make a Box Pleated Valance

1. Follow steps 1 and 2 for *Shirred Valance* above.

Box Pleated Valance

2. Along raw edge on right side of fabric, measure off and mark 1″ for seam allowance.

3. Mark off four sections in the following order. Each section should contain three times the length of a side. (Substitute individual measurements.)

    a.   3 times measurement of Side of Chair
    b.   3 times measurement of Front of Chair
    c.   3 times measurement of Side of Chair
    d.   3 times measurement of Back of Chair

4. Allow 1″ for seam allowance on other end.

5. Since the front of the chair is most important, the general width of the box pleats will be determined by the number of pleats it is convenient to fit into the front. On an average chair, from 7 to 11 pleats are used. An average chair which measures 28″ across the front will be used as an example. To fit other chairs, substitute individual measurements. Work as follows: Since the length of the front of the chair is 28″, section b marked off on the valance will be 84″. The following

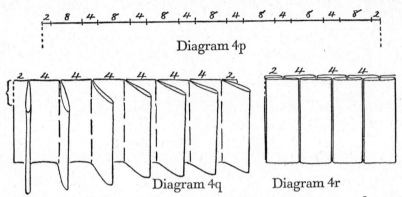

Diagram 4p

Diagram 4q   Diagram 4r

measurements for pleating the valance are determined:

a. Amount between pleats—28″ (length of front
of chair)

b. Amount for pleats—56″ (2 times length of
front of chair)

c. Number of pleats—7

d. Amount for each pleat—8″ (Step b ÷ by
Step c)

e. Amount between each pleat—4″ (Step a ÷
by Step c)

Divide section b as shown in *diagram 4p.* The 2″
(half of space between pleats) space on each end is
for the lap of the pleat on the corner.

6. If the side is the same length as the front or is
evenly divisible by 4″ (the figure in step 5e above) the
side pleats may be measured and marked in the same
way. If this is not possible, there will usually not be
more than 4″ (figure in step 5e) difference between
the two measurements. In this case, figure out the
amount of fabric for each pleat and amount of fabric

between pleat, following step 5 above. Substitute length of side of chair and use the same number of pleats.

7. To make the box pleats, baste together the markings of the 8″ pleat sections (*diagram 4q*).

8. Press pleats open into box pleats, equal amounts on each side of seam (*diagram 4r*). Baste and stitch in place along the raw edge.

9. Pin valance under turned edge of cover (on chair), adjusting to hang evenly.

10. Remove from chair, baste in place and edge stitch cover to valance.

To Make a Valance with a Box Pleat at Each Corner

Valance with Pleated Corners

1. See steps 1 and 2 for *Shirred Valance*, page 160.

2. Along raw edge on right side allow 1″ for seam allowance, then measure off 5″.

3. On the 5″ line make a fold and bring fold back to 1″ line, making an inverted pleat. Baste.

4. Pin valance under fold of cover (on chair) at one side of opening and bring fabric around to next corner. Mark. Measure two 5″ spaces, bring corner marking to first 5″ mark. Then bring second 5″ mark to meet this fold, making an inverted box pleat.

5. At each succeeding corner make a 10″ inverted box pleat in the same manner, pinning securely.

6. At the other side of the opening, make a 5″ pleat to match the first pleat made and leave 1″ for seam.

7. Remove valance from chair, baste pleats evenly,

press and stitch pleats together across the raw edge.

8. Pin valance under fold edge of cover and adjust to hang evenly.

9. Remove cover from chair, baste and stitch cover to valance along the fold edge.

How to Cover the Loose Cushion

Covering
Loose Cushion

1. Seam pieces cut for boxing strip (see page 154) together to make piece long enough to sew all around the cushion. Press seams open.

2. When welting is being used, baste welting to right side of upper and lower cushion pieces, raw edges together.

3. Begin to pin boxing strip to the middle of one side of upper piece of cushion. If a bound seam is being used, pin piece wrong sides together. If boxed or welted seams are used, right sides are pinned together.

4. Baste a 1″ seam for a joining, stitch, press.

5. When joining seam is made, baste pinned edges of strip to cushion, taking a ½″ seam.

6. Baste under piece of cushion to boxing strip just one half the distance around the cushion (half way along one side, all around the next side and half way along the next side).

7. Stitch basted seams, using cording foot for welted seams.

8. Finish opening as in step 8 under finish for *Bound Edge*, page 157. The extension is placed on the under piece of cushion, the facing on the boxing strip (*diagram 4s*).

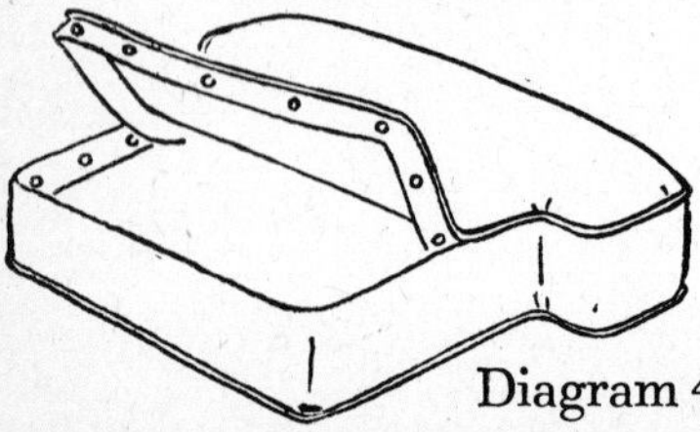

Diagram 4s

5. Bag of Tricks

Fashion has its own brand of magic, and every well-dressed woman could teach Houdini a trick or two. Only instead of taking rabbits out of her sleeve, she reaches into her bureau or closet and comes out with a dazzling new collar, a delightful little hat. And presto-chango! before you can say "needle-and-thread," a tailored town dress becomes a fluffy ingénue, a workaday suit a vamp. In the twinkling of an eye last year's dud is transformed into this year's darling. Try it and see for yourself how versatile the simplest wardrobe can be made. It's the most inexpensive magic in the world — a collection of simple-to-sew accessories is all you need.

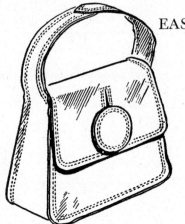

EASY-TO-MAKE ACCESSORIES

Felt Bag

(illustration on frontispiece)

Materials: Felt—⅝ yd.; lining fabric—½ yd.; interlining (strong, heavy unbleached muslin or drill cloth)—1½ yds.

Directions for cutting: (*see figure 4*, page 29, for directions on how to enlarge and use patterns).

Button—6 pieces, *pattern IXa*—2 felt, 4 interlining. Trim off ⅜" on all edges of one interlining piece and ¾" on all edges of three interlining pieces.

Back and Flap—3 pieces, *pattern IXb*—1 felt, 2 interlining. Trim off ⅜" on all edges of one interlining piece and ¾" on all edges of other interlining piece.

Reinforcement for Top of Bag—2 pieces of interlining, 2⅜" x 8".

Flap Facing—1 piece of felt, *pattern IXc*.

Front—3 pieces, *pattern IXd*—1 felt, 2 interlining. Trim off ⅜" on all edges of one interlining piece and ¾" on all edges of the other.

Gusset and Handle Piece—10 pieces, *pattern IXe*—2 felt, 8 interlining. Trim off ⅜" on all edges of the two interlining pieces, a ¾" on all edges of six interlining pieces.

Handle Facing—2 pieces of felt, *pattern IXf*.

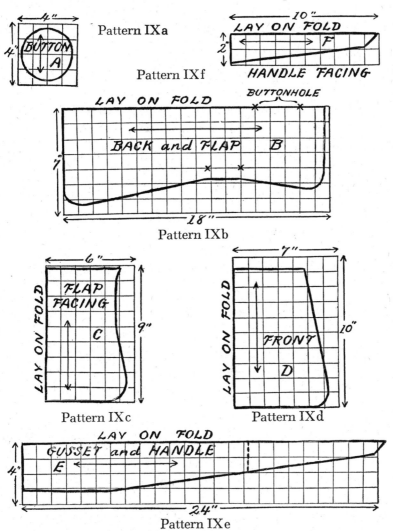

Pattern IXa

Pattern IXf

Pattern IXb

Pattern IXc

Pattern IXd

Pattern IXe

Lining for Front and Back—2 pieces of lining fabric, pattern IXd.

Lining for Gusset—2 pieces of lining fabric, *pattern IXe* to dotted line.

Directions for Making: (Press each piece of interlining

and fabric as it is prepared. Use a dry press cloth under a dampened press cloth and a moderately hot iron.)

1. Baste all the interlining pieces for each section together, the larger piece underneath with edges extending evenly. On the Gusset and Handle interlining, make two sets of four pieces, each consisting of one larger and three smaller pieces. After they are basted, run rows of stitching about 1″ apart lengthwise and crosswise through all thicknesses for firmness.

2. Baste together the two pieces for reinforcement for the top. Baste this double piece to the *Back and Flap* interlining at the narrowest part (on smaller interlining side). Make rows of stitching as above.

3. Note position of buttonhole on interlining. Draw a line between X's. Cut away ¼″ of interlining on all sides of mark.

4. Take felt *Back and Flap* piece. Baste the prepared interlining ½″ from edge to the wrong side of felt piece.

5. Take felt *Flap Facing*. Baste it to the top of Back and Flap section on the interlining side. Around the edge of the facing, stitch the two sections together with two rows of stitching, one row ½″ and one row ⅜″ from edge. Catch bottom of Flap Facing to interlining with hand sewing.

6. On right side of *Back and Flap* section make two rows of stitching, one row ⅛″ and one row ¼″ on each side of buttonhole mark. Slash between stitchings through all thicknesses.

7. Take felt *Front* piece. Baste the prepared interlin-

ing ½″ from edge to the wrong side of felt piece. Along top edge make two rows of stitching, one row ½″ and one row ⅜″ from edge.

8. Take the two sets of interlining of *Gusset and Handle* piece. Lap the wider ends one over the other for ½″ and stitch across this lapping once or twice. This makes one continuous piece.

9. Take the two felt pieces of *Gusset and Handle* section. Seam them together across the wide ends and press the seam open. Baste the prepared interlining ½″ from edge to wrong side of fabric.

10. Take two felt pieces for *Handle Facing*. Baste them to the tops of Gusset and Handle section on the interlining side. Around the edge of the facing only, stitch the two sections together with two rows of stitching, one row ½″ and one row ⅜″ from edge.

11. Now the bag is ready to be put together. Matching centers, baste the Gusset first to the Front and then to the Back. Stitch together with two rows of stitching, one row ½″ and one row ⅜″ from edge. Connect stitchings at Handle.

12. Make Button by enclosing interlining between 2 fabric pieces and join with two rows of stitching, one row ½″ and one row ⅜″ from edge. Attach to bag to meet buttonhole.

13. Lap one handle end over the other 3″ and sew together invisibly.

14. Sew lining pieces together and insert wrong side to wrong side. Turn in raw edge and hem to bag along upper edge.

Collars and Dickeys

Since the charm of neckwear is its crisp freshness, the prime requisite for fabrics is that they should launder well. Piqué, handkerchief linen, dress linen, organdie, gingham, broadcloth, dress silks and rayons are suitable.

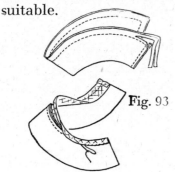

Fig. 93

Figure 93 — To make a detachable collar, place pieces of collar right side to right side. Pin, baste and stitch around outer edge, making a plain seam ½" wide *(see figure 20,* page 36). Trim seams to ¼", clip corners, if any. Turn to right side. Crease along seam line, baste close to crease and press. Baste a strip of bias 1" wide, cut from fabric *(see figures 48–51,* page 48), or of bias trim *(see figure 52,* page 49) to raw edge, right side to right side, turning in ends. Stitch ¼" from edge. Turn under free edge and slip stitch *(see figure 39,* page 41) to seam line. Press.

Figure 94 — To whip on lace edging or insertion, place right side of lace against right side of finished edge of garment, edge to edge. Work with lace towards body, easing the lace slightly between the thumb and forefinger, while taking small shallow whip stitches close together.

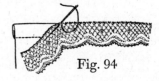

Fig. 94

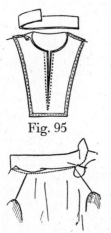

Fig. 95

Figure 95 — To make a slashed opening with a convertible collar, mark position of slash for opening and center of facing with basting lines, but do not cut. Baste center of facing to marked slash line, right side to right side. Using a very small stitch, stitch ⅛" to each side of basting, tapering to a point at bottom. Stitch twice around point where seam is very narrow. Make a narrow machine hem around edges of facing *(see figures 27–29,* page 37). Slash opening and turn facing to wrong side. Crease along seam line, baste close to crease, press. Cut a straight piece of fabric 5" wide and equal in length to the neckline, allowing 1" for seams. Fold through center lengthwise and stitch a ½" seam at both ends. Turn collar to right side and press. Baste and stitch one edge of collar to neckline (and facing) on wrong side, edge to edge (½" seam). Fold in raw edge of collar on right side and slip stitch *(see figure 39,* page 41) to seam. Press.

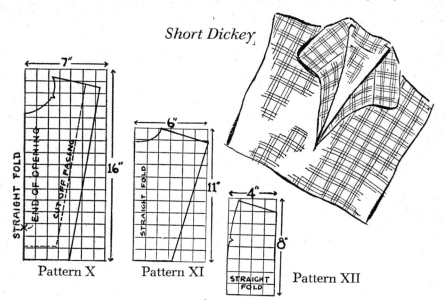

Short Dickey

Pattern X   Pattern XI   Pattern XII

Material: Fabric—½ yd.

Directions for Cutting: (see figure 4, page 29). Front—
1 piece, *pattern No. X;* facing—1 piece, *pattern No. X*
(see cut-off line); back—1 piece, *pattern No. XI;* collar
—2 pieces, *pattern No. XII.*

Directions for Making:

1.   Stitch back and fronts together at shoulder seams
with a plain seam *(see figure 20,* page 36).

2.   Make a slashed opening with a convertible collar *(figure 95).*

3.   Finish all outer edges with a narrow hem *(see
figures 27–29,* page 37).

4.   If buttons are desired, make a thread loop about
4″ from top on right side and two more at 2″ intervals
below *(see figure 101,* page 176).

5.   Sew buttons (⅜″ size) to opposite edge.

Two Dickeys

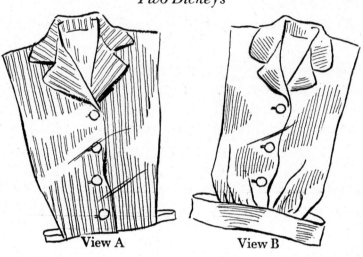

View A   View B

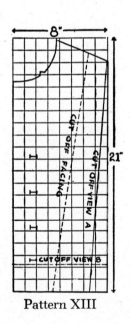

Pattern XIII

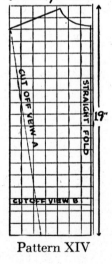

Pattern XIV

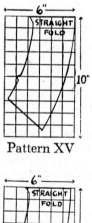

Pattern XV

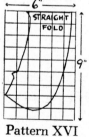

Pattern XVI

Material: Fabric — 1 yd. (for each dickey); buttons (½" size)— 4 (View A), 3 (View B); elastic — 9" (View A).

Directions for Cutting: (*see figure 4*, page 29). Note that the different revers, as well as the facing, have special cut-off lines that are clearly marked on the patterns. Observe these lines when cutting.

View A *Regulation Dickey*	*View B* *Band Bottom Dickey*
Fronts — 2 pieces	same
Pattern No. XIII	
Back — 1 piece	same
Pattern No. XIV	
Facing — 2 pieces	same
Pattern No. XIII (cut-off at facing line)	
Collar — 2 pieces	2 pieces
Pattern No. XV	*Pattern No. XVI*
	Waistband 2 pieces, each 7" x 17"

View A — Regulation Dickey

1. Mark buttonholes on outside of right front according to position marked (*see figure 98*, page 174).

2. Stitch fronts to back along shoulders, making a plain seam (*see figure 20*, page 36).

3. Make corded or welted buttonholes (*figure 99*) as far as applying facing. To make worked buttonholes (*figure 100*) do so after facing has been applied.

4. Make notched collar as shown according to either *figure 96 or 97*.

5. Finish buttonholes as in *figure 99*, or make worked buttonholes (*figure 100*). Sew buttons on left

Fig. 96

Figure 96 — To make a notched collar by attaching under collar to garment and collar to facing, stitch under collar to neckline of garment, right side to right side, edge to edge, center of collar matching center back, and matching any notches. At ends of collar and at shoulder seam, clip garment the width of the seam. Press so that both seam edges are turned toward collar edge in back and opened out flat in front. Make a narrow machine hem on the shoulder and outside edges of facing pieces *(see figures 27–29,* page 37). Stitch the outer collar to the two front facing pieces of the blouse, matching notches at the front edge of the collar. At ends of collar, clip facing the width of the seam. Press seam open. Fit the facing and collar to the garment, right side to right side. Baste and stitch. Trim seams to ¼". Clip away seam at corners. Turn front facing and outer collar to the wrong side, crease along seam line, baste close to crease, press. Turn under the raw edge of the collar and slip stitch to seam line *(see figure 39,* page 41).

Notched Collar

Figure 97 — To make a notched collar by making the entire collar separately, finish collar except neckline edge. Match center back of collar to center back of garment on outside and baste to neckline. Make a narrow hem on the shoulder and outside edges of facing pieces. Apply facing to front and neckline, right sides together, over the collar. Baste and stitch. Trim seams to ¼" and clip away seam at corners. Baste and stitch a 1½" strip of bias, folded through the center, at the back of the neck on seam line. Turn facing and bias at neck to wrong side. Slip stitch to garment *(see figure 39,* page 41).

Fig. 97

Figure 98 — To mark buttonholes, mark on the right side on the thread of the goods with a running stitch in contrasting thread. Use an H-shaped marking, the center line to mark the direction, the end marks to define the length. The distance from the edge of the garment is one half the diameter of the button to be used plus the seam allowance. The allowance for a buttonhole is ⅛" longer than the diameter of the button. Measure exactly. To measure the distance between buttonholes, use a Hem Gauge, *see figure 46,* page 44.

Fig. 98

Fig. 99

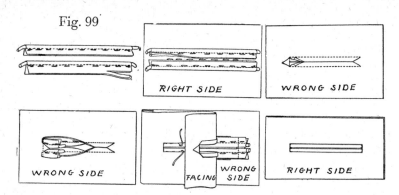

RIGHT SIDE   WRONG SIDE

WRONG SIDE   FACING   WRONG SIDE   RIGHT SIDE

Figure 99 — The bound buttonhole made with a strip of material is a professional finish, sometimes known as a welt buttonhole. Measure and mark as shown in *figure 98.* Cut a bias strip (*see figures 48–49,* page 48) of fabric ¾″ wide and long enough to allow for all the buttonholes. (Each buttonhole requires two strips of fabric, ¾″ longer than buttonhole marking.) For a corded buttonhole, make a cording by inserting No. 12 cable cord in bias strip (*see figure 87,* page 82). For a welted buttonhole, fold strip in half lengthwise, right side out and stitch ⅛″ from fold. Trim raw edges of strip (in either case) to within ⅛″ of stitching and cut into strips ¾″ longer than buttonhole marking. Baste strips on right side of garment with raw edges on marked line of buttonhole. Stitch along stitching line of strips, exactly the length of the buttonhole marking. Start stitching in center, stitch to one end, then back to opposite end and back to center. From wrong side, slash along marking line to within ⅛″ of ends, then clip diagonally to the corners. Bring strips through slashed opening to inside of garment. Be careful not to strain ends. Press. Stitch triangular sections at ends to cording. Make this a double stitching for strength. Press. Place facing over buttonhole, pin and baste carefully around buttonhole. Slash through from right side to get correct position, then continue on wrong side to within ⅛″ of ends, clip diagonally to corners. Turn under slashed edges of facing and slip stitch (*see figure 39,* page 41) to back of buttonhole along stitching line.

Buttonholes

Figure 100 — To make a worked buttonhole, measure as directed in *figure 98.* Stitch around marking by machine, using a small stitch to reinforce the buttonhole. Slash on marked line with a sharp scissors. Finish with closely worked buttonhole stitches.

To make a buttonhole stitch, thread the needle with a double thread. Hold buttonhole over forefinger and work from right to left, from the inside corner. Take a few running stitches from left to right to anchor thread at starting point. Bring the needle through from the wrong side just below stitching line, but do not draw it all the way through. Hold the thread near the fabric over the forefinger with the middle finger. Draw the thread near the needle to the right and then to the left under the needle. Pull the needle through and draw up the loop thus made. Work around the outside corner (toward edge of garment) in a fan-shaped curve. Finish at end with up-and-down stitches, secured by buttonhole stitches.

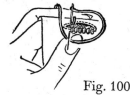

Fig. 100

front to match buttonholes *(see figure 102)*.

6. Finish sides of dickey with narrow hems *(see figures 27–29, page 37)*.

7. Make ½″ machine stitched hem along lower edges. Join back and front by inserting 4½″ of elastic at each side in open ends of hem.

View B — Band Bottom Dickey

1. Follow steps 1 to 6 under *View A*, above.

2. Turn under and press ½″ around all sides of waistband pieces. Fold in half lengthwise and mark centers. On lower edge of fronts, 2″ in from side edges, gather 3″ sections to 2″. Button fronts together and pin at lower edge. Insert front and back in each band, matching centers (see illustration, page 172). Baste all around band. Edge stitch *(see figure 38, page 41)* through all thicknesses.

3. Fasten front band to back with hooks and eyes *(figure 103)* or snaps *(figure 104)*.

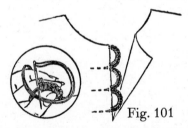

Fig. 101

Figure 101 — To make a thread loop, mark off diameter of button on edge of garment where desired. These spaces may be adjacent or separated. Make three stitches, joining one marking to the other, inserting a pencil to keep the loops the same size. Cover these foundation stitches with buttonhole stitches *(figure 100)*.

Figure 102 — To sew on buttons, mark position with pins. Use a double thread. Hide the knot under the button by pushing the needle through from the right side. Place the button in position. If it has holes, lay a pin across the top to keep the thread loose and sew back and forth across the pin. By winding the thread between the button and fabric, a shank is formed, permitting the buttonhole to slip easily.

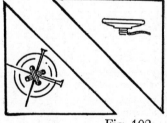

Fig. 102

Figure 103 — To sew on hooks and
eyes, use a double thread and an over-
and-over stitch through holes. Sew over
hook near top, to hold it down. The
curved eye extends slightly beyond the
edge of the opening. The straight metal
bar or thread loop *(figure 101)* is placed
on the seamline.

Fig. 103

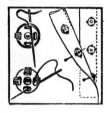

Fig. 104

Figure 104—To sew on snap fasteners,
use a double thread and conceal knot
under snap. Use an over-and-over stitch.
Sew each hole separately and carry
thread under snap to next hole. Attach
flat side of snap first. Hold the garment
closed and put a pin through the hole
in snap to mark location of other half.
Place snaps not more than 2″ apart.

Pointed or Round Collar

Material: ¼ yd. (see page 170 for fabrics) . . . *Directions for Cutting:* 2 pieces, *pattern No. XVII* (*see figure 4*, page 29) . . . *Directions for Making: See figure 93*, page 170, for making a detachable collar . . . *Suggested finishes:* A lace edging (*see figure 94*, page 170), a plain or corded piping (*see figures 86 and 89*, pages 72 and 83), a scalloped edge. (Mark edge of round collar with scallops. Make collar in usual way. Slash seam between scallops before turning.)

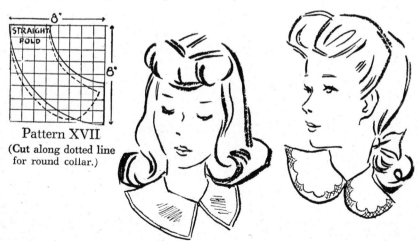

Pattern XVII
(**Cut** along dotted line
for round collar.)

Dirndl
(illustration, page 12)

Materials: Striped taffeta, 39″ wide. (Measure from waistline to floor and add 3″. Double this measurement to find out how much fabric you need.) Muslin, ⅛ yd.

Directions for Cutting: (*See diagram 5a* opposite for cutting layout for this dirndl and *figure 4*, page 29, for making and using patterns). Cut fabric into two equal pieces. Cut 14″ off the width of one piece. From this piece cut the peplum (*pattern No. XVIII*) in two pieces as shown in *diagram 5a*. From this piece, the waistband 4″ wide is also cut. The length of waistband equals your waistband measure plus 3″ for seam allowance. It is cut in two pieces. There is sufficient fabric if piecing is necessary.

Directions for Making: (½″ seams are allowed)

Press all seams as you make garment. Seam skirt on both sides. One side is left open 7″ for placket. Finish placket (*see figure 126*, page 215). Gather top of skirt (*see figure 31*, page 38). Seam pieces of the peplum, roll hem bottom edge, and gather top edge to 8¼″. Baste to back, matching centers. Cut piece of muslin 4″ wide and the same length as the waistband. Baste the muslin to the wrong side of one piece of waistband. Seam the two pieces right sides together along one long side and two short ends and turn to right side. Apply belt (*see figure 32*, page 38; *figure 135*, page 218), including peplum. Slip stitch raw side edges of peplum to skirt along stripe. Turn up hem.

The short drawstring dirndl below is made of denim. The length
of a regular skirt plus 6″ should
be doubled for amount of fabric.
Turn in 3″ top and bottom. Make
a 1″ casing at top and draw cable
cord through (about 2 yds.
needed).

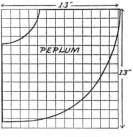

Pattern XVIII

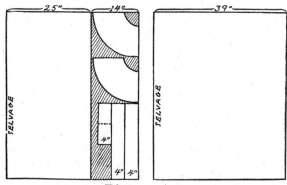

Diagram 5a

Espadrilles
Sizes 6 or 7

Material: Printed cotton—⅜ yd.; grosgrain ribbon—3¼ yds.; small pieces of felt, crinoline and toweling (scraps may be used since quantities needed are so small) . . . *Directions for Cutting:* (*see figure 4,* page 29) add ½" around pattern edges for seam allowance; 4 pieces, *pattern No. XIX*—1 fabric, 1 toweling, 1 crinoline, 1 felt; 2 bias strips (*see figures 48 to 51,* pages 48 and 49), 1" x 24" for binding; 1½" x 18" for loops. *Directions for Making:* (1 espadrille) Fold 1½" x 18" bias strip with right side inside and seam long edges. Turn to right side and cut in six equal pieces. Place three sole pieces together, fabric on top, then toweling and crinoline. Baste loops on fabric side as shown (see marks). Apply bias all around (*see figure 53,* page 49) catching in loops. Sew felt sole to bottom and lace as shown.

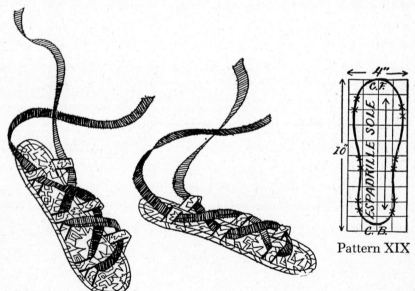

Pattern XIX

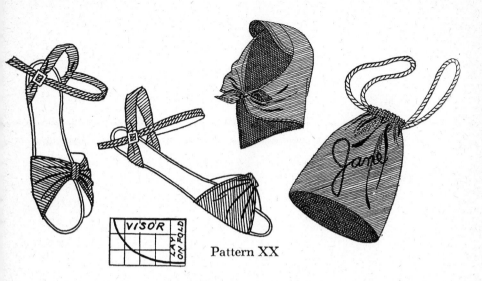

VISOR / LAY ON FOLD

Pattern XX

Sandals, Bag, Kerchief

Materials: Denim—1¼ yds.; heavy cable cord, 2 yds.; 2 small buckles, 2 cork inner soles, 2 pieces of felt, 4″ x 10″.

Directions для Cutting: (*see figure 4,* page 29). *Kerchief*—4 pieces, *pattern No. XX*—2 fabric (add ½″ around pattern edges for seam allowance), 2 crinoline (no seam allowance); 1 triangle (½ of 27″ square). *Bag,* 2 pieces, 16½″ x 19½″ (one piece could be cut of water proof fabric); 2 fabric circles 13″ in diameter; 1 cardboard circle, 12″ in diameter. *Sandals,* 4 pieces, 4″ x 4″ (fronts); 2 bias strips, 2″ x 8½″ (back strap); 2 straight strips, 1½″ x 12½″ (ankle straps and 3″ for center tab on front piece); 2 pieces of felt cut to fit cork inner soles. *Directions for Making*—Observe the drawings closely. There are no special problems in making this set.

Quartet in Leopard Cloth

Materials: Leopard cloth—1 yd.; lining fabric—1 yd. (bag, hat, scarf, mittens); crinoline—¼ yd. (hat); elastic 1½″ wide—⅛ yd. (mittens); 2 pieces of brown felt, 6″ x 9″ (mittens).

Directions for Cutting: (*see figure 4*, page 29). When cutting add ½″ around all pattern edges for seam

allowance. *Hat-Crown*, 3 pieces, *pattern XXIa*, 1 fabric, 1 lining, 1 crinoline; *Side-Crown*, 3 pieces, *pattern XXIb*, cut from same fabrics . . . *Bag*, 4 pieces, *pattern XXIc*, 2 fabric, 2 lining; for tab, 2 pieces (1¼″ x 5½″), 1 fabric, 1 lining for strips . . . *Ascot*, 2 pieces, *pattern XXId*, 1 fabric, 1 lining . . . *Mittens*, 6 pieces, *pattern XXIe*, 2 fabric (remember that it must be cut so that there is one right and one left), 2 lining, 2 felt (no seam allowance.

Directions for Making: These articles involve no particular difficulties. For the hat the crinoline is basted to the fabric and then it is treated as one piece. On the mittens, stitch the fabric and lining right side to right side, except on bottom edge. Turn to right side, press and slip stitch opening. Stitch the elastic about 1½″ from lower edge (see pattern) on wrong side of felt. Place fabric and felt wrong sides together and join with whipping stitches.

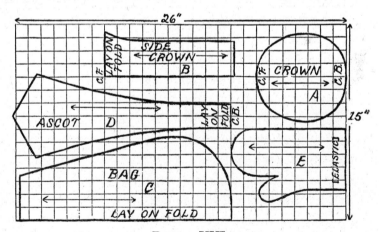

Pattern XXI

6. Pattern for Success

Who killed Cock Robin has always been much less of an enigma to the average woman than solving the mysteries of a pattern. For some reason many women shy away from commercial patterns under the impression, apparently, that they're deep enigmas. Actually, following a pattern presents no more difficulties than learning the multiplication tables, and once you've mastered it, you'll think you've always known how. Needless to say, it's an essential part of any woman's sewing education, especially today when patterns are more attractive than they ever were. The woman who wants the fashionable clothes of the moment is half way to having them if she makes herself pattern-wise. When you've finished the chapter that follows, you should be able to cut any pattern your heart desires.

SELECTION OF PATTERN AND FABRIC

When making clothing, commercial patterns pro- *Selection of*
vide fashions in the current trend which have been *Pattern*
designed to fit certain definite sizes. Even for those
with the ability and the desire to design their own
clothing, a commercial pattern makes a fine starting
point.

For successful dressmaking, the correct size of pattern is essential. The most important measurements
in choosing a pattern are the waist, bust and hip measurements. See page 188 for directions for taking these
measurements. Check the measurements with the size
information given on every pattern envelope. If they
do not coincide with any one standard size, it is advisable to choose a pattern according to bust measurement, as the adjustment of the waist and hip is rela-
tively easy. A skirt is always purchased by the waist
measurement.

In order to have successful results in sewing, it is
not enough to buy a pattern of the correct size. Another important consideration is the fabric from which
the pattern is to be made. It is a mistake to think that
any fabric may be used with any pattern. Patterns are
designed with definite types of garments in mind, and
pattern companies employ experts to give all the necessary information to insure success. On the envelope
of some commercial patterns is a list of suitable fabrics.
It is well to be guided by these suggestions. Chapter
13, beginning on page 287, gives descriptions of various
types of fabrics and suitable uses. This chapter also
discusses various finishes and descriptive terms used

on labels, to insure more intelligent purchasing of durable fabrics.

There is usually more than one view pictured on the pattern envelope. Before buying fabric, first choose the view to be made. On the back of the pattern envelope there is a chart of yardage requirements for each view in all sizes.

For convenience some patterns also list the necessary notions. Use the guide for correct thread and needles for specific fabrics on page 315. The thread should be slightly darker than the fabric, because thread, when worked into fabric, appears lighter.

The minimum equipment necessary for sewing is given on page 15. Before beginning to cut, consult page 306 on the preparation of fabric for cutting to see whether shrinking the fabric is necessary.

EXPLANATION OF COMMERCIAL PATTERN

Commercial Pattern

When beginning to cut, first take out the worksheet that comes with the pattern. Part of the worksheet is devoted to pattern layouts showing the sewer how to lay out the pattern on the fabric in the most economical way. Each view of the pattern has its own group of layouts for all sizes in various widths of fabric. Pick out the layout of the view and size desired and circle it so that it may be referred to readily whenever necessary. Following this layout, unfold the pattern and check each piece against the layout. If the piece is to be used, mark it plainly in pencil with its correct name. Fold together all the pieces which are not needed and return them to the pattern envelope.

Every pattern has certain marks that must be understood. On some patterns, directions are printed, but on most patterns various sized perforations indicate markings. Look for the mark which indicates the *seam allowance*. This will usually be a line of marks or perforations from ½" to ⅝" in from edge. *Notches* are nicks in the edge of the pattern and are most important because they mark the points at which the various pieces must fit together exactly. *Darts* are sometimes used to take in fullness at the back of the neck, the front shoulder, the top of the sleeve, the elbow, the underarm and waistline. They are wide at the seam edge and taper to a point in the body of the garment. Darts are clearly marked on the pattern. *Tucks, pleats and gathers* are also used to take in fullness but they are not stitched to a point as in the case of a dart. Observe how they are indicated. Somewhere on the pattern there will be some sort of a distinctive mark, not used for anything else, which will indicate *the straight of the goods*. These marks must always fall on a lengthwise thread of the fabric (*see figure 5*, page 29). There can be no exception to this rule. Never cut a piece with these marks placed otherwise in order to save material. The garment will not hang properly if the pattern is not cut with the straight of the goods properly set.

ALTERATION OF PATTERN

Before placing the pattern on the fabric it will be necessary to give some thought to the fit of the pattern. The pattern was bought by the bust or waist

Alteration of Pattern

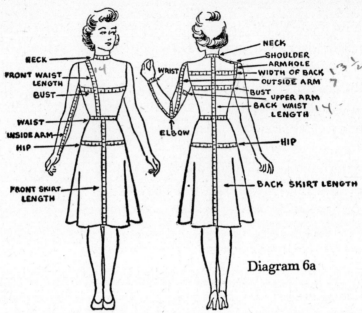

Diagram 6a

measurement. The rest of the measurements of the pattern have been designed to coincide with these measurements which are based on an average size. Most figures differ considerably from the average. It is best to alter the pattern before cutting, in order to reduce to a minimum the alterations necessary when the sewing begins.

To know where adjustments will be necessary, it is helpful to have a complete chart of individual measurements. Some adjustments are more easily made by checking the pattern measurements against individual measurements.

How to Take Individual Measurements

Taking Measurements   A list of the necessary measurements follows, with instructions as to how to take them. In the space at the right, under the caption *Individual Measurements,* note measurements for ready reference whenever buying or altering a pattern. Have someone assist in taking the measurements as it is impossible to do it alone. Remove dress and mark true waistline by tying a tape or ribbon around it. Take all measurements around body easily except waist, since this is the only part of a garment which is fitted snugly. See *diagram 6a* for where to take measurements.

$13\frac{1}{2}$

Front Measurements *Individual Measurements*

1. *Neck* — around neck at the level of the hollow of $13\frac{1}{2}$
the neck in front and the base of the neck in back.
2. *Bust* — around fullest part of the bust, about 1" 32
below armhole, and a little higher in back; take measurement from back.
3. *Waist* — around natural waistline. $26\frac{1}{2}$
4. *Hip* — around body about 7" below waistline at 36
fullest part of hips.
5. *Front Waist Length* — from center of shoulder to 14
waistline over fullest part of bust.
6. *Front Skirt Length* — from waistline to desired $24\frac{1}{2}$
length.

Back Measurements

1. *Width of Back* — from armhole to armhole, 5" below base of neck. Armhole should come well over shoulder blade in fleshy part between arm bone and shoulder blade.
2. *Back Waist Length* — from base of neck to waistline.
3. *Back Skirt Length* — from waistline to desired length.

Arm and Shoulder Measurements

1. *Shoulder* — from base of neck to top of arm bone $4\frac{1}{2}$
in shoulder, a little to the back of center.
2. *Armhole* — around top of arm over bone in shoulder from 1" below armpit.
3. *Outside Arm* — from shoulder to wrist, around elbow, with arm bent.
4. *Inside Arm* — from armpit to wrist with arm straight.
5. *Upper Arm* — around fullest part.
6. *Elbow* — around elbow with arm bent. $9\frac{1}{2}$
7. *Wrist* — around wrist, just above hand.

If alterations are made in the pattern before cutting, there will be much less difficulty in fitting after it has been cut. Pattern pieces are pinned together and tried on to see where alterations are necessary but it is usually most satisfactory to make actual adjustments on the flat pattern. When preparing pattern to try on, look carefully at the pattern and the worksheet. Pin in all darts, pleats and tucks. Gathered sections should be folded and pinned into small pleats. Pin together sections of waist, skirt and sleeve separately, matching notches. Place pins parallel to edges at seam line. To prevent tearing, do not pin too close to armhole at underarm seam of the waist or sleeve.

Making Alterations on the Waist Pattern

Try on the waist first with dress removed. Directions for the more ordinary adjustments follow.

If the Waist Pattern is Too Long or Too Short

Measure how much longer or shorter it is than the normal waistline by comparing the Waist Length measurements on page 189 with similar measurements taken on pattern. The seam allowance should not be included in measuring pattern. Three inches above the waist, on both back and front of pattern, draw a horizontal line across the pattern. This line should be at right angles to the lengthwise grain, which is plainly marked on the pattern by some special perforation or line.

If the waist pattern is too long, measure up from this line and mark at two or three points a distance equal to the amount which the pattern needs to be shortened. Using these marks as a guide, draw another line parallel to the first. Bring first line to meet second, making a tuck, and pin *(diagram 6b).* When the pattern is placed on the fabric, be sure that the side seam is cut as shown by the dotted line. Check to be sure that the back and front have been shortened the same amount.

If the waist pattern is too short, cut along the horizontal line on both back and front. Pin tissue paper to the edge of the top piece of the pattern. From this edge measure down and mark a distance equal to the amount the pattern needs to be lengthened. Following these marks, draw a horizontal line on the tissue paper. Pin the lower piece to this line *(diagram 6c).* Cut off excess tissue paper even with side edge. Check to be sure that the back and front have been lengthened the same amount.

Diagram 6b   Diagram 6c

If the Shoulder of the Pattern is Too Long

A normal shoulder extends from the base of the neck to the top of arm bone at the tip of the shoulder. When the shoulder of the pattern is too long, measure the length of the shoulder of the pattern between seam allowance markings of the neck and armhole. From this subtract the individual Shoulder measurement (page 189) to see how much adjustment is necessary. Pin a piece of tissue paper under the waist front pattern so that it protrudes beyond shoulder and armhole edge. Draw around shoulder and armhole. At center of armhole slash in about 1". At center of shoulder draw a line down to meet the slash at the armhole and slash *(diagram 6d)*. Remove the slashed piece. From the armhole end of the shoulder line drawn on the tissue paper, mark off the distance of the adjustment. Replace the slashed piece. Keep the edge at center of armhole at its regular position on the marked armhole line, but swing the top corner inward to the point marked *(diagram 6e)*. Pin slashed piece to tissue and pattern. Make a straight edge along the shoulder as indicated by the solid line. Trim away tissue paper. Repeat with waist back of pattern.

Diagram 6d   Diagram 6e   Diagram 6f

If the Shoulder of the Pattern is Too Short

If the person who is being fitted has broad shoulders, the shoulders of the pattern are apt to be short. If so, measure the length of the shoulder of the pattern between seam allowance markings of the neck and armhole. Subtract this from the individual Shoulder measurement (page 189) to see how much adjustment is necessary. Follow the same procedure as if the shoulder of the pattern were too long (above) up to removing the slashed piece. Then, on the shoulder line drawn on the tissue paper, make an extension equal to the distance of the adjustment. Replace the slashed piece. Keep the edge at center of armhole at its regular position on the marked armhole line, but swing the top corner outward to the marked point *(diagram 6f)*. Pin slashed piece to tissue and pattern. Make a straight edge along shoulder as indicated by the solid line. Trim away tissue paper. Repeat with waist back of pattern.

If Shoulders Are Square

If the shoulders of the person being fitted are square, the pattern will wrinkle from the shoulder toward the neckline when it is tried on. If it has only a slight wrinkle, let out the shoulder seam at the armhole while the pattern is being tried on, to see if wrinkle will disappear. If this is not enough, remove pattern and pin a small piece of tissue to the seam edges of both front and back shoulders, graduating from nothing at the neckline to about 1″ at the armhole *(diagram 6g)*. Repin shoulder seam and try on the pattern again, adjusting until wrinkle disappears. Graduate the amount added to shoulder at armhole edge to the regular seam allowance at the neck edge. Trim tissue paper, allowing regular seam allowance from new shoulder line (pinned line). Build up underarm, as shown, the amount added to the shoulder.

Diagram 6g   Diagram 6h   Diagram 6i

If Shoulders Are Sloping

If the shoulders of the person being fitted are sloping, the pattern will wrinkle from the armhole to the neck when it is tried on. Below the shoulder line pin in a shallow dart near the shoulder seam line, beginning at the armhole and graduating to nothing near the neck *(diagram 6h)*. Do this on both the back and the front. Adjust the dart until the pattern lies perfectly smooth. If the armhole is too small as a result of this alteration, at the lower edge of the armhole trim off an amount equal to the amount taken up in the dart.

If Bust is High

A high bust will cause the pattern to pull up at the center when it is tried on. Measure how much shorter the center point of the waist is than the normal waistline. Take off the pattern and unpin. On the front only, unpin the darts at the side. At the bust line draw a horizontal line across the pattern at right angles to the mark of the lengthwise grain. Cut on this line. Pin tissue paper to the edge of the top piece of the pattern *(diagram 6i)*. From this edge measure and mark in a few places a distance equal to the amount the waist needs to be lengthened. Following these marks, draw a horizontal line on the tissue paper and pin lower piece to this line. Cut off excess tissue paper. Repin darts and mark a new dart the same length as darts already in pattern where the extra tissue was inserted, including all of it at side edge. Repin darts and seams and try on. Adjust if necessary.

If Chest is Flat

A flat chest will cause a dip in the center front and wrinkles at the underarm of the front when pattern is tried on. To remove wrinkles and lift lower edge, take a dart in the center front above the bust line, tapering to nothing at the side seam just under the arm *(diagram 6j)*. Remove pattern and pin tissue paper under the center front and straighten the edge as indicated by solid line.

If Shoulders Are Round

Rounded shoulders will cause the pattern to pull up from bottom at center of back and pull away from the neck when it is tried on. If this defect is evident,

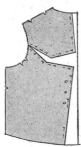

Diagram 6j   Diagram 6k

mark back armhole edge a little less than half the distance from top. Mark center back about 8″ down from neck edge. Draw a line from edge of back at right angles to lengthwise grain about two-thirds of the way across pattern. Draw line down to meet this from armhole mark. Slash along line, stopping just short of mark at armhole edge. Spread tissue paper under back, pinning and trimming it around shoulder, armhole and under arm seam, allowing it to protrude at neck, center back and bottom. Pin front and back together again at shoulder and under arm seam. Try on the pattern. Mark the center back line with pins on the tissue paper and arrange and pin slash so that pattern comes to proper lower edge *(diagram 6k)*. To make the pattern lie flat, it will be necessary to make pleats at the neck and at the lower edges. Trim away excess paper. The slight extra fullness at neck and lower edge may be taken in by tiny darts.

If Neck is Large or Small

To make neckline larger, trim off necessary amount from neck edge. Remember that a seam allowance must be kept. To make neckline smaller, insert a piece of tissue paper under neck edge and recut higher. If neckline is changed, adjust collar to match. Take a tuck to make the collar smaller; slash and make an insertion of tissue paper to make the collar the necessary amount larger.

Making Alterations on the Skirt Pattern

When all the adjustments have been made in the waist, pin the skirt pieces together and pin up the hem allowance. Fit skirt separately and make adjustments.

If a Straight Skirt Pattern Is Too Long or Too Short

Measure how much longer or shorter skirt is than normal. If it is only about 1″ too long, turn the excess up at the hem. Otherwise, remove the pattern and unpin. Below the hipline make a pleat to shorten the necessary amount (*dia-*

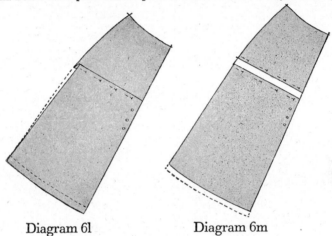

Diagram 6l   Diagram 6m

gram 6l), or make a slash and insertion to lengthen (*diagram 6m)* in the same manner as for waist pattern which is too short (see page 190). The dotted line on the side indicates the edge to be followed in cutting.

If a Flared Skirt Pattern Is Too Long or Too Short

Measure how much longer or shorter skirt is than normal. To make it longer, merely add necessary amount at hemline when cutting. Continue line of flare at sides to new hemline. To make skirt shorter cut off desired amount at lower edge. Slash pattern through center from hem almost to top. Pin cut-off hem section over pattern and spread slash to fit it (*diagram 6n).*

If Pattern is Too Small at Waistline and Hips

If the pattern does not come to the center at the waistline and hip, measure how much short of the center they are. The hipline is about 7″ down from waistline. Take off pattern and unpin. Draw a line parallel to the grain line from hem to waist about one third of the distance from side to center. Slash on the line and insert tissue paper (*diagram 6o)* in same manner as for waist

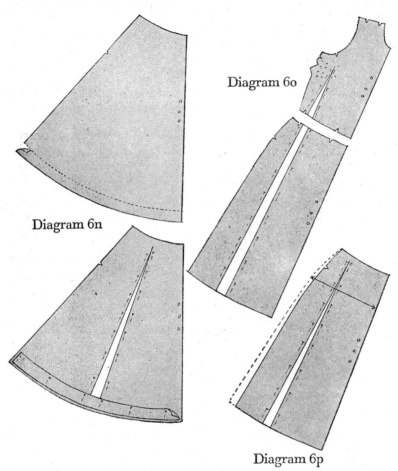

Diagram 6o

Diagram 6n

Diagram 6p

pattern which is too short (page 190). If the skirt is joined to a waist, the waist must be slashed to correspond. Slash from the lower edge to about 2" below the armhole and insert paper to hold slash open the same amount that top of skirt was spread.

If Hips Are Large and Waistline Normal

Try on the pattern. The pattern will not come to the center at the hip. Measure to find out how much allowance is necessary to make pattern reach center. Slash in the same manner as before, stopping slash just short of the waistline. Insert tissue paper to hold slash apart *(diagram 6p)*. Make sure that the extra measurement at the hipline is correct, and let the rest fall naturally.

To allow for this in another way, when cutting skirt add the extra amount from the hipline all the way to the lower edge. From the hipline up, taper off to nothing at the waist.

Diagram 6q

Diagram 6r

If Skirt Pattern Pulls Up in Front

Measure the amount by which the dress is short. If this is slight, raise the center back until the side seam hangs straight *(diagram 6q)*. If the amount is considerable in a two-piece dress, add one half the amount at waistline (half at lower center front of waist and half at top center front of skirt, tapering off to the regular seam allowance at the side). Add the other half at the lower edge of skirt *(diagram 6r)*.

Making Alterations on the Sleeve

When trying on pattern do not try to pin all the way into the armhole. Just pin seam line to seam line on the upper half of the sleeve seam.

If Sleeve Pattern is Too Long or Too Short

Measure sleeve pattern from center at top along lengthwise grain marking to lower edge. Do not include seam allowances. Compare this measurement with Outside Arm measurement (page 189). Length is adjusted by a pleat to shorten *(diagram 6s)*, or an insertion above and below the elbow to lengthen *(diagram 6t)*. Handle in the same manner as for the waist pattern (page 190).

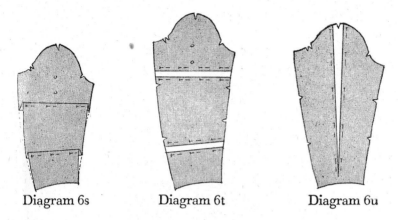

| Diagram 6s | Diagram 6t | Diagram 6u |

If Top of Arm is Larger than Normal

To find out how much is needed to adjust size of sleeve, compare Armhole and Upper Arm measurements (page 189) with similar pattern measurements. Seam allowances should not be measured on pattern. Slash through center the length of the sleeve pattern, stopping just before reaching wrist. Use tissue paper to hold slash apart the required distance *(diagram 6u).*

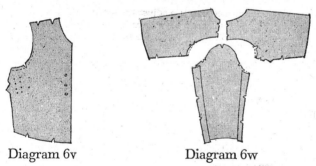

| Diagram 6v | Diagram 6w |

To Adjust Armhole for Both Methods

When the sleeve is made larger, the armhole must also be adjusted. Cut the armhole as indicated by taking off half of the amount added on the front and half on the back *(diagram 6v).*

If Arm is Very Thin

To make the sleeve smaller, take tucks at the sides of the sleeve parallel to the grain line *(diagram 6w)* to make sleeve correspond to Upper Arm measurement (page 189). Add to the armhole the same amount taken from the sleeve, half to the back and half to the front.

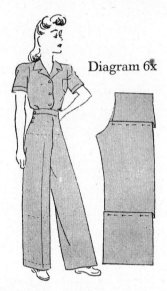

Diagram 6x

Making Alterations on Patterns for Slacks or Shorts
If the Pattern is Too Long or Too Short

Measure the amount necessary to adjust the length. Make a tuck to shorten *(diagram 6x)*, or slash and make insertions to lengthen at the points marked with a dotted line *(diagram 6x)*. Make these in the same manner as for the waist pattern (page 190).

CUTTING OUT A PATTERN
Pinning the Pattern to the Fabric

Pinning Pattern   Use the pattern layout on the worksheet suitable to the view chosen, the width of the fabric and the size — the layout circled previously when pattern pieces were removed from envelope (page 186). Follow this chart exactly. A beginner who attempts to shift or rearrange is apt to forget that sleeves cut separately must be made to fit opposite arms. No additional space is needed between pieces when pinning, since the seam allowance is included in the pattern. An exception is made for cutting a coat or a garment of heavy fabric and for fabrics which fray easily. Here a 1″ allowance is made on side seams to allow for any alterations.

Fabrics with a design, a stripe, a check, a plaid or a nap, must have special consideration and require more yardage than plain fabric. When a design points in one direction, the top edges of all the pattern pieces must point in one direction. When stripes, checks and plaids are used, the closings and seams must match, and the sleeves must match the blouse. This is accomplished by making sure that corresponding notches on pieces which are joined together are laid on the stripes in exactly the same manner in each place where the pattern piece is applied *(diagram 6y)*. Occasionally,

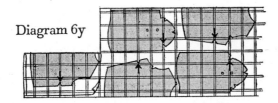

Diagram 6y

a stripe or a plaid will have a repeat, that is, certain grouping of stripes or plaids will repeat themselves at regular intervals. In this case even more care must be used in placing corresponding notches on the same stripe in a repeat. When there is an irregular repeat the top edges of all the pattern pieces must all face in one way. On a napped or pile surface (see pages 290 and 291), there is an up and down. This is determined by brushing a hand over the surface. On both surfaces, patterns must be placed so that top edges are all in the same direction. On the napped surface the smooth way must run upward in the garment, but on a pile surface either way may be used as desired.

Press all wrinkles and creases from fabric. Straighten top edge as shown in *figures 6 and 7*, page 32. Pin every piece in place as indicated on layout before cutting (*diagram 6z*). On each pattern piece, pin the marks

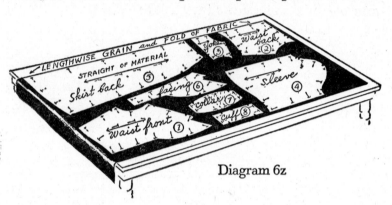

Diagram 6z

which indicate the straight lengthwise grain on a lengthwise thread. Then smooth the pattern out toward the edge. Pins are put in at right angles to edge (*figure 8*, page 33) closer together along curves than along straight edges. If part of the pattern is laid on a fold, pin the edge that lies along the fold first.

Cutting Out the Pattern

Cutting out Pattern   Use bent trimming shears (dressmaker's shears) (see page 310) for cutting. They will make long clean strokes. Cut notches out rather than in as shown on the pattern. The seam allowance is thus kept intact.

Marking the Fabric

Marking Fabric   Do not remove the pattern pieces from the fabric until each piece has been marked for stitching. The pattern is marked as follows:

1. Mark all perforations which indicate seams, darts, pleats, pocket, and buttonhole locations. There are several methods of marking perforations: tailor's tacks *(figure 105)*, carbon paper with tracing wheel *(figure 106)*, chalked thread *(figure 107)* and chalking perforations marked with pins *(figure 108)*.

Fig. 105

Figure 105 — To make tailor's tacks for marking fabric, use a double thread. Make a looped back stitch in each perforation and join perforations with a long stitch. Clip the latter and remove pattern. Separate the two thicknesses of the fabric slightly and cut the threads.

Fig. 106

Figure 106 — To mark with a tracing wheel, do not trace directly on the table. Be sure it has a protective covering such as a marking board or layers of newspaper. Cottons and linens may be traced directly through pattern. When marking with a tracing wheel on wool fabrics, use white or yellow carbon paper. Fasten a piece of this carbon with wax side up to a card table or marking board. Lay the cut-out portion of the garment fabric side down over the carbon. Run the tracing wheel along marking lines on pattern. The lines will appear as a series of tiny white dots. Remove pattern, but keep the two pieces of fabric pinned together. Now turn marked piece uppermost, place unmarked piece against the carbon and run tracing wheel along the white line of dots. This marks second piece of fabric just as the first was marked.

Fig. 107

Figure 107 — To mark with chalked thread, thread a needle with a short thread, rub thread over chalk and draw it through and out of perforations. Renew the chalk each time the thread is drawn through.

2. Run a marking basting along all center folds, whether back, front, collar, skirt or yoke (*figure 109*). Always consult pattern directions to find out what perforations indicate the center front when the garment has a front closing. On the sleeve begin from the marking which indicates the top of the sleeve and run a line of basting on a lengthwise thread down about 8″. About 3″ under the armhole, make a line of basting on a crosswise thread. Each of these lines will be perpendicular to the other.

3. Mark armhole and neckline with a running stitch along seam line (*figure 109*). It is most important that these lines should not be stretched. Always work on them with great care, especially the neck. It is advisable to machine stitch around these edges if the fabric is particularly sheer.

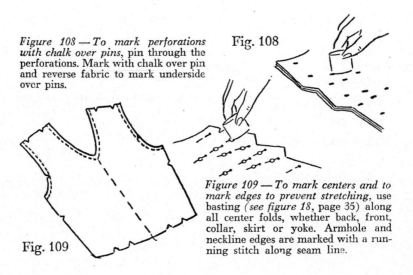

Figure 108 — To mark perforations with chalk over pins, pin through the perforations. Mark with chalk over pin and reverse fabric to mark underside over pins.

Fig. 108

Figure 109 — To mark centers and to mark edges to prevent stretching, use basting (*see figure 18*, page 35) along all center folds, whether back, front, collar, skirt or yoke. Armhole and neckline edges are marked with a running stitch along seam line.

Fig. 109

7. On the Make

Nothing about you is as eloquent as the way you look. Your clothes reflect your personality, tell the story of your taste. It's in your hands whether they tell an attractive story, one that makes people like to look at you, makes you proud to look at yourself. That doesn't mean you have to spend a fortune on your clothes, but it does mean that they must be becoming, fit like the proverbial dream. Nobody knows or cares how much your dress or your blouse cost, but what does matter is the finesse with which it's put together. In this chapter you will get to the bottom of every dressmaker's trick, learn to look-like-a-million and do it for a song.

GENERAL PROCEDURE IN MAKING
A GARMENT

General Procedure

(For details on steps 1–5, see Chapter 6, page 184.)

1. Select the pattern and fabric, matching findings (page 186) at the same time. 2. According to view of pattern chosen, determine pieces of pattern to be used. 3. Alter pattern, if necessary. 4. Follow pattern layout in cutting fabric, being careful to check straight of goods. 5. See that all perforations, notches and markings are made. 6. Work on a table. 7. Pin before basting, inserting pins at right angles. On seams match notches, pin ends and then pin in between (see page 207 for details on bastings). 8. Before stitching the seams, test the machine stitch and the tension on a sample piece of the fabric used (see page 22). See chart on page 315 for correct needle and thread sizes to be used with every fabric.

Specific instructions on how to make a skirt, a blouse and a dress follow. In studying the steps, it will be observed that there is a certain similar routine in each one. For successful results, this order of procedure should be followed in making any garment.

Two words which occur frequently are fitting and pressing. Pressing is discussed on page 221, and fitting on page 223. Without careful attention to these two details, the garment will look "homemade."

When making any garment, basting, darts, pleats, seams, necklines, plackets, belts, pockets and hems are mentioned. Various finishes for all of these constructions are discussed, beginning on page 207. At each

*Basic Dress —
Suggestions for
making given on
following page.*

*Basic Skirt and Blouse—
Suggestions for making
given on following page.*

stage of the procedure turn to this reference section and choose the construction best suited to the garment.

Steps in Making a Skirt

Steps in
Making Garments   For each construction, see reference section, beginning on page 207.
1. Stitch any seams and baste all darts and pleats that are part of the actual construction of the front and back. 2. Pin and baste skirt together along side seam markings, allowing opening at left side for placket. 3. Try on skirt right side out for first fitting (see page 223). 4. Stitch darts and seams and press. 5. Finish placket and press. 6. Finish seams. 7. Apply belt to top of skirt and press. 8. Try on for second fitting (see page 225). 9. Turn up and finish hem. 10. Sew fastenings on skirt. 11. Press skirt.

Steps in Making a Blouse

For each construction, see reference section, beginning on page 207.
1. Baste all darts, pleats and gathers that are part of the actual construction of the front and back. 2. Pin and baste blouse together along seam markings at underarm and shoulder. 3. Try on blouse right side out for first fitting (see page 224). 4. Stitch darts and seams, press. 5. Finish seams. 6. Make pockets and buttonholes (if they are welted or corded) and press. 7. Apply facing and collar and press. 8. Finish welted buttonholes, or make worked buttonholes. 9. Sew on buttons. 10. Stitch, press and finish sleeve seam. 11. Pin and baste sleeve into blouse. 12. Try on for second fitting (see page 225). 13. Sew in sleeve, finish seam and press. 14. Make and put in shoulder pads. 15. Try on for third fitting (see page 226). 16. Finish lower edge of sleeve. 17. Finish lower edge of blouse. 18. Press blouse.

Steps in Making a Dress

For each construction, see reference section, beginning on page 207.
1. Stitch any seams and baste all darts, pleats and gathers that are part of the actual construction of the front and back pieces of dress. When there is a special construction on the skirt, such as the pockets on the dress illustrated, make the skirt front as directed in the pattern. 2. Pin and baste skirt and blouse pieces together separately along seam markings and try on right side out for first fitting (see page 223). 3. Stitch darts, gathers or pleats, underarm and side seams, shoulder seams and press. 4. Make pockets and buttonholes (if they are welted or corded) and press. 5. Apply facing and collar and press. 6. Finish welted buttonholes or make worked buttonholes. 7. Sew on buttons. 8. Stitch and press sleeve seams. Pin and baste sleeve into blouse. 9. Turn top edge of skirt to wrong side along seam line and baste along edge. 10. Pin skirt to waist along waistline, matching center front and back as well as side seams. Between center and side points distribute fullness as indicated. Baste. 11. Try on for second fitting (see page 226). 12. Stitch waistline seam along edge and press. 13. Sew in sleeves, finish seams and press. 14. Make and put in shoulder pads. 15. Finish side placket of dress. 16. Make belt. 17. Try on dress for third fitting (see page 226). 18. Finish lower edge of sleeves. 19. Turn up hem and finish. 20. Make belt loops. 21. Press dress.

SEWING DETAILS

Basting

Basting is used to hold fabric in place for machine stitching, fitting or *Basting* other finishing. Pin before basting *(see figure 9, page 34)*. Use a single knotted thread. Uneven basting is the basting generally used as a quick guide line where there is no particular strain *(see figure 18, page 35)*. Even basting and slip basting used in fitting are described in *figures 110 and 111*. To remove bastings, see *figure 19*, page 36.

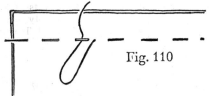

Figure 110 — Even basting is used as a firm basting for fitting or stitching. Make stitches and spaces about ¼" long.

Fig. 110

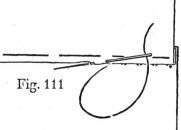

Figure 111 — Slip basting is done on the right side of a garment, when making alterations which have been marked on the right side and when matching plaids. One marking line is folded and laid against the other. Pin. Slip needle along inside fold, push it through and pick up a few threads on the opposite side. Draw thread through and repeat.

Fig. 111

Darts

Darts are used to take in the fullness of a garment at various points, usually *Darts* at back of neck, shoulder, underarm, waistline, top and elbow of sleeve *(diagram 7a)*. They make a garment fit properly and bring it into the

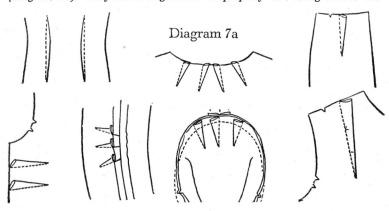

Diagram 7a

correct grain. Darts are also used for decoration. Fitting darts are stitched on the wrong side, decorative darts on the right. *Figure 112* shows how darts are marked, stitched and finished. Darts at the shoulder, the back of the neck, the top of the sleeve and the waistline are pressed toward the center. Darts in the elbow and underarm are pressed up.

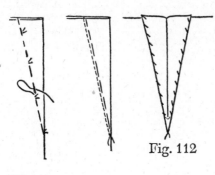

Fig. 112

Figure 112 — To make darts, mark with tailor's tacks or tailor's chalk (see page 201). Tailor's tacks show on both sides of the fabric, making it easier to work on either side. Baste marks together. Start stitching from the point of the dart, leaving long thread ends, and stitch up to wide end. Tie thread ends together at point, or thread them into needle and secure with an over-and-over stitch. On a heavy fabric, slash dart through the center, press open and overcast edges *(see figure 41, page 42).*

Pleats

Pleats   When pleats are indicated in a garment, do not sew the side seams before the pleats are laid. If the section containing the pleats has joining seams, these should be completed before the pleats are made. Side pleats are pleated in one direction *(diagram 7b).* A box pleat consists of two side pleats folded in opposite directions *(diagram 7c).* An inverted pleat consists of two side pleats folded to face each other *(diagram 7d).*

Pleats may be made on the straight of the goods or on the bias. The pattern markings indicating pleats should be followed very closely as they are carefully placed so that the pleats will not twist when completed. Study the directions to be sure which marking indicates the fold line. Make the mark-

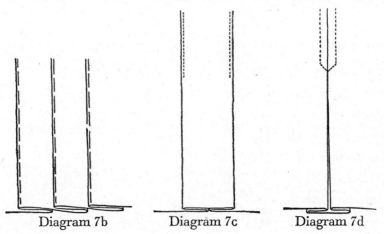

Diagram 7b   Diagram 7c   Diagram 7d

ings for the pleats in two different colors, one for the fold line and one for the line to which the fold is brought. When pleats are made on the straight of the goods, these two lines should each follow one straight lengthwise thread from the top to the bottom. See *figures 113 and 114* for making and stitching pleats. Before stitching, it is wise, in the case of a skirt, to fit the side seams. If waistline is very small, sometimes a better fit may be obtained by lapping the pleats a little more at the top. If there is a seam at the fold of a pleat, see *figure 115* for putting in the hem. To keep the inverted pleats in shape, it is helpful to stitch the fold on the wrong side very close to the edge from the top to the hemline.

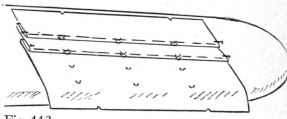

Figure 113 — To make pleats, lay fabric on table and fold on marking line indicating fold. Pin, baste, press. Pin fabric to ironing board. Matching marks, pin fold at top and bottom. Pin at intervals, matching marks carefully. Press pleat as soon as completed. Use a moist pressing cloth, even on cotton. For wool, use a moist cloth and a dry cloth (see page 220). Baste along pressed fold. Repeat for each pleat.

Fig. 113

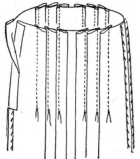

Figure 114 — To stitch pleats, stitch along fold from the top to the point indicated by pattern markings. Pleats may be stitched at the edge or in about the width of a presser foot and brought to a point. The threads should be brought through to the wrong side and firmly tied.

Fig. 114

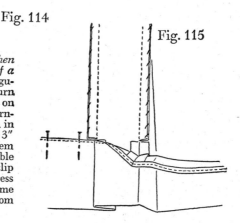

Fig. 115

Figure 115—To make hem when there is a seam at the fold of a pleat, mark for hem in the regular manner (see page 42). Turn skirt wrong side out, place it on ironing board and before turning hem, press open the seam in the fold of the pleat to about 3″ above marking. When the hem has been finished in a suitable manner (see page 220), clip seam just above hem and press exposed portion back in the same direction as before. Press from wrong side.

Gathers

Gathers   Details on making gathers and applying them to edges are given on page 38. There should always be at least two rows of gathers, and they should be evenly distributed. Shirring consists of several rows of gathers, the number depending on the position. Around the neck three to five rows are ample. Ten to fifteen rows may be used around the waist. A piece of fabric is usually placed on the wrong side under the shirring to hold shirring in place. This is known as a stay piece. Shirring may be done by machine stitching with an elastic thread in the bobbin. Do not stretch the elastic thread when it is wound on the bobbin.

Seams

Seams   The plain seam is the basic seam. It is made by pinning, basting and stitching together two pieces of fabric on the wrong side (see figure 20, page 36). Ordinarily this involves only two straight edges of fabric. When applying a bias edge to a straight edge, work with bias piece on top of straight piece. A curved seam is clipped to allow it to lie flat. There are certain instances where one side of a seam may be slightly longer than the other. Care must be taken to ease the longer side to the shorter one so that no tucks are formed (see figure 61, page 52). This is most likely to occur when stitching shoulder, underarm, sleeve and armhole seams. A lapped seam is used to join skirt to waist or to apply a yoke over fullness (figure 116). In addition to the plain seam, the seams most generally used are the French seam (see figure 40, page 42) and the flat fell seam (see figure 35, page 40).

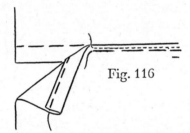

Fig. 116

Figure 116 — For a lapped seam, fold under seam allowance on top piece (skirt or yoke) and baste. Place fold on seam line of adjoining piece. Pin, baste, stitch.

After the stitching is completed, bastings are removed (see figure 19, page 36), and the seam is pressed. Raw edges of seams are finished in the following ways, depending on the type of fabric or garment and sometimes on convenience and speed: an overcast or double overcast seam (figure 41, page 42), a pinked seam (figure 117), a turned seam (figure 118), a top stitched seam (figure 119). A double stitched seam is necessary on a very sheer fabric when seam must be as strong as possible but almost invisible (figure 120).

Necklines

Necklines   A neckline without a collar may be round, V-necked, square or slashed. The most satisfactory finish for these necklines is a fitted facing or a mitered facing (see figures 36 and 37, page 40).
For the simplest method of applying a faced collar to a neckline, see figure 121. A popular finish for a neckline is a notched collar with a facing (see fig-

Figure 117 — Pinked seams are used on woolens, silks, cottons or rayons that do not fray easily. Use pinking shears, sewing machine pinking attachment (see machine manual), or ordinary shears. To pink with ordinary shears, pinch edge of seam between thumb and forefinger, cut notches into seam, edge to edge, being careful not to cut too near the stitching line.

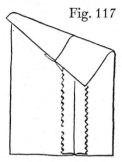

Fig. 117

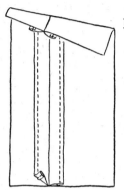

Fig. 118

Figure 118 — A turned seam is used on silk or rayon crepes, or other non-transparent light-weight fabrics. Seam should be at least ¾″ wide. Press seam open. Turn raw edge under ⅛″. Baste, holding seam free from garment. Stitch close to edge.

Fig. 119

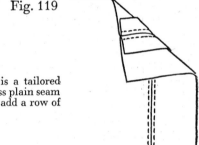

Figure 119 — A top-stitched seam is a tailored seam, used on skirts and dresses. Press plain seam open and, on right side of garment, add a row of stitching on each side of seam.

Fig. 120

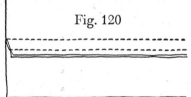

Figure 120 — A double stitched seam is used on sheer fabrics. Press edges together and, holding them free from garment, stitch seams together ⅜″ from seam. Trim. Overcast edges if they fray (*see figure 41, page 42*).

Figure 121 — To apply a faced collar to a neckline, baste collar wrong side down to right side of neck edge. Cut a matching bias strip ¾″ longer than collar and about 1″ wide (*figures 48–50, page 48*). Bias trim may also be used. Baste the bias strip, right side down and edge to edge with collar, and stitch along top edge of bias through all thicknesses. Turn in ends and opposite edge of strip. Blind hem to seam on inside of garment (*figure 30, page 38*).

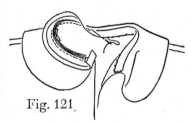

Fig. 121

ures 96 and 97, page 174). On a slashed neckline a straight collar is both simple and attractive (figure 95, page 170).

These necklines may also be finished with bias binding or bias trim. To bind a neck edge or slash, see figure 53, page 49. Stretch binding when turning point of slash. For a V-neck make a true miter at the point.

Closings

Closings   There are several types of closings. Buttons and buttonholes are the most ordinary. Buttonholes may be worked (figure 100, page 175), or they may be corded or welted (figure 99, page 175). When using buttonholes, the buttons must be sewed on securely (figure 102, page 176). Worked thread loops (figure 101, page 176) are also used with buttons. Snap fasteners (figure 104, page 177), or hooks and eyes (figure 103, page 177) are used for invisible closings. Zippers are a modern and convenient method of closing. One of the most common uses of the zipper is in the slashed opening at the back or front of the neck (figure 122).

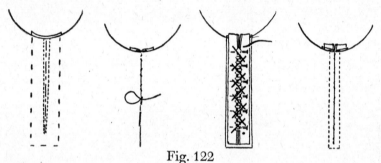

Fig. 122

Figure 122 — To apply a zipper in a slashed neck opening so that it is concealed, mark opening with basting thread the length of zipper plus ½" for top finish. Cut a piece of fabric 1½" wide and 1" longer than marking. Apply right side of piece to right side of fabric directly over marking. Baste in place. Machine stitch on wrong side as shown, using a small stitch. Stitch ⅛" from marking at top and taper to a point at end of marking. Stitch twice around point to prevent pulling out. Slash on marking line to point. Turn facing to inside, baste and press. Baste edges of slash together with a slip basting (see figure 111) as shown. Place center of closed zipper right side down exactly over basted opening on wrong side of garment. Top of pull should come ½" from edge of fabric. Pin and baste zipper in place as shown. Stitch from right side. Make allowance for extra width of zipper slider and continue stitching at that width as shown. Trim facing even with edge of tape and overcast edges together (see figure 41, page 42). Conceal top tape ends in neck finish.

Pockets

Pockets   Pockets add interesting detail to all types of garments. The size, shape and placing are important matters in the construction. A patch pocket is the easiest. On a tailored suit the patch pocket is frequently lined (figure 123). The welt pocket (figure 124) is a simple tailored pocket and is suitable for both suits and dresses. The welt may be of contrasting fabric, if desired.

Fig. 123

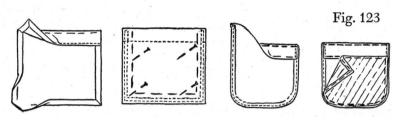

Figure 123 — For a patch pocket with a self hem or a lining, cut fabric ½"
wider and 1½" longer than the length of finished pocket. Shape the bottom as
desired. Cut lining same size. Turn under raw edges of pocket ¼", clipping
any corners, baste, press. Turn in 1" hem at top, baste, press. For pocket with
self hem, stitch hem. Pin, baste and stitch pocket to garment around edge.
(Another row of stitching ¼" inside covers the raw edge and prevents collection of lint.) For lined pocket, at each end of hem slip stitch edges of hem and
pocket together *(see figure 39, page 41)*. On lining, turn under ⅛" more than
seam allowance, baste, press, trim to ¼". Place lining against pocket, wrong
sides together, bottom edges together, pin. Turn under, pin and trim at top
so that lining covers raw edge of hem by ½". Baste, slip stitch, press and apply
to garment in regular way.

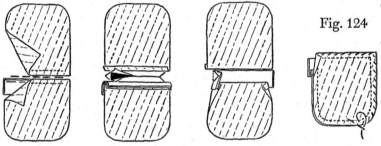

Fig. 124

Figure 124 — For a welt pocket, cut a welt piece on the straight of the goods,
1" longer than the pocket opening and three times the width of the finished
welt. A good average width is ½" finished.

On right side of garment, make a line of basting to indicate the length and
position of the pocket. Fold welt piece in half on length, right side out, press.
Place welt on lower side of marking with raw edge on marking line and
baste at a distance from the marking line equal to one third the width of the
welt from raw edge to fold.

Cut two pocket pieces from same or lining fabric, each 1" wider than the
marked opening and of a suitable length. The top piece should be longer than
the under piece, by the width of the finished welt. Place on garment as shown,
right side to right side. Baste both pieces the same distance from raw edges as
welt was basted. Stitch both pieces along basting the length of the marking.
Bring ends of thread through to wrong side and tie.

Hold back the edges of pocket pieces and welt and trim to ¼". Slash along
pocket marking to within ½" of ends, then diagonally as shown. Turn both
pocket pieces and all raw edges through the opening to wrong side. Press top
seam edges up and lower ones down. Baste and stitch pieces together, sewing
through slashed triangles. Make a second stitching around pockets, close to
edge, and overcast. Press.

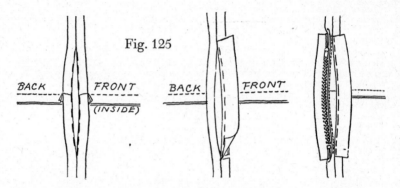

Fig. 125

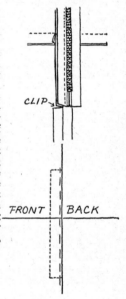

*Figure 125 — To make a zipper closing on dress or
skirt placket,* cut a facing strip of fabric 1½" wide and
1" longer than opening. On wrong side of garment,
mark seam allowances on both edges with bastings.
Trim front seam allowance to ½". Baste facing to front
of opening, right sides together, edge to edge. Stitch
from one end of opening to the other so that stitching
line is continuous with that of side seam. Trim seam.
Turn facing in at seam line and press. At back of opening, fold seam allowance ⅛" away from marking towards raw edge, continuing fold ¾" above and below
opening. Baste and press. Pin and baste back edge of
opening to zipper tape, close to metal. On skirt, place
zipper ½" below top of skirt. Ease fabric to tape so that
metal will lie flat. Stitch close to edge with cording
foot. Extend stitching beyond opening to ends of tape
at both ends. At ends of tape, clip back seam allowance
in to seam so that it will lie flat. On right side, pin front
edge of placket to seam line and baste firmly. Stitch
front of placket to tape on right side, using cording
foot. Make allowance for the extra width of the zipper
slider and continue stitching at that width. On skirt,
conceal tape ends in belt.

Plackets

Plackets

A dress placket should be in the left underarm seam. It must be long enough
to slip the garment on easily, usually from 7" to 10" long, 3" to 4" above
waistline, 4" to 6" below waistline. The placket should be carefully handled
to prevent stretching or bulging. Zippers are comfortable and convenient in
dress plackets *(figure 125)*. Since zippers are not always available at the
present time, plackets with snap fasteners and even buttons are a necessity
(figure 126).

A skirt placket is made in the left side seam and is usually 7" long. Skirt
plackets are made the same as dress plackets.

*Figure 126 — To make a faced snap-fastener placket
on dress or skirt*, cut two strips of fabric for facings,
one 3" wide, the other 1½" wide, both 1" longer
than placket opening. If dress has blouse fullness or
is darted or gathered at the waistline, the facing
strips are cut on the bias. On wrong side of garment,
mark seam allowances on both edges of opening with
bastings. At each end of placket ½" from opening,
clip back and front seam allowances in to seam so
that they will lie flat. Be careful not to cut stitches of
seam. Trim seam allowances to ½". Baste 1½"
facing to front of opening, right sides together, edge
to edge. Stitch from one end of opening to the other
so that stitching line is continuous with that of seam
line. Trim seam. Turn facing in along seam line,
baste and press. Turn under raw edge of facing ¼"
and stitch close to edge, then slip stitch *(see figure
39*, page 41) edge to dress. Stitch 3" facing to back
of opening in the same manner. Do not trim seam.
Press seam toward raw edge of facing. Fold facing,
¾" from seam line. Baste along fold. Press. Turn
raw edges under ¼", stitch close to edge and press.
Slip stitch along stitching line. Sew hook and eye at
waistline and snaps quite close together along rest
of placket (see page 177).

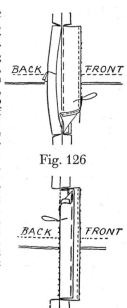

Fig. 126

Sleeves

The suggestions on sleeves are given for the regulation type. When another
type is used, the pattern will give further instructions. Baste and stitch sleeve
as in *figure 127*. Even the plainest sleeve has an allowance for fullness at the
top, to make top of sleeve conform to the shape of the shoulder without drawing. This must be eased into the armhole without gathers showing. To pin
and baste a plain sleeve into armhole, *see figure 128*, and for stitching, *see figure 129*. The sleeve may be finished with a plain hem, or a cuff, *figure 130*.
A tight sleeve with an opening at the wrist is finished as in *figures 131 and
132*. A continuous placket is the best finish for a full sleeve with a wrist band,
figure 133. In the current fashion, shoulder pads are frequently used and may
be made as shown in *figure 134*.

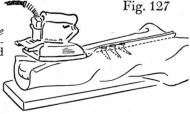

Fig. 127

*Figure 127—Baste and stitch the sleeve
seam* from bottom up with elbow fullness on top. Press open on sleeve board
(see page 222).

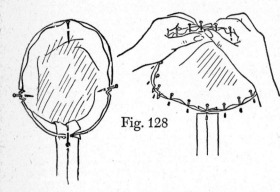

Fig. 128

Figure 128—To set a plain sleeve in an armhole, have sleeve right side out and work from wrong side of garment. Working on sleeve side fit sleeve around the armhole. Match underarm seam to underarm seam, top of sleeve marking to shoulder seam, and match notches. Even the plainest sleeve has slight fullness at the top which must be eased in *(see figure 61,* page 52). When easing-in process is difficult on woolens, *see diagram 8p,* page 234.

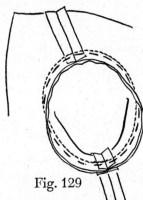

Figure 129—When stitching the sleeve in, keep the sleeve side up. Start stitching at the underarm seam and let the beginning and end of stitching overlap about 1″. See page 222 for directions for pressing sleeves.

Fig. 130

Fig. 129

Figure 130 — To finish a sleeve with a turned-back cuff, first make cuff by stitching together ends of a straight piece the length of edge of sleeve plus 1″ and twice desired finished width plus 1″. Stitch one edge of cuff to wrong side of sleeve, edge to edge, right sides together. Trim seam. Turn free edge under ½″, baste, slip stitch to seam and press. Turn back cuff to conceal seam.

Figure 131 — To finish a long tight sleeve with seam binding and snap fasteners, clip back seam allowance in to seam ½″ above top of opening, being careful not to cut stitches. On back seam, turn ⅛″ to wrong side, baste, press. Turn up hem, baste, press and trim to ⅜″. On front seam, turn regular seam allowance to wrong side. Baste, press, trim to ⅜″ and clip corners. Starting at clipping of back seam, place seam binding on fold edge of back opening. Baste down edge of back opening, around edge of hem, and up front edge of opening, mitering corners. Slip stitch both edges of binding to sleeve *(see figure 39,* page 41). Press. Sew on snap fasteners *(see figure 104,* page 177).

Fig. 131

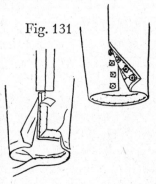

Figure 132 — To make a zipper closing in a long tight sleeve, baste two sides of opening together as if for finished seam. Press open. Place center of closed zipper, right side down, exactly over basted seam. Top of pull should come ½" from lower edge of sleeve. Pin and baste zipper in place as shown. Stitch from right side. Make allowance for extra width of the zipper slider and continue stitching at that width as shown. Note that stitching extends only as far as top of pull. Trim seam allowance even with edges of tape and overcast together *(see figure 41, page 42)*. Conceal tape ends in edge finish. Turn down tape ends and apply seam binding as shown.

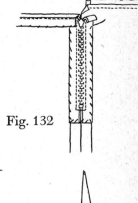

Fig. 132

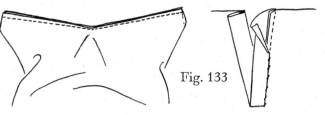

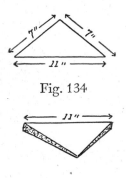

Fig. 133

Figure 133 — To finish a sleeve with a continuous bound placket with wrist band, make a 4" slash, 3½" from underarm seam on the back of the sleeve. For placket, cut strip on straight of goods, 2" wide and 1" longer than twice the length of opening. Starting at one edge of sleeve, place right side of binding against right side of sleeve, edge to edge. Pin. About 1" from point of slash, slip the sleeve in from the edge of binding ⅛". Baste (¼" seam), tapering basting to ⅛" at point of slash. Stitch. Press the seams toward edge of binding. Turn binding to wrong side. Turn raw edge under ¼", baste close to edge and press. Blind hem to sleeve along stitching line *(see figure 30, page 38)*. Front of placket is folded back on seam line and pressed. Back is allowed to extend. Gather edge of sleeve to fit wrist band.

Fig. 134

Figure 134—Shoulder pads may be made according to directions furnished with every pattern in which they are used. These pads will conform to the current fashion. A good standard shoulder pad is made by cutting four triangles according to dimensions given in the figure. Place two triangles, right sides together. Stitch along long side only (½" seam). Trim, press seam open. Fold on stitching line, wrong sides together. Place cotton batting between two triangles, making padding about ½" thick at long side and thinning the layer gradually until it is reduced to nothing at point of triangle opposite long side. The size of the pad may be varied to suit your own taste by inserting more or less padding. Match and pin raw edges and bind (see figure 56, page 50).

Belts

Belt   Before a belt is applied to the skirt, the seams and placket are stitched and finished. Although skirts are frequently made with a fabric belt (*figure 135*), many still prefer to finish the top of the skirt with belting (*figure 136*). Commercial belting from 1½″ to 2″ wide is generally preferred. It should have body but not be too stiff.

A separate fabric belt (*figure 137*) is cut on the length of the fabric and on the straight of the goods. The width depends upon the fashion, the garment and the suitability of the width to the individual. To stiffen the belt, an interlining of heavy muslin is used.

The belt may be fastened with a button and buttonhole, or by means of a buckle. These buckles are often covered with the fabric of the garment (*figure 138*). When attaching buckle, an eyelet is made in the belt for the prong (*figure 139*). The finished belt is held in place by means of thread belt loops (*figure 140*). It is sometimes attached at side seams with French tacks (*see figure 92, page 127*).

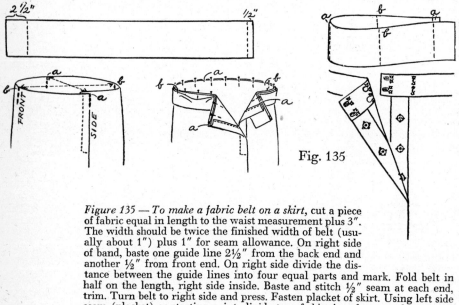

Fig. 135

Figure 135 — To make a fabric belt on a skirt, cut a piece of fabric equal in length to the waist measurement plus 3″. The width should be twice the finished width of belt (usually about 1″) plus 1″ for seam allowance. On right side of band, baste one guide line 2½″ from the back end and another ½″ from front end. On right side divide the distance between the guide lines into four equal parts and mark. Fold belt in half on the length, right side inside. Baste and stitch ½″ seam at each end, trim. Turn belt to right side and press. Fasten placket of skirt. Using left side seam (placket) as starting point, divide top of skirt into four equal parts and mark. Open placket and, beginning at front, apply belt to skirt, right side to right side and edge to edge; match and pin markings on belt to markings on skirt. Two inches should be free at the back. Pin space between markings so that any fullness in skirt is eased evenly to belt (*see figure 61, page 52*). Baste and stitch, taking a ½″ seam. Trim and press seam up. On wrong side of belt, turn free edge of belt under ½″ and blind hem along seam line (*see figure 30, page 38*). Sew snaps and hooks and eyes as shown (*see figures 103 and 104, page 177*).

Figure 136 — To apply belting, turn under ½″ along raw edge of skirt top and placket and baste. Make ¾″ hem at one end of belting. Apply belting to turned edge of skirt with the hemmed end of belting, wrong side up, at inside edge of front placket facing. Pin and baste belting all around edge to the end of the facing of placket in back. Cut belting ¾″ beyond edge of skirt. Turn the extra piece back for a hem. Stitch around the top of the skirt. Apply hooks and eyes as shown *(see figure 103, page 177).*

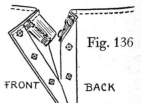

Fig. 136

FRONT   BACK

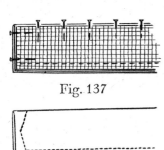

Fig. 137

Figure 137 — To make a separate fabric belt, cut a piece of fabric equal in length to waist measurement plus 6″ and twice as wide as desired finished width, plus 1″ for seams. Cut an interlining of heavy muslin the desired finished width, plus ½″ seam allowance. Fold belt in half lengthwise right side inside and pin edges together. On one side of belt, pin edge of interlining even with raw edges of belt. Baste through all thicknesses ½″ from edge. To make one end pointed, mark as shown. Beginning at center fold, stitch around point and continue stitching the length of the belt on the seam line. Do not stitch straight end. Trim seam. Turn belt to right side *(figure 33, page 39).*

Figure 138 — To cover a buckle, place it right side down on the wrong side of fabric and trace around the inside and outside edge. Allow ¼″ seam on each edge. Clip inside edge at corners. Catch stitch edges together *(see figure 91, page 124).* Cut and clip back piece in same manner, fold raw edges to wrong side and place on buckle. Whip stitch *(see figure 62, page 60).*

Fig. 138

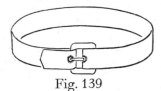

Fig. 139

Figure 139 — To attach a prong buckle to a belt, make a hole in belt 1½″ from straight end. Use a stiletto (see page 312) and make hole large enough to slip the prong through. Finish as a worked buttonhole *(see figure 100, page 175).* Place buckle on belt with prong through hole. Turn in raw edges at end and slip stitch straight end to belt *(see figure 39, page 41).* Slip pointed end through buckle and draw through to fit waistline. At the point where the prong meets the belt, make a hole in belt and finish as before.

Figure 140 — To make thread belt loops, use double thread, knot ends and insert needle through side seam half the width of belt below waistline. Reinforce this point with small buttonhole stitch *(see figure 100, page 175).* Take another stitch at same point but do not draw the thread through to complete the stitch. This leaves a loop at end near work. Place thumb and forefinger in loop. Using forefinger, draw thread through loop, thus making another loop. Draw this loop out and tighten the first one. Continue chain of loops to desired length. Pass needle through last loop and draw thread tightly to close chain. Insert needle in seam at same distance above waistline, draw through to wrong side and fasten securely.

Fig. 140

WAISTLINE

SIDE SEAM

Hems

Hems   A hem is in almost all cases handsewn and invisible from right side. A slip stitch *(figure 39*, page 41) or a blind stitch *(figure 30*, page 38) are the ideal stitches to use for hemming. A hem is marked and turned as described in *figures 42-46*, page 42. Before hand sewing the hem edge, it must be finished. The usual method is to finish with silk or rayon seam binding or bias binding, *figure 141*. For light fabrics, especially cottons, the top edge may be turned in and edge stitched, *figure 47*, page 44. For heavy fabrics the pinked hem makes a neat finish *(figure 142)* and the machine stitched hem *(figure 143)* makes a trim finish. A circular hem has a special treatment *(figure 144)*.

Figure 141 — A hem may be finished with bias binding or seam binding. Bias binding is used on heavy wools and cottons. Silk or rayon seam binding is used on lightweight wools, silks and rayons. Apply with running stitch or a machine stitch. Lay hem in place, matching seam of hem to seam of garment. Pin, baste and blind hem stitch free edge of binding to garment *(see figure 30*, page 38).

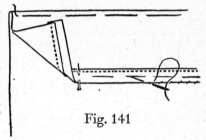

Fig. 141

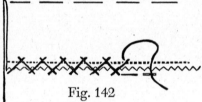

Fig. 142

Figure 142 — For a pinked edge finish on a hem, trim edge to even width with pinking shears or pink by hand *(see figure 117*, page 211). Stitch close to pinked edge. Baste hem. Catch stitch *(see figure 91*, page 124).

Figure 143 — A hem finished with several rows of stitching is good for firm fabrics. Trim hem to ½". Baste. Shrink out excess fullness (see page 223). Make three to five rows of stitching around hem edge. Trim raw edge close to stitching line.

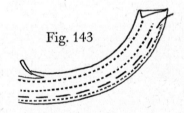

Fig. 143

Fig. 144

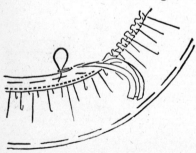

Figure 144 — To finish a circular hem, stitch ¼" from raw edge, using a loose machine stitch. Draw bobbin thread up, gathering hem slightly to fit garment. Match seams of hem to seams of garment. Distribute fullness evenly and as much as possible have the grain of hem match the grain of skirt. Fasten thread. Shrink out fullness (see page 223). Finish raw edge as in *figure 141.*

PRESSING

Since success or failure in sewing often depends on the pressing during the making. See page 313 for descriptions of the pressing equipment mentioned. *Pressing*

General Instructions

1. Always test the temperature of the iron on a scrap of fabric before pressing (belt or inside of hem), even if iron has an automatic regulator. 2. Never rest iron on fabric. Keep it moving constantly to avoid marking, always following the straight grain *(see figure 5, page 30)*. 3. While pressing, always smooth garment into correct shape so that fabric is not stretched or creased.

Press Cloths

For use with a regular iron, have three pressing cloths, one of cheesecloth, one of muslin, and one of drill cloth. Remove all sizing by rinsing fabric before using. A steam iron needs no press cloths. Uses for the different cloths are given with instructions for pressing specific fabrics.

Pressing Fabrics

1. *Cotton* — Press on right side, sponge lightly and press with moderately hot iron. If sheen appears on test scrap, use damp muslin pressing cloth. To remove wrinkles on sheer cottons, use cheesecloth, almost dry, ironing with a very moderate iron.

2. *Linen* — Press on wrong side. Sponge lightly and press with moderately hot iron.

3. *Rayon and Silk* — Press on wrong side with moderately warm iron. Special care must be exercised with rayon fabrics because some are completely dissolved by excessive heat. When moisture is necessary, first cover garment with a dry drill cloth. Then place a damp muslin cloth on top. The steam will penetrate drill cloth without leaving a sheen on fabric.

4. *Wool* — Press on wrong side and cover with a damp muslin pressing cloth. Press with moderate iron until cloth is almost dry. This steams fabric. Replace damp cloth with dry cloth. Continue pressing until almost dry. Pressing woolen garments until they are completely dry gives a sheen to garment.

5. *Velvet or Velveteen* — Press on wrong side. Place right side of fabric down on needle board, press on wrong side with moderate iron *(diagram 7e)*. To steam velvet, stand a hot iron on end and cover with a damp press cloth *(diagram 7f)*. After the seams have been opened, the wrong side of the fabric should be passed over the steaming press cloth. Hold fabric loosely so that it will not mark.

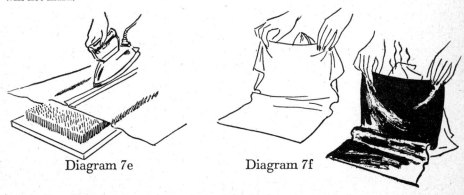

Diagram 7e   Diagram 7f

Pressing Rules

1. Press seams immediately after stitching. Do not wait until garment is completed.

2. Press all seams up from bottom or in towards center of garment, except at waistline.

3. Straight seams are usually opened out flat and pressed on a regular ironing board.

4. Underarm seams on sleeve, sleeve finishes, and other small seams are more easily pressed on a sleeve board (*diagram 7g*).

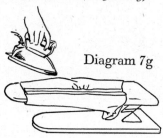

Diagram 7g

5. Seams at armhole are usually pressed toward the neck except when the fabric is exceptionally heavy, or when a coat is to be lined. Then they are pressed open. These seams may be pressed more easily over a tailor's cushion which is also used for all curved seams (*diagram 7h*).

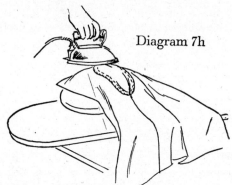

Diagram 7h

6. Press darts on light fabrics to one side, either up or towards center. On heavy fabrics slash darts and press open.

7. Do not press gathers flat. Lift portion of garment while working point of iron into them. Do a little at a time.

8. The lower edge of the hem should be pressed to give a firm, true hemline before marking the width of the hem, and again after the final sewing. Always press a hem from the bottom up, never around the bottom of the skirt. Steam out basting thread marks by pressing them lightly on the wrong side.

9. Shrinking out excess fullness at top of sleeves and at the hemline is done with an iron and a press cloth, or with a steam iron. Place the top of the sleeve over a tailor's cushion *(diagram 7i)*. Apply the moisture directly or by means of a dampened press cloth according to the type of fabric, as directed above, then press. The hem is placed flat on a regular ironing board before the seam binding is sewed on and pressed in the same way.

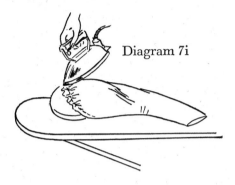

Diagram 7i

FITTING

If the pattern has been altered carefully, fitting should not be difficult. To *Fitting* refit, the seams are repinned with pins placed parallel to the body. The fitting may be done on a form which conforms to the measurement of the person to be fitted (see page 312). Otherwise it is done on the person for whom the garment is being made; in this case it is helpful to have the assistance of another person.

When it is not possible to use a form or to have another person's help, the dress is placed on the person to be fitted, and, with the help of a full length mirror, corrections are noted and indicated. The garment is then taken off and adjustments are pinned. The garment is put on again and another check made, and this is repeated until all corrections are complete.

First Fitting

Skirt (separate, or part of a dress)

Pin in corrections according to directions which follow. Then remove skirt and mark new seam lines with tailor's chalk or basting. If alterations are not too great, seams may be rebasted immediately by matching new markings. If alterations are considerable, take out side seam bastings, fold skirt pieces in half and check alterations to make sure that they are evenly made. Rebaste and try on skirt to recheck fitting.

Try on skirt right side out with darts, gathers, pleats and seams basted. Pin belt or strip of fabric snugly around waist at natural waistline. To this, pin the skirt at the waistline seam marking. Make sure that markings at center front and back are at center of body and perpendicular to the floor. Pin placket at regular seam allowance.

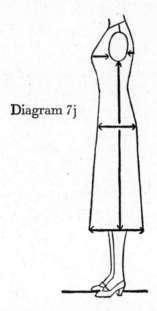

Diagram 7j

See if the lengthwise seams appear straight and perpendicular to the floor. If the side seams swing forward, raise back of skirt slightly to bring back into line. If side seam is too far forward or backward, shift seam slightly by taking more from back or front. See if crosswise grain around hips is parallel to the floor. Raise or lower the waist seam line until the grain is correct at the hipline.

See if the fit around the hips allows for sitting down comfortably. If the skirt is let out or taken in at the hipline, continue seam at same width from hipline to lower edge.

Blouse (separate, or part of a dress)

When working on a form, alterations on the blouse are pinned on the right side of the blouse. When pinning on self, it may be easier to work on left side. After alterations are pinned on one side, remove blouse and mark new lines with basting or tailor's chalk. Take blouse apart, fold front at center, wrong sides together, or match two pieces if blouse opens down the front. Pin all edges together at underarm seams, shoulder seams and armhole edges. Mark the other half according to the alterations made, using a tracing wheel or tailor's tacks (see page 201). Repeat on back of blouse. If changes have been numerous, rebaste and try on garment to check fitting again.

Try on blouse right side out, with darts, gathers, pleats and seams basted. If the blouse has a front opening, pin together at center. (Do the same if there is a back opening.) Make sure the markings at center front and back are at center of body and perpendicular to the floor.

See if the shoulder seam is a straight line from the neck to the large bone in the shoulder and if the underarm seam is perpendicular to the floor. If shoulder or underarm seam is too far forward or backward, shift either seam slightly, taking more from back or front as necessary.

See if the seam line of the armhole is correctly placed. The armhole seam line should coincide with the top of the shoulder and continue as an almost straight line, following the natural curve of the arm. The shoulder seam may be shortened by deepening the dart in the shoulder, and taking a corresponding dart in the back if necessary. The armhole should be curved to follow the curve of the armpit, making armhole at underarm come up almost to armpit. If the armhole is tight at the place of greatest curve, make small slashes into the seam allowance, being careful not to cut in too far.

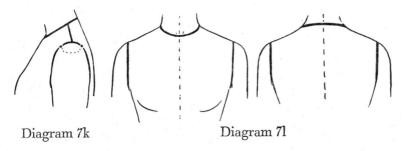

Diagram 7k   Diagram 7l

See if crosswise grain at the bust is parallel to the floor. Raise the shoulder on back or front wherever necessary to bring the blouse into correct grain and do not forget to adjust armhole accordingly.

See if the shoulder darts and under bust darts appear in a straight line, adjusting accordingly.

See if the fit across the bustline is loose enough. Let out or take in the underarm seam as necessary and remember the armhole adjustment.

See if the neckline fits snugly and smoothly. Do not twist the body when fitting the neckline at the back. Learn to judge the amount of alteration by standing in front of a mirror. If the neckline is tight at the place of the greatest curve, make small slashes into the seam allowance, being careful not to cut in too far. This slashed edge is later cut off.

Second Fitting

Separate Skirt

Check position of fastening for belt and mark hem (see page 42).

Separate Blouse

Try on blouse with sleeves basted in. See if sleeve stands up in the armhole. When the arm hangs down at the side, the sleeve hangs straight down from the top of the sleeve cap with the lengthwise grain in the upper sleeve perpendicular to the floor and the crosswise grain. When sleeves seem to twist toward the back, clip bastings at top between notches and shift sleeve slightly in order to straighten it.

Diagram 7m

Dress

Try on dress with skirt basted to the blouse and sleeves basted in. Pin placket together at marked lines.

See if waistline seam follows the natural waistline of the body. Clip bastings if necessary and raise or lower until it is correct.

See if waistline is snug and comfortable. If the seams were adjusted properly in the first fitting, there will be no difficulty about this.

Check the sleeve in exactly the same way as given for the separate blouse.

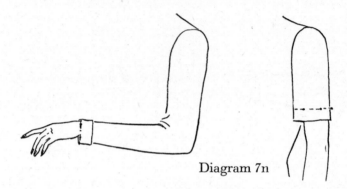

Diagram 7n

Third Fitting

Separate Blouse

Check sleeve length and make a line of pins at correct length. Bend elbow on long sleeve as this requires extra length. After removing garment, even pinned line and mark with a basting. Finish as desired.

Dress

Check sleeve length as above. Check position of belt and, with belt in place, mark hem (see page 42).

8. The Tailor's Apprentice

Fashionably speaking, this is the Tailored Age. A jacket and skirt are practically the uniform of the well-dressed woman. Morning, noon and night a suit is trim, neat, practical. A suit is versatile, adapts itself readily to any situation, from a day at the office to tea at the committee chairman's house. With a little accessory juggling, a suit can take you around the clock, across the country. It's the leading lady of this chapter in which you are thoroughly coached in the fine art of tailoring.

Successful tailoring of a jacket or a coat is the result of accuracy in cutting, fitting, basting and sewing, a thorough job of pressing, and a few tricks of the trade. The tricks of the trade are:

1. The facings of the front opening and of the collar must have a stiffening known as an interfacing. The interfacings are made of muslin, percale or light-weight canvas which should be shrunk by washing until all sizing has been removed and pressed while still damp. If, in makeovers, the old interfacing is used, do the same thing in order to renew the "body."

2. This interfacing is reinforced by means of a special diagonal basting.

3. Certain seams are taped for extra firmness.

BEFORE CUTTING THE GARMENT

Before Cutting   First alter the pattern as described on pages 186 to 197. Since most tailored garments are made of heavy fabric which is likely to tear the pattern while it is being pinned, many beginners find it advantageous to cut the garment in unbleached muslin first. All the marks of the pattern are transferred to this muslin garment by means of tailor's tacks or tailor's chalk (*see figures 105 and 108,* page 201). If there is no seam at the center back, mark center back with a basting. Baste all darts and gathers into muslin garment and baste pieces together. Put on muslin garment and fit it (see page 223), making allowances for the fact that a lining is to be inserted. This muslin pattern may be kept and used as a master pattern, making it easy to alter other patterns.

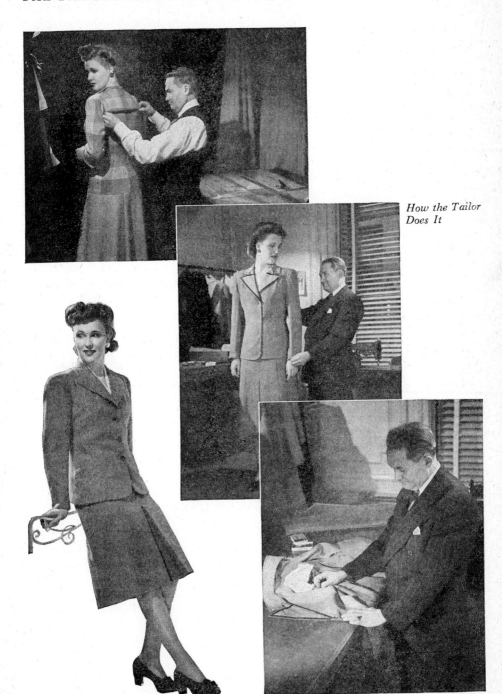

*How the Tailor
Does It*

CUTTING DIRECTIONS

Garment and Sleeves

Follow instructions for placing pattern on fabric and marking given on
pages 198 to 202. Special care should be taken when cutting woolens, because,
although they are heavier, they must hang correctly. When cutting the collar,
the upper piece should be placed so that the center fold lies on the straight
lengthwise grain. The under piece or the facing is placed on the true bias. The
pattern marks will show clearly how to do this correctly. When cutting, increase seam allowance on side seams to 1″ in all cases.

When using a muslin pattern, rip it apart, press and cut as if from a paper
pattern. When the pattern directions instruct that a piece should be cut on a
fold, fold the muslin pattern to correspond with original paper pattern. This
is usually done on the back or the collar. Transfer all marks from the muslin
to the fabric. If alterations have been made, it is the new marks that are transferred. To do this, place pins on the muslin side through all the marks so that
they penetrate all thicknesses to the opposite side. Mark on fabric side with
chalk. Remove muslin. Pin through marks just made and chalk on the other
side.

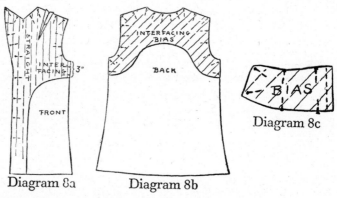

Diagram 8c

Diagram 8a   Diagram 8b

Interfacings

The interfacings for the jacket may be cut from a paper pattern or from the
muslin. *Diagrams 8a, 8b and 8c* indicate interfacings. The two front pieces are
cut on the straight of the goods and the back is cut all in one piece on the bias.
If desired, interfacing may be cut from facing pattern. The collar interfacing
is cut from the under collar pattern and is also cut on the bias.

Front of Lining

Cut from the regular pattern for the front minus the part covered by the
front facing. Consult pattern guide sheet for marks which indicate the cutting
line for lining. Pin, mark and cut the lining, allowing ½″ excess on all seams
to allow for adjustment for padding.

When the muslin pattern is used, fold it back along the line where the facing
ends and use this portion for a pattern.

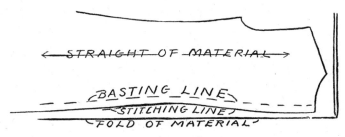

Diagram 8d

Back of Lining (with center seam)

Place back pattern on folded fabric with center edge of pattern ½" from fold *(diagram 8d)*. Pin and mark as for original garment. Mark center back edge of pattern on fabric. At center back, cut ½" farther out than the mark just made. The extra inch thus given at center back is used for a pleat. Cut around remainder of pattern, ½" farther out than regular seam allowance.

Back of Lining (with fold at center back)

Place back pattern on a folded fabric with center edge of pattern ½" in from fold. Pin all around and mark as for original garment. Mark center back edge of pattern on fabric. Leave center fold uncut. Cut around pattern ½" farther out than regular seam allowance. This extra inch at center back is used for a pleat.

Sleeves

The sleeves are cut exactly as the original garment except for the extra seam allowance.

Interlining

See directions on page 236.

MAKING THE GARMENT

Fitting

Sewing Directions

When the garment has been cut, baste all darts and seams in body of garment and try on for fitting. Instructions on fitting, basting and stitching begin on page 204.

Applying the Interfacing to Body

After the body and shoulder seams of the garment have been sewed and pressed open, the interfacing is applied. If there are any darts in the interfacing, make them on the right side, stitch, slash through center and press open. Place garment wrong side out flat on a table or on a form. Apply interfacing to corresponding parts of garment wrong sides together; match darts, if any, and tack them together. Pin first down center and then pin all around edges. Baste ¼" in from seam line on shoulders and underarm and ¼" from edge along armhole and front. Cut away seam allowance of interfacing at

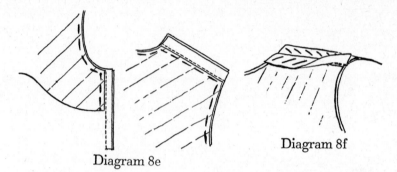

Diagram 8f

Diagram 8e

shoulder and underarm *(diagram 8e)* and catch the seam to the interfacing with diagonal stitches *(diagram 8f)*.

Turn garment to right side and try it on. Pin fronts together where top button will come. The lapels fall back, revealing natural roll of the collar. Mark the length of the roll with pins *(diagram 8g)*.

Remove garment and turn to wrong side, ¼" beyond line of pins toward armhole, run a basting line and remove pins. Using basting line as a guide, secure the two fabrics together with diagonal stitches about ½" long *(diagrams 8h and 8i)*. Use thread to match the garment fabric because the stitches

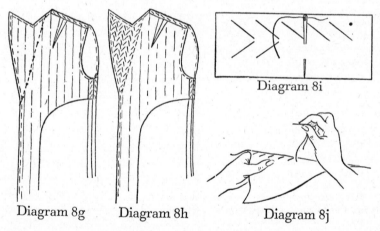

Diagram 8i

Diagram 8g   Diagram 8h   Diagram 8j

catch through. Work from the inside out toward the edge with the rever rolled over the hand, holding the rever easily, so that it will roll *(diagram 8j)*. Do not diagonal stitch seam allowance. When this section is entirely covered with diagonal bastings, check the lapels to see that they are even. They are apt to contract a little from handling. To measure them, make a cardboard pattern of the lapel from original pattern. Mark and cut off seam allowance. Apply this pattern to the interfacing side of lapel, matching shoulders and center edges below lapels and mark around it. The marking line is the new seam line.

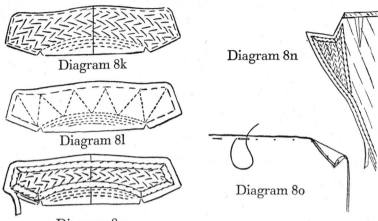

Diagram 8k

Diagram 8n

Diagram 8l

Diagram 8o

Diagram 8m

Applying Interfacing to Collar

Place under piece of collar (facing) and interfacing wrong sides together. Baste together all around at seam line. Inside seam allowance from notch to notch make a curved row of machine stitching which, at the center, reaches about ⅓ of the way up the collar. Make several rows inside this row about ¼" apart *(diagram 8k)*. There are two methods of stitching the remaining part of collar. In the first method, use top line of curved stitching as a guide and cover the rest of the collar with diagonal bastings, keeping within the seam line *(diagram 8k)*. In the second method, stitch by machine as shown *(diagram 8l)*.

Taping the Seams

Shrink and press twill tape, ½" wide. Tape is generally applied around revers, down front of jacket, around edge and at roll of under collar. Baste tape so that outer edge is on seam line. Hold it tight at bias parts and miter corners *(diagrams 8m and 8n)*. Whip *(see figure 62, page 60)* both edges of tape to interfacing. Trim away seam allowance of interfacing.

Applying Collar and Facings

Baste and stitch under piece of collar to jacket *(see figure 96, page 174)*. Press seam open, clip seam allowance to make collar lie flat.

Baste and stitch upper section of collar to front facings, right sides together. Clip. Pin facings and upper collar to jacket and under collar, right sides together. Baste, using outer edge of tape as a guide line. To stitch, begin at edge of facing at hem line on inside of jacket. Stitch up, around the collar and down the opposite side to the same point on the opposite side, using outer edge of tape as a guide line. Clip lower edge and trim. Press seam open all around, using a tailor's cushion (see page 313). Clip corners. Trim seams. Turn facing to wrong side on seam line. Baste close to seam. Press. To prevent facing from rolling to right side, the entire outer edge may be machine stitched close to edge. If this is not suitable, sew close to edge with a back and blind stitch *(diagram 8o)*, beginning at lower edge of facing. At beginning of roll of lapel, work on underside of lapel.

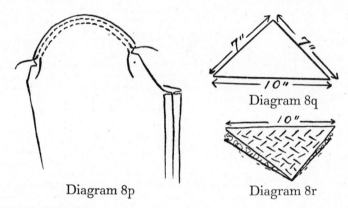

Diagram 8p   Diagram 8r

Diagram 8q

Making Hem

Turn up hem on jacket, pink raw edge or run machine stitching close to edge and catch stitch (see figure 91, page 124). Baste inner edge of facing to inside of jacket, turning rever out while doing so to make sure it is not too tight. Catch stitch to jacket.

Setting a Two-piece Sleeve into Jacket

Match and stitch seams of sleeves. Press seams open, using tailor's cushion to shape. At top of sleeve cap, gather along seam line between notches (see figure 31, page 38). Gather a second line ¼" nearer edge (diagram 8p). Turn sleeve to right side. Set into armhole. Match the two sets of underarm perforations, the shoulder seam and top sleeve perforations, and corresponding sleeve and armhole notches (see figure 128, page 216). Work from the sleeve side. Pin around underarm from notch to notch. Draw gathers of sleeve cap to fit armhole, fasten. Distribute gathers evenly. Pin all around. Try on and check fit of sleeve (see page 225). Remove sleeve from armhole. Turn to wrong side, place the gathered edge over a tailor's cushion and shrink out all fullness of gathers (see page 223). Turn to right side. Place sleeve in armhole, match perforations and notches, as above. Check fit. Baste. Stitch. Turn up hem of sleeve and pink raw edge, or machine stitch close to edge, catch stitch.

Pressing the Jacket

Before the shoulder pads and lining are put in, the jacket should have a final pressing (see page 221). Armhole seams should be pressed open. It is advisable to have this pressing done by a tailor.

Making the Shoulder Pads

From thin muslin cut 4 triangles, following dimensions given (diagram 8q). Place a layer of cotton batting on one triangle, make padding about ½" thick at 10" side, and thin the layer gradually until it is reduced to nothing at the point opposite (diagram 8r). Place a second triangle on top, matching long side to long side. Secure 3 layers together with large diagonal stitches. Place pad in shoulder of jacket with 10" side projecting slightly into sleeve cap, adjust to fit, tack at 3 points of triangle.

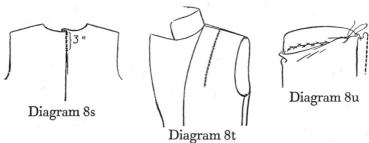

Diagram 8s

Diagram 8t

Diagram 8u

Making Lining

On back with fitted center seam, place pieces right sides together and baste along mark of center back edge. Stitch *(see diagram 8d)*. Trim. Clip seam. To make pleat, baste along center back mark for original seam allowance *(see diagram 8d)*. Press basted seam toward right section. Turn to right side and catch stitch pleat 3″ down from neck edge *(diagram 8s)*. Do not remove bastings.

On back with a fold at center back to make pleat, baste along center back mark. Press basted seam toward right section. Turn to right side, catch stitch pleat 3″ from neck edge *(diagram 8s)*. Do not remove bastings.

Putting Lining into Jacket

Put jacket on form or on table, wrong side out. Place front lining in jacket first, wrong sides together. Match the armhole seam marking of the lining to the armhole seam of the jacket and pin. Do the same at underarm, working from top, easing the fabric. Pin to seam line. Do the same at shoulder. Turn raw front edge under ½″ and baste. Pin this fold over raw edge of facing. Fold dart allowance under toward center, pin. Try jacket on, lining side out, and check to see that lining fits smoothly, but not tightly. If necessary, re-adjust shoulder and underarm seams to accommodate excess padding. Mark these seam lines with basting. Catch stitch darts *(diagram 8t)*. On back, match and pin center of lining to center of jacket the length of the garment. On shoulder and side seams fold raw edges of lining under on seam line and match folded edge to seam line of front and pin. Clip, turn under raw edges of neck and pin. Try on jacket to check fit. Make adjustments necessary with pins. Remove jacket and slip stitch *(see figure 39, page 41)* at underarm seams, shoulders, front and neckline seams. Baste around armhole on seam allowance.

Turn sleeve wrong side out. Slip lining on, right side out. Match seams, notches and perforations. Pin lining to sleeve along seams. Fold raw edges of armhole under on seam line and match folded edge to seam line of jacket. Check fit. Slip stitch seam.

Hemming Lining of Jacket and Sleeve

Put jacket on and pin lining to jacket about 3″ above hem, all around. Baste lining to jacket around this line. Turn up hem of lining ½″ shorter than hem of jacket. Baste. Press. Trim to ¾″. Set lining edge ½″ up from jacket edge and slip stitch to jacket *(diagram 8u)*. Remove bastings at center back of lining.

Dad's striped shirt makes a fetching bathing suit (right) with a sarong skirt and a bra top. Commercial patterns furnish many choices of design. Two of his white shirts make this year's favorite beach coat (left), the cholo. The little ruffle is in the front only.

9. Repeat Performance

If you are smart and thrifty, you will refuse to keep a lot of unused clothes hanging in the back of your closet. You know the skeletons we mean: "the material's in wonderful condition but" or "the bodice is old-fashioned" or "the sleeves are rubbed kind of thin." That's no excuse. Your old clothes and your husband's too, can be restyled and remodelled so your best friend wouldn't know them. Put your ingenuity to work — let an old suit, a discarded evening dress act as a challenge to your skill. Don't be surprised if the repeat performance is as good or better than the original.

GENERAL RECOMMENDATIONS

When It is Worth While to Make Over

General Directions
for Make-Overs

When making over clothing, the first consideration is whether the fabric is in sufficiently good condition to warrant the time to be spent on it.

Woolen fabric may often be turned to the wrong side if outer part is worn. Even when a fabric has a pronounced right and wrong side, it may often be reversed with good results. Small holes and tears may be darned or covered with a decorative detail.

Cottons, silks and rayons should be held up to the light to see weak spots around the places where tears or breaks have already occurred. It may still be possible to use remaining fabric.

Cleaning

It is preferable to have garments washed or dry cleaned before starting to rip.

To Rip or Not to Rip

Whenever the size of a garment permits, it is advisable to cut it apart at the seams. When the garment is to be ripped, two methods are generally used.

Method No. I — Clip a thread and rip out a few stitches with the head of a needle until there is enough to grasp. Pull the thread until it breaks. Turn the seam over and pull the thread on the other side until it breaks. Continue this method of working from one side to the other until the seam is ripped. This method has the advantage of not leaving any threads in the seams.

Method No. II — Rip seams with a stiff one-edged razor blade or better still, buy a gadget in which a two-edged razor blade may be screwed.

Preparation of Fabric

After fabric has been ripped, it should be pressed carefully. It may be desirable to mark the straight of the goods as well as the right and wrong side of each section. Then the fabric is ready for the pattern. It is laid on and cut as if the fabric were new (page 198).

Cutting

Follow general cutting directions on page 198.

Sewing and Finishing

Follow pattern guide and consult index for directions for particular finishes.

CUT UPS

There's a simple as ABC trick for stretching a slim budget to cover an active family. Don't waste or discard anything. Make clothing do time, twice, thrice, before you let it get away from you. A tired dress can be rejuvenated with a bit from the scrap bag or it can be made into a jumper, a vivacious swimming suit, a gay pinafore. Cutting up isn't just fun, it's smart!

1. When the skirt of a dress is too narrow, add new skirt at waistline or slightly below in contrasting fabric.

2. Make a jerkin or a jumper from a dress which is worn out under the arms.

3. To make dress larger, insert contrasting panel in front.

4. When the waist or the skirt of a dress is out of date, make it over in a new style in contrasting fabric.

5. Make a playsuit from a summer dress which is too short.

6. If shoulders are out of date, add contrasting yoke and sleeves.

For all these restyling suggestions, use commercial patterns chosen to fit in with existing style of garment and type of change desired.

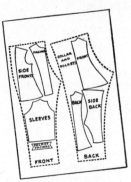

Make a child's coat
from white flannels.

LITTLE SHAVERS

There's plenty of life in those old clothes of dad's. All
they need to give them a new lease on life is a little head-
work and some deft surgery with the scissors. Trousers for
your young son, a small girl's coat, slacks for you, all kinds
of clothes for all sorts of small fry are lurking among the
discards in your closet. Get to work and make them go
to work!

Use commercial patterns chosen to fit in with limitations of fabric. The layouts give suggestions as to how
pieces can be laid out for cutting.

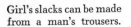

Girl's slacks can be made
from a man's trousers.

This boy's suit was once a man's suit.

This girl's coat had its beginning as an overcoat.

This boy's coat was originally a man's topcoat.

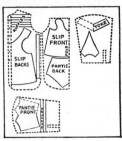

Panty and Slip
from a Man's Shirt

TALE OF A SHIRT

Remember the fairy tale of a thousand and one stories? Well, dad's old shirts aren't quite up to that many, but they can give a good account of themselves. Take the worn shirts off his back and make them into blouses and suits.

For making all of these clothes, use commercial patterns chosen to fit in with the limitation of fabric in shirt. The layouts give suggestions as to how pieces can be laid out for cutting.

Smocked Dress
from Two Shirts

Child's Pinafore
from a Shirt

Blouse from
Two Shirts

Boy's Blouse
from a Shirt

Child's Sun suit and
Bonnet from a Shirt

Child's Overalls
from a Shirt

Here's a useful piece of wardrobe magic. Canny cutting turns a man's top coat into the sort of casual topper every woman loves. Use a commercial pattern. Refer to Chapter 8 for tailoring.

A two-for-one trick worth trying on a spring reefer that has seen better days is to divide it into a chic bolero and skirt ensemble. You can find a suitable design in any pattern book.

MAKING A MAN'S SUIT INTO
A WOMAN'S SUIT

In addition to the general considerations which pertain to all makeovers, there are certain specific problems involved in making over a man's suit.

Consideration of Size

When making a man's suit into a woman's suit, size is an important consideration. The suit must be larger than the woman for whom the suit is planned.

Keeping Any of the Tailoring

The tailoring along the front edges and the pockets may be kept. If it is retained, the pattern bought must resemble as nearly as possible the original suit. The jacket will have to be completely ripped: 1. If buttonholes are changed to the right side (men's suits button to the left). 2. If worn fabric is to be turned. 3. If a double-breasted coat is being used. 4. If the existing tailoring is too exaggerated.

Cleaning and Ripping

When sending the suit to be cleaned, instruct the tailor not to press the crease in the trousers. See page 238 for methods of ripping and pattern layouts (pages 247 and 249) for specific instructions.

Choosing a Pattern

Few patterns have been designed for makeovers, so the purpose of the two layouts presented is to show how suit patterns of an ordinary type may be adapted with a few minor alterations. When purchasing a suit pattern for remodelling, remember that men's suits in general have certain characteristics: a seam down the back, two darts at the waist, a side pocket on the left, and frequently flap pockets, so select a pattern with these characteristics.

The limitations of fabric in the trousers make it necessary for the skirt to be fairly straight. A kick pleat or a slight flare is the only fullness that can be expected.

Lining

Usually it is not advisable to use the old lining. Rayon twill is a very serviceable fabric to use, although silk and other rayons may be used.

When lining is used, see pages 230 and 231 for cutting directions and page 235 for instructions on finishing.

Interfacings

The collar and facings must have interfacings. The interfacing already on the suit may be used. If that seems too heavy, a lightweight muslin or canvas may be used. The fabric is shrunk before using by washing and pressing while still damp. Do the same with the old interfacing, if it is used, so as to renew the "body." Cut interfacing for front facings from same pattern as front facings on the straight grain. Cut the interfacing for the collar from under collar pattern, cutting on the bias (*see figure 48*, page 48). This makes the collar lie more smoothly. See pages 230 and 231 for directions.

General Directions on Cutting

1. Pin together corresponding parts of ripped suit, same sides of fabric together.

2. Take out pattern pieces needed. Note perforations for straight of goods. Mark them with a colored pencil, as it is most important that these perforations be laid on the lengthwise grain (*see figure 5*, page 30).

3. Where there is a dart on the pattern at front shoulder, pin it up, matching perforations. This permits the pattern to fit into the original armhole with less overlapping. Notice on pattern layout that this dart is allowed for elsewhere.

4. Using the layout and the instructions given for each layout, depending on type of pattern, cut out pattern.

5. In the instructions which follow, certain words have special meanings: (a) *Lay pattern on the fabric* means that in doing so you must match the perforations for the straight of the goods to the lengthwise grain (see page 30). (b) *Mark* means mark darts, seam allowances and other indicated points with tailor's tacks or tailor's chalk (*see figures 105 and 108*, page 201). (c) *Cut* means cut around pattern, cutting notches away from pattern.

LAYOUT No. I

Jacket

When Tailoring Is Retained
On this jacket some of the original tailoring is to be retained, so a pattern is picked which resembles the original as closely as possible (see page 247). The pockets, the two front darts and the front edges from the collar joining just above the lapels are not ripped. The outer edge stitching is ripped down to the tip of the lapel and from the bottom up to the first button. The interfacing is trimmed to the edge of the coat facing.

Back of Coat (Jacket Back)

Lay pattern on back sections of coat as shown. Mark seam allowances and shoulder darts, but disregard darts at waistline. Cut around pattern and cut off extra piece of pattern.

Front of Coat (Jacket Front)

Each side will be cut separately, since the tailoring is retained. Lay pattern (dart at shoulder already pinned) on front section as shown, front edges together, and marking for pockets in line with pockets already in coat. The

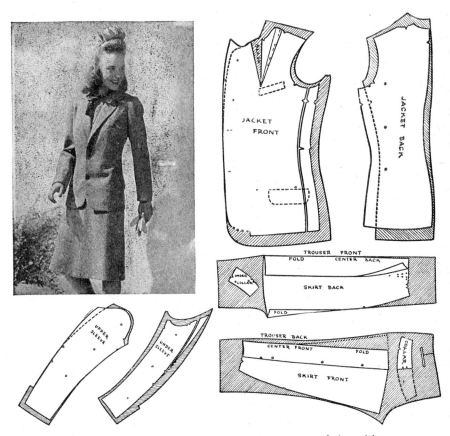

pockets on coat will be a little farther back than on pattern, or their position may be a little higher or lower. This makes no difference, nor does it matter if the lapel point of pattern projects a little beyond fabric. Pin pattern in a few places. To make pattern lie flat, a new dart must be cut from the neckline as shown. Draw a line from bottom perforation of pinned dart to the neckline, parallel to dart already in lower part of coat, and cut along this line. Smooth pattern out and pin around it. Add piece cut from back, as shown, matching notches. To make it lie flat, slash at inner edge at waistline and pleat at outer edge, as shown. Pin, mark (do not forget new dart at shoulder) and cut around pattern except at front edges. Transfer notches at side seam to outer edge.

Skirt

The pattern for this skirt is made with inverted pleats at center back and center front. To change this to a four-gored skirt, turn under pleat extensions on both back and front ½″ beyond pleat perforations towards center edge. The ½″ is for seam allowance.

Back of Trousers (Skirt Front)—Upper Collar is also cut from this section.

Lay skirt front pattern on back section of trousers as shown. Pin. To allow additional fullness as indicated by dotted portion of diagram, measure down 11" from top edge along fold of pattern and mark. Continue line of lower edge of pattern to edge of fabric with a basting. Connect end of this line with point marked above, as shown. This is cutting line. Mark and cut. After skirt front is cut, take one of remaining pieces and fold on lengthwise grain. Place upper collar pattern with perforations on fold. Mark and cut.

Front of Trousers (Skirt Back)—Under Collar is also cut from this section.

Lay patterns on front sections of trousers, as shown. If skirt pattern exceeds width of fabric, turn it back at side seam as shown, graduating in to hipline. Pin, mark and cut.

Sleeves

Lay patterns on sleeve sections as shown. Cut off the pattern piece that extends beyond the fabric of the upper sleeve and pin to under sleeve as indicated. When pinning, notice that a small amount of width is added to keep the outer line curved. Mark and cut.

Belt

Cut belt from any remaining fabric. Piece at side seams if necessary. If fabric is heavy, face with lining material.

Lining and Interfacings

See instructions for *Lining and Interfacings*, page 245.

Sewing and Finishing

Follow pattern guide and see Chapter 8, page 227, for instruction on the special processes used in tailoring. The skirt is seamed at center back, center front and sides, and finished as usual. Hints on how to finish the front and the collar of the jacket of this suit, in which the tailoring has been retained, are as follows:

1. Seam under section of collar to jacket, right side to right side, and press.

2. Turn facing out over the right side of jacket and at lower edge of jacket, stitch facing and front together, continuing original seam.

3. At neck edge, stitch upper section of collar to facings (the collar will be placed under the facings, right side of collar to right side of facings). Press seam open.

4. Sew upper and under sections of collar together, continuing the stitching down the edge of the rever, and keeping an even line until it merges with old seam.

5. Trim seams, clip corners and turn facing to inside of jacket.

6. Baste around outer edge of collar and rever and lower edge of jacket. Press. Finish edges with stitching the same as original front edge stitching on suit. To hide ends of thread, leave long enough ends when finishing off machine stitching to thread a needle and bring the ends through to the inside of jacket.

7. Turn lower hem and catch stitch to coat (*see figure 91*, page 124).

8. Baste inner edge of facing to inside of jacket, turning rever out while doing so, to make sure that it is not too tight. Catch stitch to jacket.

LAYOUT No. II

Jacket

Suit Entirely   For this jacket in which the coat was entirely ripped and turned, a pattern
Remade   with patch pockets has been selected so that the pocket slashes might be covered

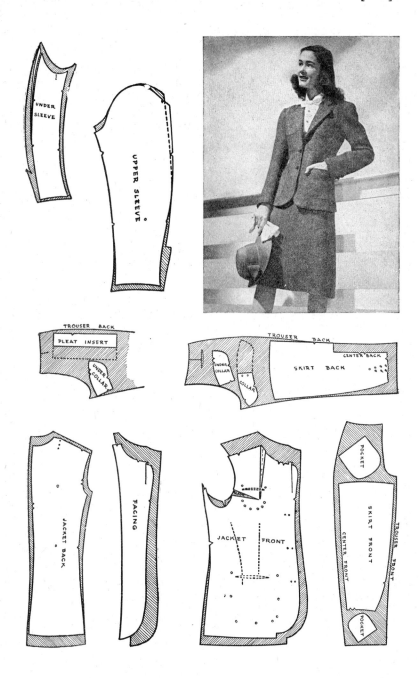

by patch pockets. The two front darts have been retained and sewed in on the other side. The dotted lines on the jacket front indicate the pockets and darts on the original suit. The perforations indicate the placing of pockets on re-modelled suit.

Back of Coat (Jacket Back)

There is no special problem. Pin pattern to back sections of coat, mark and cut.

Front of Coat (Jacket Front)

1. Both sides may be cut at one time. Lay pattern (dart at shoulder already pinned) on front coat sections as shown, so that front edge comes just to the buttonholes. The buttonholes may run a little into the seam allowance, but this is of no consequence. Pocket perforations should come above the pocket slash. Pin pattern in a few places.

2. To make pattern lie flat, a new dart must be cut from the armhole to lower perforation of shoulder dart as indicated. It should come below pocket slash.

3. Smooth pattern out and pin all around. If rever of pattern extends out a little too far, take a small pleat in it, graduating it as shown. Mark seam allow-ances and new dart. Disregard waistline darts on pattern. When fitting coat, it may be necessary to take in existing darts a little.

Front Facings

Lay pattern on so that front edge is in back of buttonholes. If rever of jacket front was made smaller by a pleat, take the same pleat in the facing as was taken in the front. Pin, mark and cut. It makes no difference if facings are a little narrower than the pattern. Allow the extra amount on the lining.

Skirt

Front of Trousers (Skirt Front)—Pockets are also cut from this section.

1. Lay skirt front on front sections of trousers as shown. Be sure it is far enough from the edge to allow for seam at outer edge and far enough down so that pockets may be cut from piece above. Pin, mark and cut.

2. Pin pockets on remaining pieces as indicated. In a herringbone tweed, a nice effect is produced by cutting on the bias as shown. Pockets may also be cut straight.

Back of Trousers (Skirt Back)—Collars and Pleat Insert are also cut from this section.

1. Lay skirt back on back sections of trousers so that pleat extension is on lengthwise grain of fabric. Pin, mark and cut.

2. From one of two remaining pieces the collars are cut. Pattern pieces are shown in proper position. From the other piece the pleat insert is cut with the center back on a lengthwise fold.

Sleeves — See instructions for *Sleeves* under *Layout No. 1*, page 248.

Belt — See instructions for *Belt* under *Layout No. 1*, page 248.

Lining and Interfacings — See instructions for *Lining and Interfacings*, page 245.

Sewing and Finishing — Follow pattern guide and see Chapter 8, page 227, for instruction on the special processes used in tailoring. To close pocket open-ings, cut strips of lining ¾″ wide and length of opening plus 1½″. Baste ½″ turn under on all sides. Baste on right side over openings and stitch around edge. These strips will be hidden by pockets.

10. Stork Set

It's the inalienable right of every baby to look adorable. And it's the privilege of every mother, aunt, grandmother and friend-of-the-family to make sure of this. Whether it's for your own special bundle of bliss or somebody else's blessed event, making things for a baby with your own hands comes under the department of pure pleasure. Fortunately, there's no limit to what a brand new baby needs to make it comfortable and happy. Everybody can sew to her heart's content, baby will reap the benefits and say thank you with an irresistible gurgle.

BABY CLOTHES TO MAKE

Baby's Slip

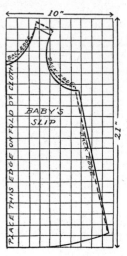

Pattern XXII

Baby Clothes

Material: Batiste or nainsook—¾ yd.; pearl buttons (¼″ size)—4.

Directions for Cutting: 2 pieces, *pattern No. XXII (see figure 4,* page 29, for directions for enlarging pattern from diagram).

Directions for Making:

1. Baste front and back wrong sides together and finish sides with French seams *(see figure 40,* page 42).

2. Cut bias strips ¾″ wide and join to make a strip 1½ yds. long *(see figures 48–51,* page 48). Face neck and armhole edges as in *figure 60,* page 52. Take ³⁄₁₆″ seams.

3. At shoulder edges make ⅝″ hems. On back shoulder edges, make worked buttonholes *(see figure*

101, page 176), ³⁄₁₆″ from edge, to fit buttons. On
front edges, sew buttons to correspond *(see figure 103,
page 177)*.

4.   At bottom edge, turn up 3″ hem, slip stitch *(see
figure 39,* page 41).

Baby's Sacque or Wrapper

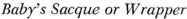

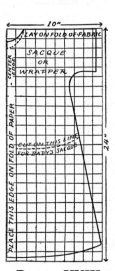

Pattern XXIII

Material: Sacque—Albatross, challis, outing flannel
or terry cloth—¾ yd.; satin ribbon (½″ wide)—2½
yds. *Wrapper*—Outing flannel, wool or part wool flannel, cotton bird'seye—1½ yds.; satin ribbon (½″ wide)
—1½ yds.

Directions for Making Pattern: Fold a piece of wrapping paper 24″x24″ in half. Mark off *pattern No. XXIII*
(actual size) on paper with center edge against fold
(see figure 4, page 29, for directions for enlarging pattern from diagram). Cut through 2 layers of paper
around all edges, except center edge that is laid on fold

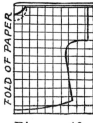

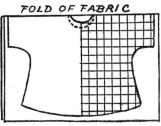

Diagram 10a   Diagram 10b

(diagram 10a). Cut along back neckline. Mark front (lower) neckline on paper.

Directions for Cutting: Fold fabric in half crosswise, right sides out. Lay shoulder edges of *pattern No. XXIII* on fold *(diagram 10b).* Pin. Mark front neckline on upper side of fabric with tailor's tacks *(see figure 105,* page 201). Cut. To make front opening, cut down center front.

Directions for Making:

1. Fold sacque or wrapper in half at shoulders, matching underarm seams, wrong sides together. Finish underarms with French seams *(figure 40,* page 42).

2. On sacque, bind all raw edges with ribbon, miter corners. This is done the same as binding with bias trim in *figure 56,* page 50. To make bow closing, cut 2 pieces of ribbon each 13" long. On each piece turn under one end and whip to sacque at neck edge *(see figure 62,* page 60).

3. On wrapper, to bind edges cut strips of bias of self fabric *(see figures 48-51,* page 48). Bind as in *figure 53,* page 49. To make bow closing, cut 4 pieces of ribbon each 13". Turn under one end of each and whip 2 pieces to wrapper at neck edge and 2 pieces 5" down from first set *(see figure 62,* page 60).

Baby's Dress

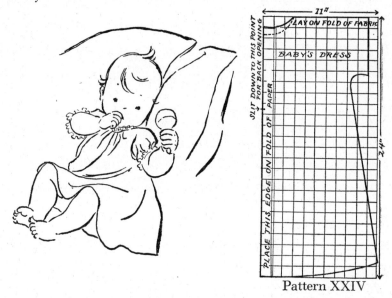

Pattern XXIV

Material: Batiste or nainsook—1¼ yds.; Valenciennes lace (¼″ wide)—1¼ yds.; entre-deux (fine)—¾ yd.; pearl buttons (¼″ size)—2.

Directions for Making Pattern: Use *pattern No. XXIV.* See *Directions for Making Sacque Pattern* on page 252. *Directions for Cutting:* See *Directions for Cutting Sacque,* page 253. Mark center front with basting line. Cut down center back to point marked on pattern.

Directions for Making:

1. Make baby placket at back opening (*figure* 145).

2. Fold dress in half at shoulders, matching underarm seams, wrong sides together. Finish underarms with French seams (*see figure 40,* page 42).

Figure 145—At end of back slash and at right angles to it, clip ⅜" to each side. On both edges of slash, turn ⅛" to wrong side, baste. Along each folded edge mark ½" at intervals. Fold both sides of opening to wrong side along marked lines, baste, slip stitch *(see figure 39, page 41)*. Lap right edge over left with fold edge of right meeting stitching line of left hem. This will form a pleat. Pin. Stitch placket closed across lower end with tiny back hand stitches *(see figure 22, page 36)*, making a square of stitches. Make one worked buttonhole *(see figure 100, page 175)* on upper part of placket, ¾" from neck edge. Make a second one 3" down from first.

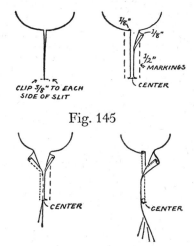

Fig. 145

Fig. 146

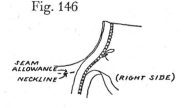

Figure 146—Trim off one edge of entre-deux. Baste entre-deux to neck edge with cut edge along seam line (½" in from raw edge). Whip *(see figure 62, page 60)* inner edge to garment. Turn to wrong side. Trim seam allowance of garment to ¼", hand roll and whip. Trim opposite edge of entre-deux.

3.   Mark center front of neck edge ½" from edge. Mark 2½" to each side of center. Gather the 5" to measure 2" *(see figures 31 and 32, page 38)*.

4.   Attach entre-deux as in *figure 146*.

5.   To apply lace edging, cut piece of lace 1½ times the neck edge. To gather lace, pull the strong thread that lies along the straight edge. Gather to fit neck edge and fasten gathering thread. Place right side of lace against right side of entre-deux, edge to edge, distributing fullness evenly. Whip edges together *(see figure 62, page 60)*. At ends of lace turn back raw edges, roll and whip.

6. One-half inch from lower edge of sleeves gather sleeves to measure 7″. Apply entre-deux as above and whip on lace. Whip ends of lace together.

7. Turn up 3″ hem at lower edge of dress and slip stitch (*see figure 39*, page 41).

GIFTS FOR THE NEW MOTHER AND BABY

Bath Towel Apron

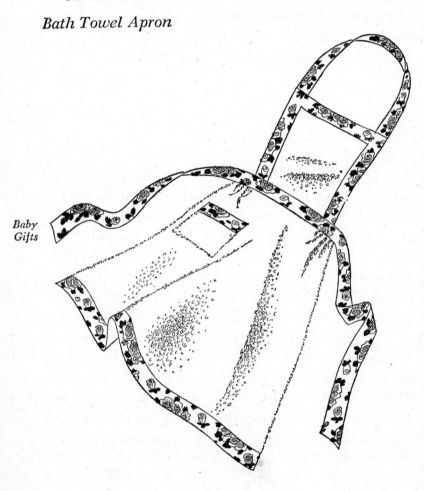

Baby Gifts

Material: Plain bath towel, 27"x42"; chintz—½ yd.
Directions for Cutting: Cut away hems on both ends of towel. *Skirt*—1 piece, 26" long x width of towel (27"); *bib*—1 piece, 10"x13"; *pocket*—1 piece, 7"x8"; *chintz* —7 strips, each 2½"x35" or 36".

Directions for Making:

1. On one 27" end of skirt, place right side of one chintz strip on wrong side of towel, edge to edge, stitch. Turn to right side on seam line, press, stitch close to edge. Turn free edge ½" to wrong side, edge stitch to towel.

2. On opposite end of towel, mark center of width. Gather this end to measure 22".

3. Piece chintz strips to make 2 strips, each 2½" x 54".

4. Place 1 strip on unfinished end of towel, right sides together, edge to edge, match center of strip to center of towel. In same manner, place right side of other long strip on wrong side of apron, edge to edge. Stitch 2 strips together along top side, including the apron, across ends, and on under side as far as sides of apron. Turn tie ends to right side and press (middle section is open and raw edges are turned in).

5. To make bib, apply strip of chintz to two 10" sides and one 13" side as in step 1. (Pleat corners diagonally to make strip lie flat.) On untrimmed side, 3" from center front, make ½" pleat on each side of bib. To sew bib to apron, insert bib in opening, matching centers. Baste and stitch all around band close to edge.

6. To make strap for bib, cut a chintz strip 2½"x20".

Fold in half lengthwise. Stitch around one end and lengthwise edge, turn. Turn in raw edges at end and slip stitch (*see figure 39*, page 41). Attach ends to top corners of bib.

7.   For pocket, cut a chintz strip 2½"x7". On one 7" edge of pocket, apply chintz as in step 1. Turn raw edges of pocket ½" to wrong side. Apply pocket to apron in desired position. Stitch around 3 sides, close to edge.

Cuddly Pig

Material: Gingham or cotton fabric—⅜ yd.; pink sateen scraps; cotton batting for stuffing; 2 shoe buttons; heavy duty mercerized sewing thread. *Directions for Cutting:* (*See figure 4*, page 29) when cutting, add ½" to all edges of pattern for seam allowance): 2 pieces, *pattern XXV a*, for sides; 1 piece, *pattern XXV b* for top; 1 piece, *pattern XXV c* for underbody; 4 pieces, *pattern XXV d* for ears (2 gingham, 2 sateen); 5 pieces, *pattern XXV e* of sateen (four for bottoms of legs and one for end of nose). *Directions for Making:* 1. Stitch the ears and lining together except edge opposite point, wrong side to wrong side. Turn right side out and press. 2. Fold both sides of ear under so that corners of open edge meet and baste down against edges of side pieces where marked. 3. Baste top piece between sides (right sides together), easing as necessary, and stitch. 4. Stitch indicated dart in nose. 5. Baste underbody in place between sides, leaving a 6″ opening for stuffing along one side, and stitch. 6. Press seams open, turn right side out and place tail of heavy cotton cord with ravelled end at back joining of sections. 7. With tiny stitches, overcast 1 pink circle around the end of the nose. 8. Stuff the pig very firmly, distributing the cotton batting with a knitting needle. 9. Slip stitch opening, then sew circles of sateen at bottom of each of the 4 legs, overcasting in tiny stitches. 10. To sew on shoe button eyes where marked on pattern, tie end of thread to 1 button and, using long needle, carry across to other eye point, fasten through eye, then back to first eye. Sew back and forth several times until a strong thread shank ties the two eyes firmly together. Fasten off.

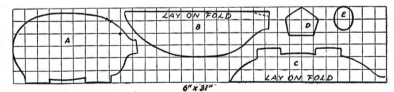

Pattern XXV

Terry Cloth Toy

Material: ¼ yd. terry cloth or towel; scraps of percale; cotton batting; embroidery floss.

Directions for Cutting: From *pattern No. XXVI* cut the number of each piece indicated on pattern. Cut all from terry cloth except paws, eyes, nose, tongue, flower, petals and 2 ear pieces (percale). Allow ⅜" around all edges for seams. Mark joining lines on body and head with running stitches.

Directions for Making:

1. Stitch both body pieces together, leaving top open. Turn. Stuff.

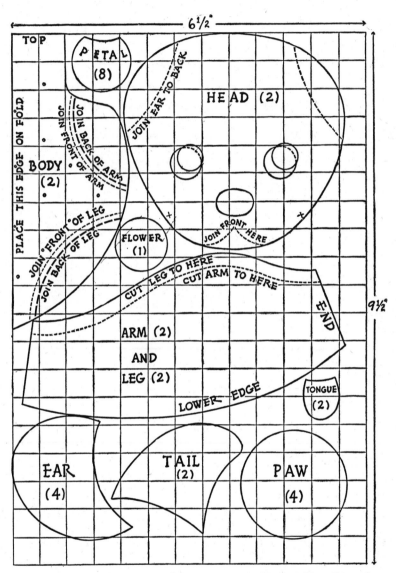

Pattern No. XXVI — See figure 4, page 29 for directions for enlarging pattern. *Draw ½″ squares instead of 1″ squares.*

2. On each arm and leg piece, stitch ends together. Stitch a paw piece into lower edge of each. Turn. Cut 4 circles of cardboard from paw pattern (no seam). Insert in end of each.

3. Stuff to within ⅜" of top edge. Turn under ⅜" and fit to body on marked lines, adjusting stuffing. Whip in place (*see figure 62*, page 60).

4. Stitch both tail pieces together, leaving straight edge open, turn, stuff, fit and stitch to back between legs as in step 3.

5. Stitch tongue around curved edge, turn, stuff. Stitch head pieces together, leaving opening between X marks, and turn. Stuff and stitch head to neck as in step 3. Turn front under on dotted line and insert tongue, tipping head before whipping down.

6. Stitch one terry ear to one percale ear around curved edge. Turn. Turn in raw edges and whip to back of head along marks.

7. Stitch petal pieces together by two's around curved edge. Turn. Gather raw edges, lap together to make flower. Tack to head and cover raw edges with center piece turned under at edge of pattern. Whip in place.

8. Cut out eye and nose pieces, allowing just enough to turn under, and appliqué in place, or embroider features. Make French knots evenly spaced to cover body. See Chapter 11.

9. Cut a strip of percale 1½"x13". Fold lengthwise, stitch along edge, turn, press and tie around neck.

11. Flossy Touches

By some strange paradox the Machine Age has only served to intensify the value we place on handcrafts. The fine linens, the exquisite French imports that used to be, the children's clothes you "oh" and "ah" at, all have handwork to distinguish them from their mass-made brethren. You can add to your needle-and-thread versatility with a repertoire of the basic embroidery stitches. You'll find no limit to their usefulness, from making a patch ornamental, a handkerchief more personal, a guest towel more inviting, to giving your wardrobe and your house furnishings, in general, a more precious look.

EMBROIDERY

Some of the basic embroidery stitches are given below. They may be combined to make attractive border designs as shown on page 267. Several embroidery and combined embroidery and appliqué designs are given on pages 268 to 270.

Basic Embroidery Stitches

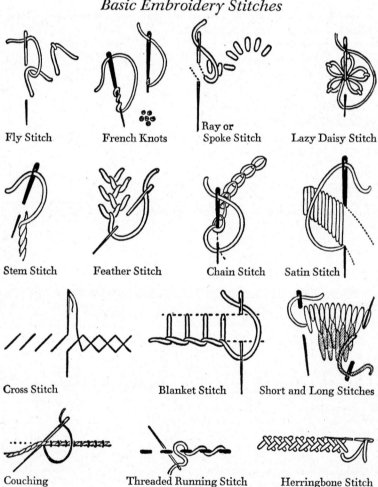

Fly Stitch   French Knots   Ray or Spoke Stitch   Lazy Daisy Stitch

Stem Stitch   Feather Stitch   Chain Stitch   Satin Stitch

Cross Stitch   Blanket Stitch   Short and Long Stitches

Couching   Threaded Running Stitch   Herringbone Stitch

Borders Made From Basic Stitches

Threaded running
stitch, lazy daisy.

Lazy daisy, French knots.

Grouped blanket
stitch, spoke stitch.

Lazy daisy, French
knots, spoke stitch.

Blanket stitch over
rug yarn, lazy daisy.

Lazy daisy stitch.

Blanket stitch, spoke
stitch, French knots.

Couching over rug
yarn, lazy daisy.

Fly stitch, French
knots, lazy daisy.

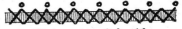

Woven cross stitch with
rug yarn, French knots.

Long and short blanket stitch.

Chain stitch, spoke stitch.

Blanket stitch, lazy daisy.

Herringbone stitch, couching.

APPLIQUÉ

Appliqué Directions   Commercial transfer patterns for appliqué may be used, or flower motifs may be cut from chintz and appliquéd as trimming on plain fabrics. To use the appliqué designs shown, trace off each part to use as a pattern. To appliqué, cut pieces from fabric, allowing ¼″ around all edges to turn under. Turn under ¼″, clipping points if necessary so piece will lie flat. Baste close to turned edge. Press. Baste pieces in place and blind stitch around edges (*see figure 30*, page 38). For embroidery stitches used to complete designs, see page 266.

Embroidery and Appliqué Designs

Appliqué Designs   Hearts and flowers — appliqué
Dots and stems — satin stitch
Leaves — short and long stitch
Veins — stem stitch
Stems — stem stitch

Large pieces — appliqué
Dots and stems — satin stitch

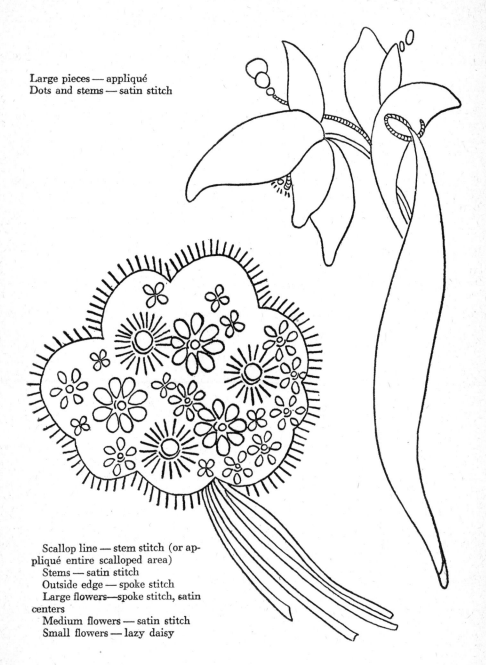

Scallop line — stem stitch (or ap-
pliqué entire scalloped area)
   Stems — satin stitch
   Outside edge — spoke stitch
   Large flowers—spoke stitch, satin
centers
   Medium flowers — satin stitch
   Small flowers — lazy daisy

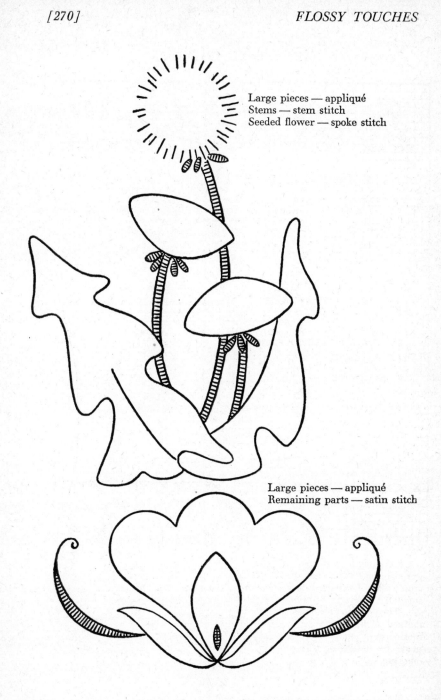

Large pieces — appliqué
Stems — stem stitch
Seeded flower — spoke stitch

Large pieces — appliqué
Remaining parts — satin stitch

MONOGRAMMING

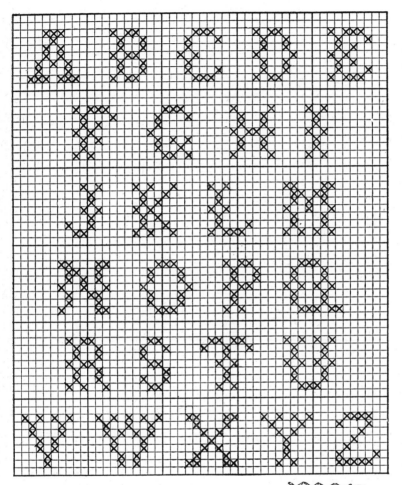

Cross Stitch Monograms

Cross stitch monograms can be made any size, depending upon the size of the cross stitch. To make letters larger or smaller, redraw in squares of desired size. The position of the stitches may be marked on the fabric, or, if threads of fabric are pronounced, stitches may be made by following threads without marking.

*Padded
Monograms*

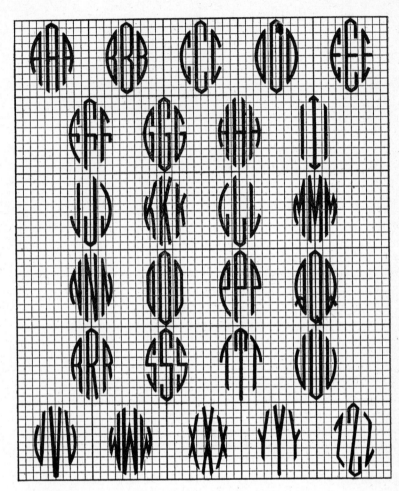

Padded monograms can be made in the size shown (suitable for linens, handkerchiefs and wearing apparel) by tracing the letters, blackening the back and transferring to fabric. Pad letters with chain stitch and cover with satin stitch closely worked (see page 266). To make letters larger, redraw on larger squares.

SMOCKING

Smocking is a decorative method of gathering fab- *Smocking* ric. It is very satisfactory for children's clothes and is also used on yokes of women's dresses. The thread used for smocking should be about the same thickness as a thread of the fabric. Embroidery floss is often used. The width of the fabric required is about 3 times the width of the finished piece.

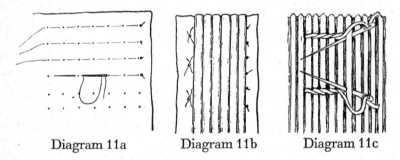

Diagram 11a   Diagram 11b   Diagram 11c

Foundation Steps

1. With a ruler and a sharp pencil, mark dots on the wrong side of fabric at equal intervals both horizontally and vertically *(diagram 11a)*, allowing ½" between each dot on heavy fabrics and ⅜" to ¼" on finer fabric.

2. Thread a needle and make a large knot at one end. Foundation stitches are made from right to left on the wrong side. Make a small straight stitch under each dot horizontally across each row *(diagram 11a)*, leaving a long end of thread at end of row.

3. Draw up the long ends of thread, making even folds on the fabric and having them lie flat *(diagram 11b)*. Tie ends of two rows securely together.

Smocking Patterns

Smocking is worked from left to right on the right side of fabric. Always start with a knot. Several patterns are given, and these patterns may be combined any number of ways.

Rope Pattern — Insert needle from wrong side through the center of first fold and in line with foundation stitches of row. Keeping the thread above the needle, make a stem stitch *(diagram 11c)* at center of each fold across top row. Fasten end securely on wrong side. When two rows of rope pattern are made, work the following row in the same manner but keep the thread below the needle, instead of above the needle *(diagram 11c)*.

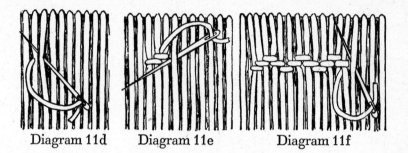

Diagram 11d   Diagram 11e   Diagram 11f

Chevron Pattern — Insert needle from wrong side through the center of first fold and in line with foundation stitches of row. Keeping thread below needle, insert needle in next fold and bring it out about ⅛″ above point where needle was inserted *(diagram 11d)*. Repeat. Keeping thread above needle, insert needle in next fold and bring it out ⅛″ below point where needle was inserted *(diagram 11e)*. Repeat. Now repeat from beginning and continue in this manner to end of row *(diagram 11f)*. If two rows of chevron pattern are made, work the next row in the same manner, reversing the position of the stitches *(diagram 11g)*.

Honeycomb Pattern — (This pattern has more elasticity than any other, and 2 rows are worked at one time.) Insert needle from wrong side through the center of first fold and in line with foundation stitches of row. Keeping thread below the needle, insert needle in second fold and bring it out at center of first fold *(diagram 11h)*. Make a similar stitch directly above previous stitch. Insert needle in same place as before on second fold and, leading it through center of fold, bring it out in line with next row of foundation stitches on second fold *(diagram 11h)*. Keeping thread above the needle, make 2 stitches as before, joining second and third folds together. Then insert needle on third fold and bring it out on line with top row of horizontal stitches on third fold *(diagram 11i)*. Repeat the last two groups of stitches alternately, always joining the next fold to the previous one as others were joined before. Make as many rows as desired.

Diagram 11g   Diagram 11h   Diagram 11i

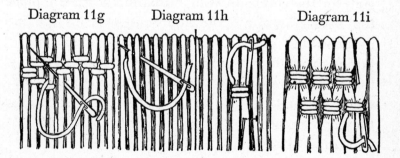

12. *Life Savers*

Clothes, like people and plants, respond to care and kind treatment. The law works in reverse, too. Neglect brings on a variety of symptoms from premature old age to complete collapse. Leave a snag in your stocking without first aid and it becomes an angry runner. Give it a stitch in time and double its life expectancy. That goes for the collar on your husband's shirt, the place that's wearing thin in the elbow of your dress, the tiny indiscernible gap in your hem, the small tear in junior's suit. If you take care of your clothes today, they'll be here to give you service tomorrow. Today when so many things are doubly precious because they're irreplaceable, this adds up to more than dollars and cents—it's plain common sense!

MENDING MADE EASY

Stockings

Mending Stockings   Mending stockings may be a preventive as well as a corrective measure. When stockings are washed, examine for worn places and repair as follows:

1.   Reinforce worn places in foot and heel with small running stitches parallel to weave.

2.   Mend split seams with an over-and-over stitch.

3.   Bring pulled threads through to wrong side and secure with tiny stitches to prevent runs.

4.   Darn holes before they become large (*figure 147*).

Fig. 147

Figure 147 — *To darn a hole*, turn stocking right side out and insert darning egg under hole. Trim ragged edges of hole. Do not use a knot and make lengthwise threads first. Leaving a short end free, take a few running stitches far enough from the hole to take in all the worn part. Turn, leaving a small loop at turning. On each succeeding row increase number of stitches so that when stitches come to the hole, they will cover it and also strengthen the worn part. Arrange stitches so that needle comes out over edges of hole. Decrease length of rows on other side of hole. Cut thread when finished and turn darn around. Weave stitches in the same way across the width over and under foundation stitches already made.

Girdles

Mending Girdles   Frequent laundering and attention to small details of reconditioning will result in much extra wear. To mend the elastic webbing, catch the end of each rubber thread that has pulled out and wrap it securely with strong thread. Darn it down into the seam or fabric where it pulled. Take care not to put needle through any rubber threads for it will cut them. For the same reason do not stitch elastic webbing on the machine. Repair the fagotted section with a catch stitch (*see figure 91*, page 124), using heavy mercerized thread doubled. To reinforce the seams, sew twill tape or satin fabric on under side. When sewing on elasticized fabric, catch stitch is always best to use because it has more "give."

Fasteners

A stitch in time will anchor a loose button, snap, hook, or eye before it comes off. See *figures 102–104*, page 176, for directions for sewing on fasteners. Very strong thread is used for sewing buttons on men's and boys' heavy clothes. A heavy variety of mercerized thread is ideal for sewing buttons on any fabric with a firm body. If there is to be unusual strain on a button, reinforce it with a piece of garment fabric, folded into a small square, by sewing it on the wrong side at the same time as the button is sewed on the right side. Small buttons are used to reinforce buttons on heavy wool fabrics.

Sewing Fasteners

Easy Aids to Good Grooming

Dangling belt loops and split seams are enemies of the well-kept look. Cut off the broken belt loop and make a new one as in *figure 140*, page 219. Split seams may be repaired as in *figure 148*. Dress shields take only a few moments to sew in but aid greatly in conserving the fabric of the dress (*figure 149*). To prevent shoulder straps of slips from being troublesome make lingerie straps (*figure 150*).

Grooming Aids

Fig. 148

Figure 148 — To mend a split seam, if possible, stitch seam from wrong side by machine. In lined coats, seam is mended with an invisible stitch from right side. Insert needle 1" from beginning of split. (Knot is clipped when mending is finished.) On opposite edge of opening and directly across, catch 2 or 3 threads on needle. Continue to catch 2 or 3 threads alternately on either side of split. Keep stitches very small. Pull thread up from time to time. Fasten off invisibly and run thread end on inside for 1" before clipping.

Figure 149 — To secure shields in desired position, use invisible stitches, taking stitches only through finished edge of shield. Tack shield at each end of curved seam to under armhole seam, leaving it loose enough that it will not pull when garment is on. Tack shield also to side and sleeve seams. For coats and suits, use dark shields or cover them with lining material.

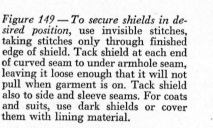

Fig. 149

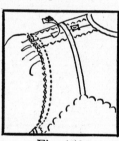

Fig. 150

Figure 150 — To make lingerie straps, either make a chain of single crochet 1½" long, or use narrow tape or narrow bands of dress fabric. Sew one end to shoulder seam half way between armhole and center of shoulder seam. Sew flat side of a small snap to free end, and other side of snap to shoulder seam directly over the top half of snap (*see figure 104,* page 177).

Turning the Collar and Cuffs on a Man's Shirt

Mending Collars and Cuffs
Often a man's shirt is in very good condition with the exception of the collar and cuffs. Turning these will mean months of extra wear (*figure 151*).

Mending Tears

Mending Tears
To mend the three ordinary types of tears, the straight tear (*figure 152*), the three-cornered tear (*figure 153*), and the diagonal tear (*figure 154*), use

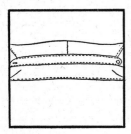
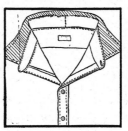

Fig. 151

Figure 151 — To turn the collar and cuffs on a man's shirt, determine exact center of collar and neckband by folding them in half, matching edge to edge and point to point. Mark center of each with pin. On wrong side of collar and on inner side of neckband, run colored bastings down the centers. Remove collar from top of neckband by ripping stitching carefully. Pull out all thread ends. Press neckband (seams still turned in) and collar. Insert reversed collar in neckband, matching centers carefully. Pin from center out, making same seam allowance as before. Do not stretch band or collar. Ease wherever necessary. Baste both sides of neckband to collar along old stitching line. Stitch by machine from inside around edge, using a small stitch. It is practical to turn cuffs only when they fold back. Remove cuff by ripping stitching across top. Press. Ease sleeve into turned cuff. Baste and stitch on outside.

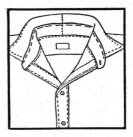

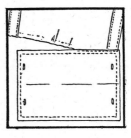

Fig. 152

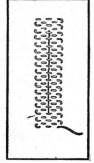

Figure 152 — To mend a straight tear, begin by bringing thread through from wrong side of garment about ¼" beyond end of tear and a little to the right, leaving a 6" end on wrong side. Following the thread of fabric, take a few rows of small running stitches back and forth. Do not darn too tightly and leave a very small loop at each turning. When reaching the tear, fit edges together and sew across opening. On one row make the stitch over edge of tear and on next row under. Continue for about ¼" beyond end. To finish, catch thread through stitches of last row and clip. Thread needle with 6" thread left hanging at beginning and catch it through stitches of at least one row. Clip closely.

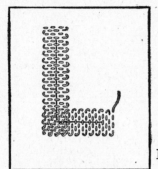

Figure 153 — To mend a three-cornered tear which is both lengthwise and crosswise, darn in same manner as for straight tear (figure 152). Stitches run at right angles to opening. Begin at one end and darn one side completely. Then begin at other end and darn that side completely. Stitches at corners thus overlap and are strengthened.

Fig. 153

Figure 154 — To mend a diagonal tear in which both lengthwise and crosswise threads are cut, darn with small running stitches parallel to lengthwise thread, but in direction of tear. Over these stitches work another set at right angles to first.

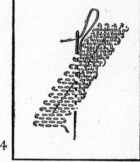

Fig. 154

a thread which matches the fabric as closely as possible. For woolens, a thread of fabric drawn from the hem or side makes a neat and inconspicuous darn. Darn on right side. Do not make a knot as there is no strain on fabric.

To reinforce a worn place on a garment, cut a piece of fabric the same as garment just a little larger than worn place. Baste to wrong side under worn spot and cover entire area as for darning a straight tear (figure 152), taking stitches through both thicknesses of fabric. On wool fabric, if a similar piece of fabric is not available, baste a piece of net under worn spot and darn as for tear.

Patches

Patches   When hole is large, a darn would be too conspicuous and not strong enough. The hole should be patched with fabric the same as garment. Cut a piece from hem or seams to obtain matching patch. If necessary, fade patch to correspond by washing in soap suds and baking soda, rinsing well and drying in the sun. A hemmed patch *(figure 155)* is the most usual. The least noticeable is an overhand patch *(figure 156).*

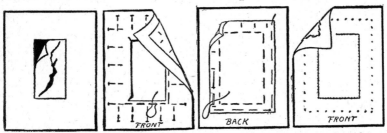

Figure 155—*To make a hemmed patch,* use threads of fabric as guide and cut away worn portion to make either a square or rectangle. Cut patch 1″ larger on all sides than hole after edges have been straightened. Pin patch in place under hole, right side showing through. Threads in patch must run same way as those in garment, and any pattern should match exactly. On right side of garment, clip corners of hole diagonally about ¼″. Turn in raw edges and baste to patch. On wrong side of garment turn in raw edges of patch ¼″ and baste to garment. Press. Stitch edges down by machine or blind hem *(see figure 30,* page 38).

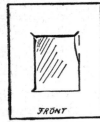 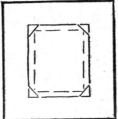 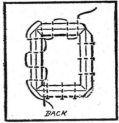

Figure 156—*To make an overhand patch,* straighten hole as for hemmed patch *(figure 155).* Clip corners diagonally for ⅜″. Turn edges under as far as possible. Baste. Press. Measure dimensions of hole with edges turned back. Carefully match grain and pattern of patch and cut it ⅜″ larger than the hole on all sides. Turn in ⅜″ allowance on one side. Press down. Do same on 3 remaining sides. With patch flat, where creases come to a point, cut off triangle of fabric. Put patch directly under hole. It should fit exactly. Pin in place with pins at right angles to folded edges. Baste with small stitches at these points. On wrong side whip patch to garment with tiny stitches *(see figure 62,* page 60). Overcast raw edges *(see figure 41,* page 42). Remove bastings. Press.

Fig. 156

 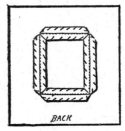

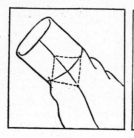 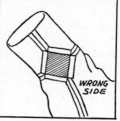 

Fig. 157

Figure 157 — To make an underarm patch, cut away worn portion in a square so that each corner comes at a seam line. Straighten edges of hole. Turn dress to wrong side. Rip seams about ½". Turn edges of hole back ½" and press. Cut patch ½" larger all around than opening. Place patch over hole right side down. Allowing ½" for seam, baste edge of patch to edge of hole. Stitch on basting line. Press seam open. Overcast raw edges *(see figure 41,* page 42).

However, this is not very strong and should be used only on fine fabrics where there is no great wear. One of the spots where there is most wear in a dress is at the underarm. Directions for a special underarm patch are given in *figure 157.*

Holes may also be cleverly hidden by means of appliqué. Cut out flowers from printed fabric, or use original patterns or commercial transfers. See Chapter 11, page 265, for designs and directions for appliqué.

TIPS ON ALTERATIONS

Shortening or Lengthening a Dress

Alterations   1. Take out old hem and remove old seam binding to use again. Press out crease mark from wrong side through a damp cloth (see page 221).

Diagram 12a   Diagram 12b

2. Put on garment, wearing shoes of a suitable heel height. Mark **new** hemline as shown in *figures 42–44*, page 42. Finish suitably. See suggestions for hem finishes, page 220. When lengthening the skirt, if, after cleaning and pressing, the line of the former hem persists in showing, choose a mercerized or silk thread of matching color and machine stitch over the mark. Do this before putting in the hem.

Shortening a Full Length Dress

1. Hem is marked with chalk or pencil ¼″ below point where dress touches floor, when it is hanging straight. Cut off on this line.

2. Stitch back ⅛″ by machine. Turn up edge another ⅛″ and slip stitch (*see figure 39*, page 41). Or hem may be roll hemmed by hand (*see figure 68*, page 68).

Shortening a Dress from the Waistline (When Lower Edge Cannot Be Altered)

1. Determine how many inches dress is to be shortened. Measure desired number of inches down from waistline all around skirt and mark with pins. Baste around marked line (*diagram 12a*).

2. Rip skirt from waist and rip placket from skirt. Mark waistline on waist with basting. Mark center back and center front of waist and skirt. Rip side seams of skirt to basting line.

3. Turn under top of skirt at basting line and, matching center points, pin to waist at waistline (*diagram 12b*).

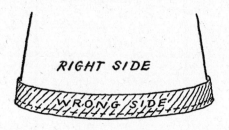

Diagram 12c

4. Put on dress and check evenness of hemline. Take up or let down as necessary by turning under more or less around top of skirt.
5. Fit side seams and mark the new side seam line with chalk or pins.
6. Remove dress. Mark fold at top of skirt.
7. Remove skirt and trim top edge ¾″ above marking line. Baste and stitch side seams along marking lines, graduating into old seams.
8. Rip old seams, press open, trim to ¾″.
9. Turn in top edge of skirt along marking line. Matching centers and side seams, pin skirt to waistline. Stitch, press, insert placket (*see figures 125 to 126, page 214*).

Lengthening a Skirt by Applying a Facing

Occasionally there is not sufficient fabric to turn up for a new hem. Under these circumstances a false hem or facing is applied. On a flared skirt a facing is made as follows:

1. Begin as in Steps 1 and 2 of *Shortening or Lengthening a Dress*, page 282.
2. Mark pinned hemline with a basting. Cut off ½″ below basting.
3. Measure around bottom of skirt. For facing, cut bias strips of a fabric similar to that in dress and join enough together so that piece equals distance around bottom of skirt (*see figures 48–51, page 48*).
4. Place piece against lower edge of garment right sides together, edge to edge, and baste. Join ends. Stitch, taking ½″ seam. Trim seam to ¼″. Press seam open (*diagram 12c*).
5. Turn back along seam line, baste, press and finish suitably. See suggestions for hem finishes, page 220. On a straight skirt, a facing is applied in the same way, except that the facing strip is cut on the straight of the goods.

Taking in a Dress at Waistline

1. Take out side seams, removing placket. Press out folds (see page 221).
2. Refit both side seams by pinning in excess fullness evenly on sides.

Diagram 12d

3. Mark new seam lines on back and front with pins placed parallel to seam. Run basting along pin line *(diagram 12d)*.

4. Place two basting lines together and sew right side seam. In same manner, sew left side seam above and below placket opening (length of zipper teeth).

5. Finish placket *(see figures 125 and 126, page 214)*.

Taking Out Bagginess at Back of Skirt

1. Take out back waistline seam and side seams of skirt, taking out placket below waistline. Press out folds (see page 221).

2. Raise back of skirt just enough to bring side seams into line (½" to ¾"), turn under top of skirt at new line, baste. Refit side seams and finish placket as above. Even hemline (see page 42).

Altering a Waistline Which is too Low

Follow the directions on *Shortening a Dress from the Waistline.*

Altering the Hem of a Coat

1. Rip lining from facing on inside of coat far enough to allow for working comfortably. Free lining from hem of coat and take out both hems. Press (see page 221). Put on coat.

2. Determine new hemline in same manner as for dress *(see figures 42–44, page 42)*. Mark new length on facing also.

3. Turn up hem on coat and facing at new line *(see figure 45, page 44)*.

4. Trim to 1½", using a gauge *(see figure 46, page 44)*. Shrink out excess fullness (see page 223). Finish raw edges by pinking, running a machine stitching close to edge, and catch stitching in place *(see figure 91, page 124)*. Or machine stitch seam binding on hem edge and blind hem *(see figure 30, page 38)*.

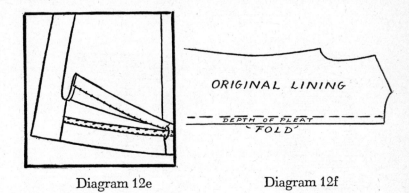

Diagram 12e   Diagram 12f

5. To finish lining, put coat on and pin lining to coat around bottom of coat about 4″ above lower edge. Baste lining to coat around this line. Turn up hem of lining 1″ shorter than hem of coat, using coat hem as a guide. Baste. Press. Make a 1″ hem and blind hem. Fold facing back in place. On a coat which is not to be lengthened again, hem of facing is trimmed to ¼″ and slip stitched (*see figure 39,* page 41) to lower edge of coat. (Do not trim facing on children's clothes.) Slip stitch lining to facing where it was ripped. Fasten lining to hem at each seam with French tacks *(diagram 12e).* French tacks are made according to *figure 92,* page 127.

Relining a Coat

Linings may be made of silk, rayon, or cotton. Rayon twill is a very durable fabric. For an average length of coat, buy, in 39″ fabric, twice the length of garment plus about 12″ for hems. Allow a little more or less according to width of fabric.

1. Do not wait until lining is too badly worn since it is necessary to use it as a pattern.

2. Before ripping out, make a cross stitch to mark (a) where sleeve joins shoulder seam, (b) about mid-point on back and front of sleeve at armhole seam, (c) corresponding places on back and front at armhole seam, (d) where dart comes at front shoulder.

3. Note depth of pleat at center back where it joins neck.

4. Rip lining out and rip pieces apart. Mark original seam allowances around all edges. Press.

5. Fold the back in half on length. Mark the depth of pleat at center back with tailor's chalk *(diagram 12f).* Cut on chalk line. For patterns use one of the back pieces, one side of front, and one sleeve (one of each sleeve piece if it is a two piece sleeve).

6. Cut lining as described on page 230. Make marks to correspond with marks made on old lining in step 2.

7. Finish lining as on page 235.

13. Material Evidence

Once upon a time, life was comparatively simple. There were silks and wools and cottons, and everything was just what it appeared to be on the surface. That was before man started playing variations on Mother Nature and created fabrics out of coal, milk and wood. That was before nylon and aralac and the rayon family came to live with us. Dry clean or wash? Hot or cold water? Hang in the shade or roll in a towel? Press on the wrong side or the right? Hot iron or warm? Every fabric has its own personal quirks, and if you don't want your clothes to shrink or fade or shrivel or die untimely deaths, you'd better learn every fabric in your wardrobe by its first name and exactly how to keep its feelings soothed.

SELECTION OF FABRICS

Selection of Fabrics   Before purchasing fabrics, consider their suitability and serviceability. Suitability of the fabric to the type of article or garment to be made may be determined from recommendations throughout this book and by consulting the Textile Chart beginning on page 292. Shopping in the stores for ideas will result in an increased appreciation of the types of fabrics and their uses. Pattern envelopes sometimes give suggestions for suitable fabrics. To select a fabric that will give serviceability in wear, it is helpful to recognize various fabrics, to know their uses, to know how to care for them, and to understand the information generally given on modern textile labels.

Textile Fibers

Fibers   Formerly, it was comparatively easy to determine the fiber content of a fabric, but today fabrics are no longer made only of natural fibers, such as cotton, linen, silk, wool. They are also made of rayon and other synthetic fibers. Rayon is the general name applied to man-made yarns of cellulose, derived from wood pulp or cotton linters (short fibers which stick to seeds). This is done by any one of three processes to make three types of rayon yarn: viscose, cellulose acetate, or cuprammonium. New synthetics, other than rayon, have found their way into popular usage, many are still being perfected, and still others will appear on the market. Some of the best known of the new synthetic yarns are:

Aralac — a synthetic fiber made from the casein

in milk. It is usually used in combination with wool, cotton or rayon and can be treated to resemble any one of them.

Nylon — a synthetic fiber made from derivatives of coal, air and water. It is strong, elastic and non-absorbent.

Vinyon — a synthetic fiber made from derivatives of coal, air and water.

Combinations of two or three fibers are not uncommon. It is desirable, therefore, to know the fiber content of a fabric and to treat it according to instructions given for the more delicate of the fibers included.

Terms Used in Describing Fabrics

Fabrics of the same fiber may differ in construction. *Fabric Terms* The differences in construction cause differences in appearance. In order to understand differences in construction, there are certain textile terms that should be understood.

WARP — the threads of a fabric that run lengthwise and parallel to the selvage.

FILLING—the threads of a fabric that run crosswise from selvage edge to selvage edge.

TWIST — the number of turns in a fiber. Usually a fabric made of tightly twisted yarns has a harder, smoother finish than one made of loosely twisted yarns.

THREAD COUNT — the number of warp and filling yarns per square inch of fabric. It is a form of measurement to designate the quality of a fabric, but does not necessarily indicate strength. However a fabric which has approximately the same thread count in warp and filling yarns will usually wear better than one having a difference in the number of warp and filling yarns.

YARN DYE — yarns or fibers dyed before they are woven into cloth.

FLOATS — the yarns that are carried across the surface of the fabric, for short intervals, and then caught in the weave at intervals. The presence of floats in fabrics affects the durability of the cloth, because they catch and snag easily.

SIZING — stiffening or dressing added to cotton or linen to give a better appearance of body or quality. This is not a permanent finish. By rubbing the fabric between the two hands over a dark cloth, the loosened sizing will show up on the dark cloth.

MERCERIZATION — the name of a process by which fibers are treated to improve the luster and add to the elasticity and strength of the thread or fabric.

NAPPING — a process whereby the fabric is passed over a revolving cylinder which is covered with wire teeth or teasels to raise the nap. The wires scratch the ends of the fibers and bring them to the surface. The nap is then clipped to a uniform length. The surface of wool fabrics and blankets is napped to cover up defects, to make them softer to touch, to increase warmth (the hairy surface entraps and holds more air).

WORSTED — yarn made from woolen fibers laid parallel to one another on the length of the strand and then highly twisted. The highly twisted yarn produces a hard and durable finish in fabrics, in contrast to the soft feel of fabrics woven from wool yarns that are not laid parallel and are not so highly twisted.

Weaves of Fabrics

Weaves   With this information, it will be easy to understand the main differences in the construction of weaves.

Diagram 13a

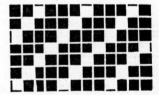

Diagram 13b

PLAIN WEAVE — A filling thread is passed over and under a warp thread, making an alternate interlacing of the two fibers *(diagram 13a)*. Plain, closely woven fibers usually make more durable fabrics. Basket weave and rib weave are variations.

TWILL WEAVE — The warp and filling threads are interlaced so that the filling thread passes over and under 2 or 3 warp threads in a fixed stagger weaving method, giving a diagonal effect *(diagram 13b)*. This weave is used to give variety to a fabric that is otherwise plain. When made of worsted yarns, it is usually very durable. On loosely woven fabrics, however, the fibers are more exposed and apt to wear more quickly. Herringbone weave is a variation.

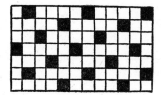

Diagram 13c

SATIN WEAVE — The filling thread passes over one and under several warp threads. The warp is thus floated (see page 289) on the surface, producing a sheen which is very decorative *(diagram 13c)*. It is not a durable fabric because the floated yarns on the surface of cloth are apt to catch and pull. Honeycomb weave is a variation.

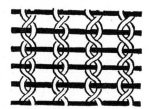

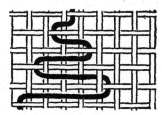

Diagram 13d   Diagram 13e

GAUZE WEAVE — There is an interlocking of 2 warp threads around 1 filling thread *(diagram 13d)*. Filling is thus held in place, and threads will not sag easily. With this weave a fabric may be loosely woven, but firm.

LAPPET WEAVE — A needle attachment on the loom weaves additional thread into the cloth at fixed intervals, from selvage to selvage *(diagram 13e)*, as in dotted Swiss.

PILE WEAVE — An extra set of warp or filling threads is interlaced into the cloth to form loops. These loops may be cut as in velvet, or left uncut as in terry cloth.

DOUBLE-CLOTH WEAVE — Two fabrics are made on the same loom, at the same time. An extra filling thread interlaces them together. Double-cloth weave is usually used in blankets.

FIGURE WEAVES — These are produced on special looms called Jacquard looms. The best known weaves of this kind are damask and brocade. A damask weave has one side on which the warp design is in high gloss, and the filling threads are dull. The other side is reversed. A brocade weave has designs woven in colors that contrast to the background. The designs are raised, and colors not used in the design are floated across the back of the fabric.

TEXTILE CHART

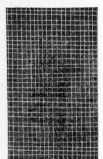

Argentine Cloth

Art linen

Astrakhan

Batiste

Name of Fabric	Uses
ALBATROSS—Soft, lightweight wool fabric in plain weave with crepe surface.	Infants' wear, negligees, linings.
ALPACA—Thin, wiry, smooth fabric. Plain or twill weave, composed of cotton warp yarns and filling yarns made from the hair of the alpaca goat.	Linings, men's and women's summer suits.
ARGENTINE CLOTH — Highly glazed cotton fabric in a plain open weave with very low thread count. Washing removes glaze or stiffening.	Curtains and closet accessories.
ARMURE — Stiff, firm rayon or silk fabric. Stripe, rib or allover design in damask weave.	Linings, neckwear, trimmings, skirts, suits, upholstery, draperies.
ART LINEN—Fabric with fine, even thread woven in a plain weave, usually made in natural or ecru color.	Embroidery, dresses, table linens, doilies, scarfs.
ASTRAKHAN — Heavy wool fabric with a pile surface that has been woven or knitted to resemble caracul or Persian lamb fur.	Women's and children's coats.
BASKET CLOTH — Cotton fabric woven in a basket weave in which two or more filling fibers pass over and under two or more warp threads. Solid surface with loose weave.	Place mats, runners, pillow covers, draperies.
BATISTE—Sheer, soft, smooth cotton, linen, or wool fabric made in plain weave.	Infants' wear, blouses, lingerie, children's dresses.
BENGALINE — Corded fabric in a plain weave with silk or rayon warp threads and heavy cotton, worsted, rayon or silk filling threads. Has a characteristic crosswise rib.	Coats, suits, dresses; draperies.

Bengaline

Bird's Eye Cloth

Name of Fabric

Uses

Buckram

BIRD'S EYE CLOTH—Linen or cotton fabric with a dot in center of a diamond design that is woven in the cloth (figure weave). Soft, absorbent.

Infants' diapers, towels.

BOBBINET—Fine or coarse net cotton fabric with characteristic six-sided meshes.

Curtains.

BOUCLÉ—Woven or knitted wool, cotton, silk or rayon with a curled or looped surface appearance.

Suits, coats.

Brocade

BROADCLOTH — (a) Cotton — Soft, closely woven, firm fabric in plain weave with warp threads more closely spaced than filling threads. Filling threads are more pronounced, showing a very fine rib. Usually mercerized finish.

Men's shirts, pajamas, shorts; women's blouses, tailored dresses, uniforms; children's suits, dresses.

(b) Silk — Closely woven lustrous fabric in plain weave.

Shirts, pajamas, sports clothes.

(c) Wool — Soft, closely woven, lustrous, napped fabric with a satin appearance. Plain weave.

Coats, dresses, suits.

BROCADE—Silk or rayon fabric in figure weave. Designs are woven in contrasting colors from the background and are raised. Frequently silver and gold threads are introduced into filling threads.

Evening dresses and wraps, housecoats, hostess dresses, upholstery.

Broadcloth — wool

BROCATELLE—Heavy silk or rayon fabric in figure weave. Extra filling yarns throw pattern into higher relief than on brocade.

Upholstery and draperies.

BUCKRAM—Stiff, open weave cotton fabric made by glueing two fabrics of plain weave together.

Interlining or stiffening used in clothing, leather goods or millinery.

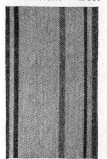
Broadcloth — silk

Bobbinet

Broadcloth — cotton

Name of Fabric

Uses

BUNTING—Soft, thin cotton or wool fabric in plain weave.

Flags, decorations.

BUTCHER'S LINEN — Bleached, crash linen with a plain weave. Rayon sometimes made to look like this.

Originally used for butcher's aprons. Now for women's suits, slacks.

CAMBRIC — (a) Cotton — White or yarn dyed fabric with plain weave and slight gloss on one side.
(b) linen—Sheer, fine linen of plain weave.

Fancy dress costumes, interlinings.

Handkerchiefs, neckwear, blouses, doilies.

Cambric

CANTON CREPE—Silk or rayon fabric with a slight cross ribbed effect. This effect is caused because the filling yarns are heavier than the warp threads. Alternating yarns of different twists form ribbed effect. Plain weave.

Dresses.

CANTON FLANNEL — Soft, warm and absorbent cotton fabric. A twill weave shows on one side and a long fleecy nap on the reverse.

Sleeping garments, infants' wear, interlinings for coats.

Canton crepe

CANVAS — Firm, fairly coarse linen or cotton fabric of plain weave.

Interlinings for coat and suit lapels.

CHALLIS — Lightweight, soft wool, cotton or rayon fabric of plain weave with no luster.

Dresses, negligees, sleeping garments.

CHAMBRAY—Smooth, soft, durable, cotton cloth of plain weave, having colored warp threads, white filling and selvages.

Men's and boys' shirts, women's dresses, children's clothes.

Challis

CHEESECLOTH — Thin, soft cotton fabric with a very low thread count, and little or no sizing. Plain weave.

Fancy dress wear, experimental draping, curtains, dust cloths.

CHEVIOT—Medium weight, slightly napped wool fabric of a twill or herringbone weave, made from wool or worsted yarns.

Coats, suits.

Chambray

Cheviot

Chiffon

Name of Fabric

Uses

CHIFFON — Thin, soft, transparent silk or rayon fabric of plain weave.

Evening gowns, blouses, lingerie.

CHINCHILLA—Soft, heavy wool fabric with a short, curly pile. Sometimes a double cloth with a plain color on curly side and a plaid back.

Coats, jackets.

CHINTZ—Plain woven fabric of fine cotton yarns. May be glazed on one side. Usually printed with floral patterns.

Draperies, slip covers, upholstery, cushions, housecoats, playclothes.

CORDUROY—Cotton fabric with pile in wide or narrow wales or ribbing running warpwise. The weave may be twill or plain.

Suits, dresses, slacks, coats, bathrobes, housecoats, children's wear, upholstery, draperies.

COVERT — Medium weight twill or plain weave cloth in wool or worsted, characterized by white flecks in cloth.

Coats, suits, jackets.

CRASH—Fabric with a rough texture made from coarse cotton, linen, rayon, or wool fibers in a plain or twill weave.

Cotton — Towels, dresses, table runners.
Linen — Towels, dresses.
Rayon — Dresses.
Wool — Dresses, coats.

CREPE—(a) Cotton—lightweight fabric of plain weave with a crinkled surface.
(b) Wool—lightweight fabric of plain or twill weave with a pebbly surface.
(c) Silk—lightweight fabric of plain weave with a slightly pebbly surface.

Children's and women's sleeping garments, negligees, underwear.

Dresses, blouses, soft suits, children's dresses.

Same uses as cotton and wool.

CREPE-BACK SATIN—Silk or rayon fabric with satin weave on one side and crepe back of hard twisted yarn. Satin appearance on one side and crepe on the other.

Dresses, blouses, lingerie, linings.

Crepe — wool

Crepe — silk

Crash

Chintz

Corduroy

Covert

Name of Fabric

Uses

CRETONNE—Strong cotton fabric in plain or figured weaves. Unglazed, printed on one or both sides. Usually heavier and coarser than chintz. Has soft, thick, filling yarn.

Curtains, slip covers, upholstery, draperies.

CRINKLE-CREPE — Silk or rayon crepe with a crinkled appearance. Plain weave.

Dresses.

Cretonne

CRINOLINE—Plain woven cotton fabric with low thread count. Heavily sized.

Millinery and stiffening in belts, shoulder pads, curtains.

DAMASK—(a) Linen—Firm glossy fabric, usually white, woven so that one side has warp designs in high gloss. Filling threads of less gloss form the background. Other side is in reverse. Durable and decorative. Figure weave.

Linen, Cotton, Cotton and Rayon — Table linen.

Crinkle crepe

(b) Cotton—Same as linen.

(c) Cotton and Rayon—Damasks are now made in a combination of cotton and rayon fibers. These come in a variety of colors.

(d) Silk or Rayon—Fabric made in one color, decorated by motifs in contrasting weave to background.

Silk or Rayon — Lightweight damasks are used for dresses, blouses, coat linings, housecoats. Heavier weight for draperies, upholstery.

Crinoline

DENIM—Sturdy cotton fabric with a twill weave. The warp yarns are closely woven, heavy and colored. The filling yarns are white. Fabric is durable and firm in construction.

Men's work clothes, children's clothes, playclothes.

Damask — cotton   *Denim*   *Dimity*

Name of Fabric

Uses

DIMITY—Fine, crisp, lightweight cotton fabric, plain weave. Several threads, laid parallel to one another and used as one at intervals in the warp, form cords in fabric. When such "heavier" threads run both lengthwise and crosswise, a checked effect results. The checked fabric wears better because of more even balance of yarns.

Curtains, lingerie, dresses, blouses.

Flannelette

DOESKIN—Soft, napped wool fabric resembling wool broadcloth. Plain weave.

Suits, coats, children's coats.

DRILL CLOTH—Coarse, firm, heavy, twilled cotton cloth. Will take rough wear.

Men's shirts, middies, blouses, suitings, linings, uniforms, press cloths.

DUCK—Strong, closely woven, heavy cotton fabric in plain weave. Lighter and finer than canvas. Serviceable, somewhat waterproof.

Uniforms, work clothes, shirts, trousers, coats, middy blouses, awnings, shower curtains.

Flannel

EIDERDOWN — Warm, fleecy, lightweight wool or cotton cloth, napped on both surfaces. Double-cloth weave.

Infants' wear, negligees, bathrobes.

FAILLE — Silk or rayon and cotton fabric of plain weave with cross ribbing made by heavy filling yarns.

Dresses, suits, millinery, jackets.

FELT — Wool fabric made by rolling and pressing wool fibers or hairs of certain furs into a mat.

Hats, belts, bags, table mats.

FILET NET—Cotton or linen net with a square mesh. Hand netted filet has a hand tied knot at each corner of the mesh square.

Curtains, tablecloths, runners.

Filet Net

FLANNEL — Soft, lightweight wool fabric in twill or plain weave, slightly napped on one side.

Men's and women's suits, coats, dresses, children's clothing.

Drill cloth

Faille

Felt

Name of Fabric	Uses

Gabardine

Gingham

Homespun

Honeycomb

FLANNELETTE — Soft cotton fabric napped on one side with plain or twill weave on reverse. It is made in white, colors, or floral designs. Absorbent, soft, warm.

Sleeping garments, infants' wear.

FRISÉ — Cotton or wool pile fabric with uncut loops.

Upholstery.

GABARDINE—Firm twilled cotton or wool fabric which has a raised diagonal rib effect on right side.

Men's and women's suits and coats, skirts, riding habits, uniforms.

GINGHAM — Yarn dyed plain woven cotton fabric made in stripes, checks and plaids. Firm and lightweight.

Dresses, children's wear, shirts, aprons, curtains, playclothes.

GLASS TOWELING — Firm plain woven white or cream colored linen with threads of colored cotton yarn at intervals to form stripes or checks in fabric.

Glass towels.

GROSGRAIN — Cotton, silk or rayon fabric of plain weave with heavy ribbed effect. Ribs are very closely spaced.

Dresses, suits, millinery.

HANDKERCHIEF LINEN — Fine, firm, soft fabric of plain weave.

Handkerchiefs, lingerie, dresses, blouses.

HOMESPUN — Soft, loosely woven, rough wool fabric in plain or twill weave. The yarns are usually of two or more colors.

Skirts, suits, coats, jackets.

HONEYCOMB — Cotton fabric with twill or plain weave. Squared, rough surface suggests cell of honeycomb. Softly spun yarns give fabric absorbent quality. Long floats of yarn make it impractical for hard wear.

Towels, bathrobes.

Huckaback

Indian Head

Name of Fabric

HUCKABACK — Cotton or linen fabric with small geometric patterns in figure weave. Prominent filling threads. Softly spun yarn gives fabric absorbent quality.

INDIAN HEAD — Trade name for sturdy, medium weight cotton fabric of plain weave.

KHAKI — Sturdy, twilled cotton fabric in olive drab color.

LAMÉ — Plainly woven or brocaded silk or rayon fabric. Gold or silver threads are mixed with silk or rayon.

LAWN—Sheer, fine, soft cotton cloth with a plain weave. Lightly starched or sized. May be printed.

LONGCLOTH — Fine, soft, closely woven cotton cloth made in a plain weave. It is bleached and lightly sized.

MADRAS — Firm, soft cotton cloth. Usually made from mercerized yarn. Fabric is usually striped or has small figures which are woven into cloth. Plain or figure weave.

MALINE — Fine net silk fabric characterized by hexagonal open mesh.

MARQUISETTE—Silk or cotton fabric with gauze weave, having open mesh appearance.

MATELASSÉ—Raised woven designs in wool, cotton, silk, or rayon fabric. Gives a blistered effect to cloth. Figure weave.

Uses

Towels.

Work clothes, sport clothes, uniforms, children's clothes, aprons.

Uniforms, work clothes, children's clothes.

Dresses, blouses, wraps, neckwear, trimmings.

Infants' wear, dresses, blouses, neckwear, underwear.

Infants' and children's dresses, underwear.

Shirts, dresses, aprons.

Veils, neckwear, evening dresses.

Glass curtains, dresses.

Dresses.

Moiré

Matelassé

Marquisette

Lamé

Lawn

Madras

Name of Fabric	Uses

Monk's Cloth

MELTON — Heavily felted wool fabric with a short nap. Plain weave.

Men's and women's overcoats and coats.

MOIRÉ — Silk or rayon fabric with "watered" effect. Made by passing cloth through heated rollers which engrave pattern on cloth. May or may not be a permanent finish. Plain weave.

Evening dresses, suits, dresses.

MONK'S CLOTH — Rough, loosely woven cotton fabric in basket weave.

Draperies, upholstery, bedspreads, pillows.

Muslin

MOUSSELINE-DE-SOIE — Transparent silk or rayon gauze-like fabric, slightly stiff and of plain weave.

Dresses, blouses, linings for lace yokes and collars.

MUSLIN—Durable, firm, plain weave cotton cloth, bleached or unbleached. In cheaper grades it is usually heavily sized. Wide widths are used for sheeting. The narrow, finer cloth is used for underwear.

Dresses, shirts, aprons, housecoats, lingerie, children's clothes.

Nainsook

NAINSOOK—Soft, lightweight cotton fabric made of fine yarns. The fabric has a plain weave and a luster on one side. Plain weave.

Handmade lingerie, infants' wear.

NINON — Sheer silk or rayon, open mesh fabric of plain weave. One of the more durable sheer cloths.

Dresses, lingerie, glass curtains, draperies.

ORGANDIE—Fine transparent cotton fabric in a plain weave. Its characteristic crisp finish may be of a permanent nature or may wash out after a few launderings, according to the manner in which the fabric has been treated.

Dresses, neckwear, curtains, bedspreads, blouses.

OUTING FLANNEL — Lightweight cotton fabric with nap on both sides. Twill or plain weave. Soft, absorbent.

Sleeping garments, infants' wear.

Ninon

Outing Flannel

Oxford shirting

Name of Fabric

OXFORD SHIRTING — Mercerized cotton fabric in a basket weave. Yarn is dyed before it is woven. Soft and absorbent.

PERCALE — Closely woven, firm cotton fabric made in a plain weave in solid colors or prints.

PERCALINE—Fine, thin, glossy percale. Finished with sizing.

PIQUÉ — Cotton fabric with cording effect running lengthwise or in novelty effects. Novelty weave.

PLISSÉ CREPE — Cotton fabric of plain weave treated with a caustic bath which causes cloth to crinkle. Crinkle only remains in fabric if not ironed.

PLUSH—Similar to velvet, but with longer pile and coarser back.

POLO CLOTH—Soft fabric made from loosely spun yarns in a twill weave. Can be napped on both sides of fabric to give more warmth. The yarns may be wool, alpaca, camel's hair.

PONGEE — Lightweight silk fabric, plainly woven of irregular yarns. Usually in natural or ivory color.

POPLIN—Cotton, silk, or wool fabric of plain weave. Warp threads are of fine yarn, giving a corded effect on crosswise grain.

Uses

Men's shirts, women's dresses.

Dresses, aprons, children's clothes, playclothes, housecoats, draperies.

Linings and foundations.

Collars, cuffs, blouses, vestees, dresses, playclothes, children's clothes.

Underwear, sleeping garments.

Coats, collars and cuffs, muffs, upholstery.

Coats, jackets.

Curtains, smocks, art needlework, linings.

Dresses, suits, coats, skirts, children's clothes.

Sateen

Rep

Poplin

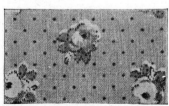

Percale

Piqué

Plissé — crepe

Satin

Seersucker

Serge

Shantung

Name of Fabric	Uses
RATINÉ — Loosely woven, rather stretchy cotton, silk, rayon or wool fabric made in plain weave. Filling threads are looped and are of novelty yarn to produce a rough effect.	Dresses, coats, suits.
REP — Firm cotton, wool, rayon, or silk fabric with heavier filling thread than warp thread. Crosswise rib is very distinct. Plain weave.	Skirts, suits, men's and boys' wear, draperies, upholstery.
SATEEN—Cotton fabric with a satin weave. A mercerized finish further increases luster.	Linings, draperies, costumes, slip covers.
SATIN—Silk or rayon fabric with a satin weave. This weave produces the sheen that is characteristic of satin.	Dresses, linings, lingerie, blouses, neckwear.
SCRIM—Light, transparent cotton fabric in open mesh, plain weave.	Curtains.
SEERSUCKER — Lightweight, washable cotton fabric in plain weave with crinkly stripes running lengthwise at alternating intervals. Crinkle is caused by slackening tension of warp yarns. Does not need to be ironed.	Dresses, children's clothes, men's suits, playclothes, underwear.
SERGE—Soft, durable wool, rayon or silk cloth made from worsted yarns. A twill weave with a diagonal effect on both sides of cloth.	Men's and women's suits and coats, dresses, skirts, middy blouses, shirts.
SHANTUNG — A heavier, rougher texture of pongee.	Dresses, suits, coats.
SURAH—Soft, lightweight silk fabric in a twill weave.	Neckties, dresses, blouses.

Swiss (dotted)

Taffeta

Name of Fabric

SWISS (DOTTED)—Fine, transparent, crisp cotton fabric in plain weave. Frequently figured with dots or small figures that are produced by a special process of weaving or by chemical application.

TAFFETA—Smooth, lustrous rayon or silk fabric of a plain weave. Iridescent effect of some taffetas is caused by difference in color of filling and warp yarns.

TERRY CLOTH — Cotton pile fabric with raised uncut loops on both sides of fabric.

TICKING—Firm, durable cotton cloth in twill weave with yarn-dyed blue and white stripes running lengthwise.

TROPICAL WORSTED — Lightweight worsted cloth in plain weave.

TULLE—Soft silk or rayon net of fine mesh.

TWEED—Rough surfaced wool fabric in plain, herringbone or twill weave. Warp thread is usually composed of a two-ply yarn which has two colors, giving a soft tone to the fabric.

VELOUR—Soft, strong, closely woven cotton, woolen, silk, rayon fabric with a pile. Somewhat like velvet.

VELVET—Silk or rayon fabric with a soft, thick, short pile on face and a plain back.

VELVETEEN—Cotton fabric with a soft, thick, short pile on face and a plain or twill back. Resembles velvet.

VOILE — Sheer cotton, silk, or rayon fabric in plain weave.

Uses

Curtains, dresses, blouses, bedspreads, neckwear.

Dresses, blouses, suits, millinery, slips, draperies, upholstery.

Bath towels, bath robes, beach robes, wash cloths.

Mattress and pillow covering, upholstery, playclothes.

Men's and women's suits.

Trimmings, veiling.

Men's and women's coats, suits and jackets, slacks, dresses.

Coats, suits, upholstery, draperies.

Dresses, suits, coats, negligees, trimmings, millinery.

Dresses, coats, suits, children's dresses, draperies, upholstery.

Dresses, blouses, curtains, lingerie.

Voile

Velveteen

Velvet

Terry cloth

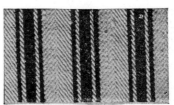

Ticking

Tweed

SHRINKING OF FABRICS BEFORE CUTTING

Shrinking   Today, cottons, linens and wools are often commercially pre-shrunk. If there is no mention of pre-shrinkage on the label, or no guarantee is given by the retailer, at least 5 per cent more yardage should be allowed on cottons, linens and wools. Shrinkage may be taken care of at home. Silk or rayon does not require any shrinkage or sponging. Rayons are apt to shrink in washing, but this shrinkage cannot be controlled by shrinking before fabric is cut. When purchasing rayon inquire as to its washability.

White cottons or linens should be folded so they will not wrinkle, then soaked in cold water for several hours. Colored cottons or linens should be rinsed in cold water. Upon removal from water, do not wring fabric; squeeze water from it. Hang on clothes line, and when nearly dry, iron on wrong side, ironing with the grain of the fabric. Fold fabric with the right side inside, selvage edges together, and filling threads straight across from edge to fold.

Wools are usually commercially pre-shrunk; however, all wool fabrics should be sponged either at home or by a reliable local tailor. To sponge at home, unfold fabric, clip selvages at intervals of 2″ all along edges. Thoroughly wet a sheet in cold water, ring it out and lay fabric smoothly on sheet. Roll sheet and fabric together and let stand over night. Unroll fabric. Press (see page 221) with the iron following the grain of the fabric. Fold fabric with the right side inside, selvage edges together, and filling threads straight across from edge to fold.

CARE OF FABRICS

Laundering and Cleaning

Consult the garment and fabric labels which advise *Cleaning* on their proper care. Before laundering any fabric not specified as washable, it should be tested first for shrinkage and color fastness. The rules for laundering are essentially the same: Squeeze gently through a lukewarm suds made of mild soap, holding fabric under water until cleaned. If necessary, use a second suds. Squeeze suds out, do not wring silk, rayon or wool. Rinse at least three times in clear lukewarm water. Squeeze out excess water. Roll in a Turkish towel and gently knead out water. When laundering cottons, warm water may be used, and they may be hung up to dry. Press as described on the label, or see page 221.

Spot and Stain Removal

Determine nature of spot and type of fabric. Treat *Spot* as promptly as possible. Test the cleansing agent first *Removal* by applying it on a small piece of fabric taken from seam. Some of the principal cleansing agents and the methods for using them are on next page. If spot cannot be removed, it is best to have garment dry cleaned immediately.

Cleansing Agents	Method

ABSORBENTS (used to remove grease spots)
a. Powdered form
    Fuller's earth
    French chalk
    Starch
	Powdered form of absorbent is used only on light-colored fabrics. Place stained part of fabric on flat surface and cover stain thickly with powdered absorbent. With circular motion rub finger gently on spot. Brush powder off fabric, repeat application until no more of stain can be absorbed. Cover with new layer of powder and allow to stand for several hours. Brush fabric thoroughly.

b. Blotting paper or brown wrapping paper	Blotting paper or brown wrapping paper will remove grease. Place paper under spot and press spot with warm iron for several minutes. Brush thoroughly and repeat if necessary.
SOLVENTS (used to remove spots from non-washable fabrics) Carbon tetrachloride—(may be purchased at drug store). This is the basis for most dry cleaning fluids.	Place fabric right side down on blotting paper. Barely moisten clean lintless cloth with solvent and apply lightly with straight strokes, working from outside of spot toward center. Light, straight strokes prevent rings in fabric. While working, blow on damp area to speed evaporation. Change blotter area and cloth as soon as they are soiled.
BLEACHES (used to remove stains which will not wash out of cottons) Sodium hypochlorite (Javelle water). It should not be used on silk, rayon or wool. Hydrogen peroxide.	*Bowl Method* Stretch spotted portion over a bowl of water. Hold fabric taut by stretching rubber band around sides of bowl. Using a glass rod, moisten stain with clear water. Apply cleansing agent, using second glass rod. Allow to set for one minute. Follow with a second application of water, using glass rod previously used for water. If necessary, apply cleansing agent with third glass rod. Rinse thoroughly with clear water. Repeat if necessary. *Blotter Method* Place spotted area over a blotter, spot side down. Using a medicine dropper, moisten stain with clear water. Apply cleansing agent, using a second medicine dropper. Follow with second application of water, using dropper formerly used for water. If necessary, apply cleansing agent with third dropper. Rinse thoroughly with clear water. Repeat if necessary.

14. Supply Depot

    You can't really be efficient about sewing unless you have the proper equipment. Naturally this is relative —you're the best judge of your own needs. If you do a little mending or put up an occasional hem, you hardly need the same tools as the woman who thinks nothing of making all her slip covers and a complete wardrobe for her whole family. It's an almost irresistible temptation to collect gadgets, but it's pointless to clutter up your sewing box or your sewing room with anything you don't actually need. Too many things get in your way, defeat your purpose, just as much as too few. So it's up to you to select from the complete list of supplies for your sewing room exactly what you need to function efficiently.

SEWING ROOM ACCESSORIES

It is not necessary for the beginner to assemble all sewing equipment at one time. It is more satisfactory to choose the necessary implements first. See page 15 for a detailed description of the necessary equipment needed to start. These should be collected in a sewing cabinet or a large sewing box so that they will all be at hand when needed. A description of desirable sewing equipment is listed below. Many of these articles may be purchased as progress in sewing warrants the use of them.

Implements Used in Cutting

8" Bent Trimmer (Dressmaker Shears)—A shears is a cutting implement at least 6" long, which has a small ring handle for the thumb, and a larger handle that is large enough for several fingers. The difference in the size of handles allows for greater leverage. A shears with bent handles insures greater accuracy and ease in cutting fabric flat on the table.

Pinking Shears — This is a shears with blade edges that are notched. It is used on firmly woven fabrics to produce an evenly notched edge that prevents ravelling. A pinked edge is a quick and easy seam finish.

Scissors — A scissors is a cutting implement from 3" to 6" long. It has 2 ring handles, both the same size, for thumb and finger. A 6" size is a convenient scissors for clipping threads, ripping, cutting through buttonholes and general fine sewing.

Razor Blade — For ripping, use a single edged blade, or a razor blade holder with a double edged blade.

Dressmaking Board — This board is used when a large flat cutting surface is otherwise unobtainable. It can be folded for storage, or opened out flat on a bed or on the floor to provide a flat surface for cutting.

Dressmaker's Pins — Fine quality brass dressmaker's pins (size 5 or 6) with sharp points that will not mar fabrics are best. Purchase by the ¼ or ½ lb. box.

Implements Used in Measuring

Tape Measure — A 60″ length oilcloth tape will give accurate measurements because it will not stretch. Be sure that the numbers start at one end on one side and at opposite end on reverse side so that measurements can be taken from either end. Metal tips at both ends will prevent fraying.

Yardstick — Be sure to get a good, durable, wooden yardstick with well-turned smooth edges and clear markings. This is used for measuring and marking long lengths, where a solid type of gauge is needed, and also for taking hems.

6″ Ruler — A 6″ ruler with markings up to 1/16″ is useful for marking seams. If it is transparent, it is possible to see the grain of the fabric.

Hem Gauge—This is convenient for marking the width of hems and all short measurements.

Hem Marker — A commercial hem marker provides an easy and convenient way to mark hems.

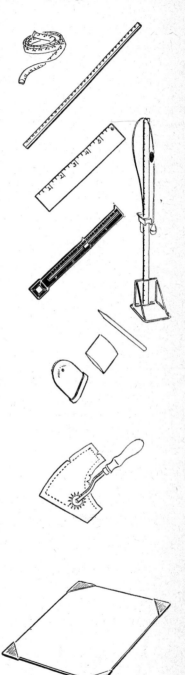

Implements Used in Marking

Tailor's Chalk — This is used to mark notches, perforations, seam allowances, and alterations. For cotton, silk, linen or synthetic fabrics, use the dry powdered variety available in a flat piece, or in pencil form. There is on the market also a plastic container that holds loose tailor's chalk. It has a small tracing wheel at the bottom, which marks the chalk on the fabric. This tracer is good for marking long distances on a flat surface. Be sure to protect surface upon which it is used with a marking board or with layers of newspaper. For marking wool, a wax chalk may be used. This is obtainable in square or pencil form. It will mark other fabrics permanently.

Tracing Wheel — This wheel with pointed edge is used to mark pattern perforations on firmly woven fabrics. It may be used with or without a tracing board, but it will mark any surface on which it is used.

Marking Board and Carbon Paper — Colored or white carbon paper may be placed between 2 layers of fabric and a marking board placed underneath. The perforations and notches on the top layer of fabric are traced with a tracing wheel through to the under layer of fabric.

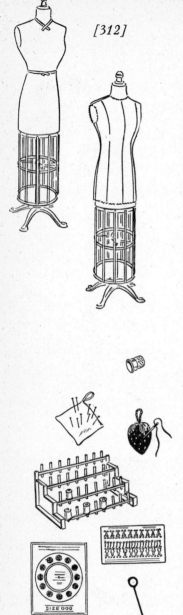

Implements Used in Fitting —

Padded Form — This form is padded to specific measurements, using as a basis a form with a knitted covering, one size smaller than the bust measurement. A dress form foundation is bought or made from a commercial pattern. This is fitted to the individual, and all seams are stitched except at center back. Curved seams are clipped, all seams are pressed and waistline is marked. The dress form is padded to the measurements of the fitted foundation, using cotton wadding or tissue paper. It is then covered with fitted foundation, padding being added or removed as necessary. Back opening edges are catch stitched *(see figure 91, page 124)* together.

Adjustable Form — These forms are made so that bust, shoulder, back, waist and hip sections can be adjusted to the measurements of the individual.

Plastic Form — This form is molded on the individual, then removed, allowed to solidify and placed on stand.

Full Length Mirror — A mirror is necessary for fitting.

Implements Used in Sewing

Sewing Machine — This is discussed on pages 21 to 26.

Needles and Thread — These are discussed in detail on page 315.

Thimble — This very important part of sewing equipment is used as a guard for the middle or "pushing" finger. It should be made of a good quality metal or plastic, and should fit the middle finger well. Sizes 7, 8 and 9 are the average adult sizes.

Pin Cushion — This is used to keep pins assembled and within easy reach. To prevent rusting of pins, the cushion should be made of a closely woven woolen fabric and stuffed with hair or ravellings from woolen fabrics.

Emery Bag — This is used to remove rust from needles. The needle is never left in the emery bag, but is merely run through it when necessary.

Spool Rack — A rack keeps spools of thread neatly arranged and within reach.

Hooks and Eyes — Black and white hooks and eyes in several sizes are useful for side placket openings on dresses and skirts.

Snaps — Black and white snaps in several sizes are useful for side placket openings on dresses and skirts.

Bias Trim Turner — This gadget is helpful for turning belts, bias bindings and cordings.

Stiletto — This is for punching holes in preparation for eyelets.

Bodkin — This is used to draw ribbon through a casing or beading.

Implements Used for Pressing

Ironing Board — A good ironing board should be well padded. Removable covers for the ironing board make it possible to have clean covers at all times.

Iron — A well constructed iron with a temperature regulator for various types of fabrics is a necessity. A cold iron is cleaned with cleansing powder which will not scratch. A hot iron is cleaned by ironing over salt on brown paper. Starch is removed by rubbing with paraffin and ironing over brown paper to remove paraffin.

Steam Iron — This iron is constructed to hold water. When heated, the steam escapes through holes in the bottom of the iron. Ironing with steam eliminates the use of a press cloth and gives a more finished look to garment.

Pressing Cloth — Cloths for pressing are usually of cheesecloth, muslin or drill cloth. Before using, all sizing should be removed by rinsing several times in clear water.

Pressing Sponge — A sponge is used to dampen cottons and linens directly, and to dampen the press cloth when pressing silk, rayon and wool.

Sleeve Board — This is used for pressing sleeve seams and small seams.

Tailor's Cushion — This is useful in pressing the curved seams of a garment. It can be made of unbleached muslin, with sizing removed by rinsing. The fabric is pressed and 2 oval shaped pieces each 9″ x 12″ are cut (see sketch). These are placed right sides together and stitched, leaving smaller end open for about 6″. It is turned to right side and stuffed with wadding until cushion is very firm. Raw edges of opening are turned in and whipped together *(see figure 41, page 42)*.

Pressing Mitten — This is used to press the curved seams of a garment. It can be made from unbleached muslin, with sizing removed by rinsing. The fabric is pressed, and two pieces, each 8½″ x 9½″, and one piece 8½″ x 13″, are cut. One end of each of the smaller pieces is shaped *(diagram 14a)*. The large piece is folded in half crosswise, and the edges opposite the fold are shaped the same way. The folded cloth is placed against one of other pieces, curved edges together and pinned all around. The two pieces are stitched together for 2″, starting 2″ in from fold edge *(diagram 14b)*. This is placed against remaining single piece, right sides together, and stitched around edge, leaving one straight edge open. Then mitten is turned, stuffed firmly, the seam allowance of opening turned in, and opening whipped together *(see figure 41, page 42)*.

Needleboard — This board is used for pressing pile fabrics.

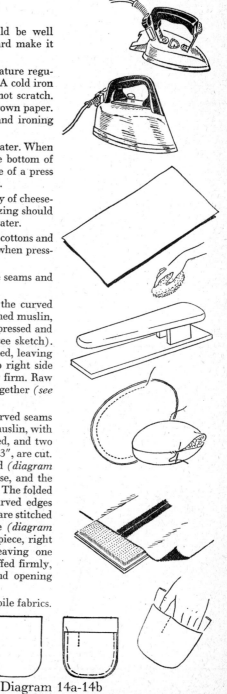

Diagram 14a-14b

Sewing Is Easier with the Correct Needle

Needles come in various sizes, small numbers indicating coarse needles, large numbers indicating fine ones. Due to wartime conditions some sizes may not be available. Assortments of sizes 3 to 9 in different kinds of needles take care of ordinary requirements.

For General Sewing

Sharps have small rounded eyes and are medium in length. Sizes 3/0 to 12.

Betweens have same size eye and diameter as sharps but are shorter in length. They are used for making short, fine stitches, as in fine handwork and tailoring. Sizes 1 to 12.

Milliners Needles have same size eye and diameter as sharps but are much longer. They are used for quick, long stitches such as basting. Sizes 1 to 12.

For Embroidery

Crewel Needles, known as *Embroidery Needles*, have long eyes to hold several strands of thread. Sizes 1 to 12.

For Darning

Cotton Darning Needles have same size eye and diameter as crewel needles but are longer for easy weaving. Sizes 1 to 10.

Yarn Darning Needles are extra coarse for mending woolens. Sizes 14 to 18.

Needle Sizes and Correct Threads for Various Fabrics

Sewing Needle Size	Type of Fabric	Thread size	Machine Needles	Machine Stitch per inch
Coarsest (3)	Heavy duck, canvas, coating.	8, 10, 12 black and white	Coarsest	8
Coarse (4, 5)	Ticking, denim, sewing buttons on heavy material.	16, 20, 24 black and white	Coarse	10, 12
Medium Coarse (6)	Cretonne, slip covers, wools, sewing buttons on medium-heavy material.	30, 36, 40 black and white. Heavy mercerized thread in colors.	Medium coarse	12
Medium (7)	Percale, gingham, rayon, linen, lightweight wool.	50, 60, 70 black and white. Mercerized in colors.	Medium	14
Medium fine (8)	Voile, lawn.	80, black and white. Mercerized in colors.	Medium fine	16, 18
Fine (9)	Organdie, batiste.	100, black and white. Mercerized in colors.	Fine	20, 22

First quality material such as the Government issues should not be wasted. The adorable coat for the little girl is made from a tar's jumper, while the small boy's suit was once his sailor-daddy's "bell bottom trousers." See the chapters on tailoring, page 227, and Repeat Performance, page 237, for helpful hints in accomplishing a make over project of this kind.

Index